MOSES MEETS ISRAEL
THE ORIGINS OF ONE GOD

By

Joseph Winsten, M.D.

RUMFORD PRESS
BOSTON, MASSACHUSETTS

MOSES MEETS ISRAEL
THE ORIGINS OF ONE GOD

Published by
Rumford Press, L.L.C.
221 North Beacon St., Boston, MA 02135

Jacket and book design, typography and electronic pagination by
Arrow Graphics, Inc., Cambridge, Massachusetts

Printed in the United States of America

Publisher's Cataloging-in-Publication
(*Provided by Quality Books, Inc.*)

Winsten, Joseph, 1925-
Moses meets Israel : the origins of one God/
by Joseph Winsten. — 1st ed.
p. cm.
Includes bibliographical references and index.
Preassigned LCCN: 98-91316
ISBN: 0-966340-60-4

1. Monotheism—Middle East—History. 2. Moses
(Biblical leader) 3. Jews—History—To 953 B.C. I. Title.

BL221.W56 1998   211.34
             QBI98-1061

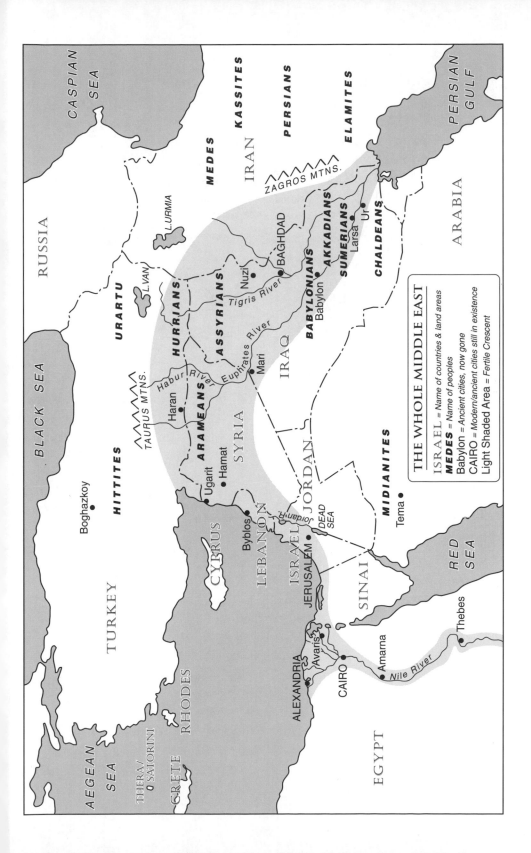

THE WHOLE MIDDLE EAST

ISRAEL = Name of countries & land areas
MEDES = Name of peoples
Babylon = Ancient cities, now gone
CAIRO = Modern/ancient cities still in existence
Light Shaded Area = Fertile Crescent

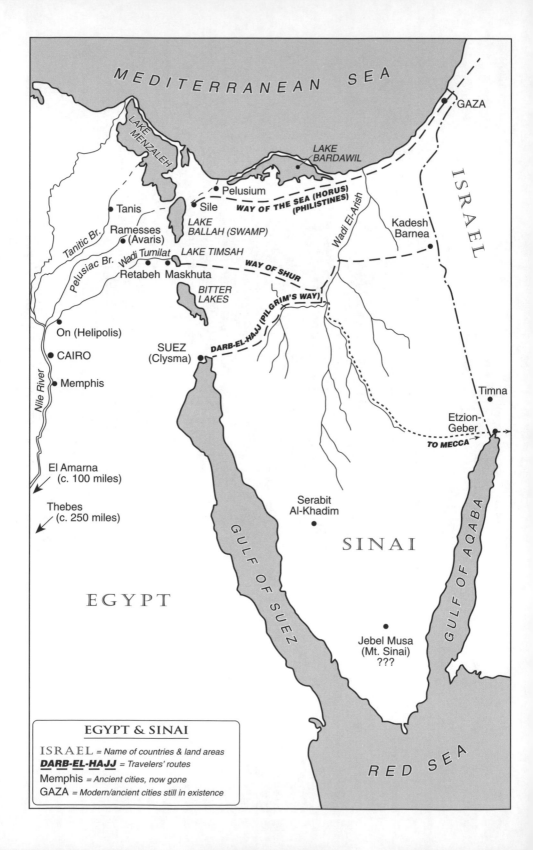

MEDITERRANEAN SEA

LAKE MENZALEH

LAKE BARDAWIL

GAZA

ISRAEL

Pelusium

Sile

WAY OF THE SEA (HORUS) (PHILISTINES)

Tanis

Ramesses (Avaris)

LAKE BALLAH (SWAMP)

Wadi El-Arish

Kadesh Barnea

Tanitic Br.

Pelusiac Br.

Wadi Tumilat

LAKE TIMSAH

Retabeh Maskhuta

WAY OF SHUR

BITTER LAKES

On (Heliopolis)

DARB-EL-HAJJ (PILGRIM'S WAY)

CAIRO

SUEZ (Clysma)

Memphis

Nile River

Timna

Etzion-Geber

TO MECCA

El Amarna (c. 100 miles)

Thebes (c. 250 miles)

Serabit Al-Khadim

SINAI

GULF OF AQABA

EGYPT

GULF OF SUEZ

Jebel Musa (Mt. Sinai) ???

RED SEA

EGYPT & SINAI

ISRAEL = Name of countries & land areas
DARB-EL-HAJJ = Travelers' routes
Memphis = Ancient cities, now gone
GAZA = Modern/ancient cities still in existence

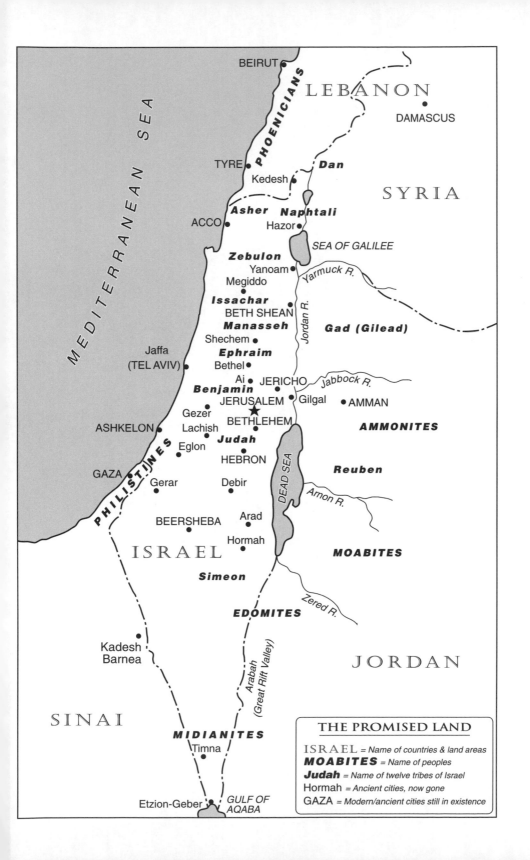

THE PROMISED LAND

ISRAEL = Name of countries & land areas
MOABITES = Name of peoples
Judah = Name of twelve tribes of Israel
Hormah = Ancient cities, now gone
GAZA = Modern/ancient cities still in existence

Contents

Foreword

Times of crisis generate strong concerns for the identification of roots and for a redefinition of the understanding of history. This is surely true in contemporary Israel with the reintroduction of such usages as Judea and Samaria to identify the geography of an area more commonly referred to as the West Bank. Such efforts are indicative of the perennial concern for the origins of Israel and the related question of when it is appropriate to identify the Jewish people.

Dr. Joseph Winsten came to know the fascination of issues such as these during the course of his studies at Brown University, studies quite distant from the medical career which he had fruitfully pursued for many years. At the same time, the skills of a surgeon informed his vision of the task and contributed to the success of the effort. His book is a tribute to his skills in assimilating a mountain of data, often conflicting, and separating out those elements that illuminate his central goals. The study of ancient Israel is a challenge to any historian who must contend with missing data of central concern and a web of summarization imposed on ancient Israel by the layers of successive generations in the first millennium B.C.E.

The intent here is not to reduce the heroes of faith to nonentities or to vaporize the major events of early Israelite history. Rather it is to be a responsible historian who can lay before a reader an understandable analysis of contemporary scholarship in language that will be comprehended by that reader. Dr. Winsten is quite prepared to add his own hypotheses when he finds supporting evidence or a reasonable logic. This study penetrates beneath the miraculous surface of the Hebrew Bible and seeks to understand the function of miracle in the life of ancient Israel.

The book presupposes that the reader shares with the author a fascination for early Israel and a recognition of the central yearning of the Jewish people for a foundation not only in Abraham, Isaac, Jacob, and especially Moses but also in the creation of the universe. It is also true, however, that the author does not tolerate fanciful visions of that foundation. In the view of Dr. Winsten an essential demythologization will permit a useful remythologization and thereby a retelling of ancient Israel's story understandable in our day.

A responsible reliance on the best scholarship of our day, a lucid style of exposition, and a firm commitment to contemporary canons of historical analysis make Dr. Winsten's book a commendable contribution to the current literature on the origins of ancient Israel.

ERNEST S. FRERICHS
Director
Program in Judaic Studies
Brown University

Preface

A serious quest for the earliest origins of Israel faces formidable hurdles: the paucity of hard data available from that time and the unabashedly doctrinaire use of facts or traditions by subsequent generations. Given the complexity of this undertaking, in which historically cogent facts have to be sought in the obscure precincts of ancient, scattered, and often contradictory details, problems of definition and identification are unavoidable. It is the interaction of bold intuition melding with disparate facts but restrained by a disciplined reason that provides a coherent history.

Ancient names, places, and words often have variant forms from different sources, changed usage, and even by scholarly choice. The words Semite or Semitic refer to all people who spoke dialects of the same language but do not specify Israelites except as they were part of that broader group.

Many names have been assigned to the land in which Israel finally settled. Canaan is used here to denote the overall area, which includes present-day southern Lebanon, southwestern Syria, western Jordan, the present State of Israel, and northeastern Sinai. Some names that were normative at certain times in the past may have no precise application today. In this book Canaan, Syro-Palestine, and Israel are essentially trivalent terms, each denoting slightly different but overlapping areas.

B.C.E. (Before the Common Era) and C.E. (Common Era), centered on year 0, differentiate the two critical time blocks of Western history and correspond to the now archaic B.C. (Before Christ) and A.D. (Anno Domini), respectively. The time periods prior to the Common Era are written in capital letters. For example, Nineteenth Century indicates B.C.E., whereas a C.E. date would appear as nineteenth century. Also, a descending range of years, such as 1200–1000, signifies B.C.E.

Three maps have been included to aid in visualizing the regions where the history of ancient Israel unfolded, and a chronology chart compares time relationships of relevant persons, institutions, and events described in this book. The glossary at the end of the book facilitates access to uncommon terms.

Appropriate biblical passages were taken mainly from the *Tanakh* (the Holy Scriptures of The Jewish Publication Society, 1985) and *The Pentateuch and Haftorahs*, 2d ed. (Soncino Press, 1969), but consultation with any other Bible can serve equally well.

*
 * *

It is extremely rare today that a person can produce a new book without some degree of midwifery, and in this context I have had a most supportive labor. I acknowledge a singular debt to the Chairman of the Program in Judaic Studies at Brown University, Professor Ernest S. Frerichs, for his generous availability, rational counsel, and unfailing good humor. Harold G. Jacobs, Jerome S. Kornreich, Joy A.W. Pratt, Italo Servi, Janet Q. Tassel, and my brother, Harold H. Winsten, contributed selfless critiques to early drafts of the manuscript. Words of gratitude can hardly express my debt to them.

And closest to me, I offer humble tribute to my wife, Nancy R. Winsten, for her technical and editorial help, as well as her patience in putting up with the occupational absentmindedness of an author-in-residence.

Lexington, Massachusetts
August 1997

Introduction

1

Western civilization weans its children on tales of heroism and selflessness. For us our religious ancestry usually came to life on Sundays, with stories of patriarchs and other heroes ladled out in jellied dollops. The reality of those fabled forefathers was never questioned; it was simply truth. Now grown to adulthood, with further experience in the world of reality, we have come to realize that those lessons were concerned less with defining historical truth than with developing a sense of moral purpose. The people of the Bible became the prototype for a meaningful existence.

The biblical traditions are among the earliest tales that fueled the storyteller's art, and they became the standard for this genre. Many of us still recall the resonant tales about our ancestors and how they altered the inchoate world of their time. The Bible has been the ultimate source of humanity's moral structure, and although its role today may seem tangential to the cares of daily living, it still has the power to arouse our yearning for personal validation.

The definitive history of early Israel has not been written yet and may never be. Events that witnessed the formation of the Western world's monotheism, reported in our only direct source, Hebrew Scripture, is colored with a heavy creedal impasto. Supporting data are few, fragmented, and equivocal and must await future archeological findings or technological innovations to open new avenues of research. The phenomenon of Israel's early development can be understood only by a reasonable and logical deployment of what facts we have.

Moses Meets Israel presents early Israel as a rational development of unique economic, political, and social factors without recourse to a divine source. Because divinity is a concept that sprang from the human brain at its beginning, along with other abstract answers to new mysteries, it would be unwarranted to assign primary cause to God. But that is precisely what primitive peoples did, fostering the contemporary dilemma of reality versus faith.

Readers will not find a new religion in this book, but neither will the revelations prompt a wholesale defection from their own religious havens. All of us who share an interest in the origin and evolution of spirituality are merely new dots in a line that began thousands of years ago and continues to grow longer. The saga of Israel, from wherever one places its beginning, had a definitive history, although we are left to only infer this from the fascinating tales in Scripture.

People living today, unlike previous generations, are repositories of vast knowledge that has been increasing geometrically. Learned verities seem to suffice only for ever shorter periods and to result in a distressingly frequent need to reassess those previous truths. Spirituality, however, fosters an ineradicable function in humankind by introducing the unknown as it drives intuitive thought. We cannot live comfortably without at least its gentlest touch.

In attempting to construct a realistic picture of Israel's early formative years, I was acutely aware of the limitations of fact and the potential subversion by personal involvement. The difficulty in applying objectivity to the traditional narratives has dogged the completion of this book. Many questions arose to keep the author awake nights: Will this book add something substantial to the massive body of existing literature? Is another book about the origin of ancient Israel justified if people are vaguely surfeited by their childhood indoctrination? More important, do I really have better answers, or will I merely accelerate the skepticism that is already widespread?

The accumulated literature is so vast that it overwhelms our capacity to assimilate it. Writers from confessional or theological disciplines are more likely to defend traditional positions, whereas academically oriented scholars tend to critique those same issues. This observation implies that even the most objective investigator cannot be totally free of unconscious motivations. The need to seek intellectual neutrality within an unremitting emotional involvement creates a paradox within every thinking person. Individuals today, highly educated and sophisticated even beyond what their own parents could imagine, find that they must either resign themselves to faith set by a vaguely discomforting mythology or remove themselves to an equally discomforting limbo. How reassuring it would be if those rootless souls could find serenity in a faith that did not violate reason!

It has been said that all human history has in it an element of mystery,[1] and *Moses Meets Israel* probes this embellishment of reality. Certainly many people lack a comprehensive knowledge about early Israel despite an almost universal acquaintance with its major actors and events. Biblical scholarship, riding the winds of scientific achievement in the past hundred years, has uncovered new and critical information. Unfortunately much of the material has been gathered in diverse fields and often languishes in specialty journals. Even when it does reach public notice, the usually minute increments of data appear irrelevant or, worse, arcane.

The Bible is the written account of the Israelites, an otherwise unremarkable people, fitfully advancing toward a uniquely ordered way of life. The Torah, comprising the first five books of the Bible, heralds the lives and acts of the pathfinders. It represents the intellectual heart of Judaism, as well as the cryptic basis of Christianity, offering a history from the beginning of the world and a constitutional guide for positive action. All of humanity is included even as it concentrates on the growth of a single family—Jacob's. Until the past two centuries the Torah remained essentially unchallenged on either the historical record or the ethical premise. But now that our society has evolved to a modest level of intellectual maturity, we must find the courage to reexamine the Torah's historicity.

The thesis of this book is that early Israel is not the seamless tale of selflessness and heroism that is taught in Sunday schools but rather the prosaic history of an unendowed people seeking a better life within the indifference of natural experience. Israel, which arose from the Semitic primordium of the ancient Near East, did not reveal any distinction until it was joined by people coming from Egypt. Whether the latter were ethnic Semites, Egyptianized Semites, Egyptians, or other is far less important than the momentous message they carried: An omnipotent but inscrutable God modulates the world with impartial justice, and all people become equal when they accept His rule. Also, God's promise of perpetual title to a land of "milk and honey" lent substance to abstraction. The miracles that attended the Exodus experience, whether natural or unnatural, simply confirmed the superior power of this new deity. Opportunity to enlist in such a beneficent contract must have been irresistible to the disestablished people they met en route or in the land itself.

The various groups that became Israel projected a common destiny while maintaining political independence. Slowly they began to merge into a single people by anthologizing a kindred heritage. Multilateral traditions were donated and accepted into a common pool. Most of these revealed the transcendence of human nature, although some were laced with examples of boorishness. But the national epic recorded them all unflinchingly. In that sense it became a document of history. Tribes were awarded separate, familial identities as they assembled into a unit that was really a loose confederation on its way to nationhood.

The first six books of Hebrew Scripture, with the exception of cult-oriented Leviticus, tell the early story of the people. The narrative tales are organized more or less chronologically but do not have the character of history in a modern sense. Hard data, such as references to persons, places, or dates that resonate with other known sources, are absent. In their place are vignettes highlighting human behaviorisms and unfamiliar references, often difficult to fathom. Miraculous theophanies punctuate the lives of heroes, investing them with a celestial grandeur that disguises reality. Yet encounters with God are commonly experienced by persons under stress. To be sure, some included behavior would be considered irrational in any era, but it creates a sense of original history, especially when there is a later gloss moderating the issue.

All Bible stories represent highly stylized historiography, although at some level each is a germ of truth. The certainty that recorded traditions were contemporaneous with their subjects, and therefore approximated reality, must be tempered by the knowledge that they were inscribed hundreds of years later. By then many emendations had been made to support and promote a creed. As we analyze the Torah, its commentaries, and related legends, we must be alert for subjective accretions to history. Hidden reality is especially likely where ambiguity, contradiction, or irrationality is found.

To approximate a balanced reconstruction of early Israel, where the stones of fact need only the mortar of reason, I have sought to correlate recent scholarship in all fields, literary and scientific, with extrabiblical data and traditional material from Scripture. I evaluated and weighted conflicting points of view, adding my own, often eclectic, analyses. I offer conclusions only when they can be supported by the judicious opinions of previous writers or at least by simple, self-evident logic. Where a firm conclusion is still elusive, each of us must rely on that ultimate human resource, reason and intuition. Ideally no reader will retreat to an earlier faith just to avoid grappling with the disconcerting implications of this book. It was written to extend, not supplant, honestly held beliefs about the origin of Israel.

In this context I must issue a warning. Some of the data and reasoning actively demythologize the traditional understanding of the words of the Bible. You may find yourself bristling at the temerity of the challenge. For this I apologize but in defense hasten to say that the project was not undertaken capriciously. Just as physicians, and especially surgeons, must prescribe unpleasant procedures to heal a patient's body, some psychic dislocation becomes inevitable when one seeks a more profound understanding of any issue. Faith and reason, being philosophically antithetical, create tension where a choice must be made. In our daily existence choices are unavoidable, and each one, like a fingerprint, is so complex that it becomes unique to the moment, the issue, and the individual. I would even suggest that such perturbation as you might experience is the by-product of a mind forced to review what has lain dormant for years, blanketed by a downy faith. If the challenge to that faith is joined, more adrenaline must flow. Experience shows that fundamental decisions cannot be avoided indefinitely, compelled as we are by the primal imperative of reason.

Thus we approach a personal philosophical dilemma. If faith, by its intrinsic demand for the forbearance of reason, compels us to deny what reason suggests, it retards intellectual growth. On the other hand, reason, by its limitless ability to qualify observation, subjects every thought and previous understanding to further review, making it difficult to form any but temporary conclusions. Fortunately the genius of human cognition makes such stark alternatives unnecessary. Personal experience, heightened by the cumulative wisdom of history, affords us a unique ability to shuttle lightly between both, without permanent affront to either. Yet the balance is tested continuously at all levels, conscious and subconscious.

Moses Meets Israel should be read as an exercise of reason in the service of a more defensible, individual faith. Even if the book does not yield new and moving insights, the loosening of ties to childhood dogma should prove salutary in itself.

A major question that will occur to the reader is the validation of important conclusions. There is a paucity of direct supporting data extrinsic to the Bible and thereby free of creedal bias. Even where external data are available, their use becomes analogic or implicative when Israel is not clearly named. The most we can hope to achieve is a sense of general validity in the biblical narratives rather than a model of incontestable "proof." Readers need not accept any statement that does not comport with their own intrinsic reason. But in fairness they must be able to intellectually defend a contrary opinion.

I hope that every reader accepts the challenge.

Notes

1. M. Noth, *The History of Israel* (New York: Harper and Row, 1960), p. 2.

Israel: "A Light to All Peoples, A Beacon for the Nations" Isa. 42:6

2

The book's title, *Moses Meets Israel*, heralds a critical juncture in the development of Western religion; Israel was conceived only when Moses approached some Semites laboring in Egypt. That joint venture, begun as the Exodus, rekindled the ember of ethical monotheism, grown cold since the Amarna Age, and ultimately engulfed the pagan world. From a tenuous beginning Israel grew to nationhood, developed a remarkable literature, and then spawned two daughter religions, Christianity and Islam. The Bible, originally Hebrew Scripture, began as the saga of a benighted people's journey to distinction, adding a universal history and a national constitution of broad, apodictic laws for enlightened behavior. Unfortunately the objective criteria for historical reportage were conspicuously subordinated to the subjective needs of a cultic structure. History was overshadowed by a burgeoning theology that for three thousand years discouraged serious question. The people slowly became aware that an extraordinary and exclusive concept of divinity had been offered to them. Their rising self-esteem was reflected in the traditions that ennobled their ancestors with portentous activity. Yet the scribes walked a fine line between recording the idealized stories as truth and the conflicting perspective of other sources. These men, charged to present a valid history of the people, recognized the intrinsic compromise they were making in modifying that history to satisfy the narcissism of a nation. It is to their everlasting credit that they included ambiguous, conflicting, and even sinister material in the national archive. Lingering concern about the Bible's truth is evident from the apologetic exegeses offered by Jewish scholars, most notably in the Middle Ages. Today our investigation of reality in biblical history benefits from the tools of technology, and interest quickens with every new discovery.

The first five books of the Bible, Leviticus excepted, purportedly describe the persons and events that created the world, founded Israel, and led them to the "land of promise." Certainly conjecture was the source of the first eleven chapters of Genesis as the onset of civilization. It was not until chapter 12 that Abraham, the named progenitor of Israel, was introduced on his way to Canaan. Two more patriarchs, Isaac and Jacob, were then added before the people found their way into Egypt, where they later met Moses.

We shall start here to examine this history critically: Which people or peoples became Israel, who the patriarchs were, when and where they appeared, and how they came to be incorporated in the sacred literature. Also, we shall trace Moses' past, what he represented to Israel, and how the remembrance of his contribution was unaccountably allowed to wither. The subsequent chapters, with supporting references, will explore these issues at length.

In the Thirteenth Century many groups living in the land of Canaan were beginning to accept monotheism and the Mosaic tradition. They are the first peoples who can be identified as Israelites with any degree of certainty. It was a long and convoluted trail that had deposited these descendants of proto-Israelites at that particular place at that particular time. Mainly Semites of the Near East, their ancestors had originally spilled out from the desert vastness of the Arabian peninsula thousands of years before. They spoke in related dialects, having first differentiated into West Semitic and Mesopotamian branches.

There were significant migratory movements between them, but both groups managed to retain discrete identities.

Among these groups were the Hab/piru, a ubiquitous people known to have lived throughout the ancient Near East and who seemed to define an early prototype of Israel. They were first recorded in the Mesopotamian region at the beginning of the Second Millennium as an essentially rootless, dispossessed class with no specific ethnicity. Not surprisingly they were mainly Semitic and constituted a politically alienated group, characterized by landlessness, outsider status, and aggressive opportunism. By the Fourteenth Century they represented a significant population within Canaan. When they were not fighting as mercenaries for various city-states, they were laying claim to the sparsely settled hill country. There is strong justification for believing that the Hab/piru were also the early Hebrews.

Three men have been identified as the progenitors of the Hebrews: Abraham, Isaac, and Jacob. The identities of these three patriarchs are beyond our reach except by the stories recorded in Genesis. Were they real men who lived earlier as ancestors of the proto-Israelites? Or were they mythical heroes constructed by later people to add depth to a genealogy that was now becoming important? We probably would be close to the truth by assuming that the answer to both questions is yes. The patriarchal legends are remarkably consonant with the known activity of the buccaneering, land-hungry Hab/piru, suggesting that these men were charismatic chieftains of especially successful groups. Although they are presented as grandfather, father, and son, they could just as well have been unknown to one another or contemporaries in geographically distinct areas within the land.

The God making promises to the patriarchs was soon construed by their descendants to be "the God of the Fathers." However, the term used, *elohim*, is clearly a plural form of the widely worshipped Canaanite god, El. This would indicate that they were not monotheists. Also, each patriarch's god had a different name, so that even if each man worshipped a single god, it was not the universal God that Moses would later introduce.

Natural disasters were common in this arid region, and movements of Semites from the Syro-Palestine area into the Nile delta for drought relief are well documented. The Egyptians were involved in international commerce during the Bronze and Iron Ages and were far more receptive to the benefits of cultural exchange than has been generally taught. They did not discourage assimilation, and indeed some persons rose to high rank and honor from the many Semitic migrations. A Joseph could become the pharaoh's confidante—even his father-in-law. Certainly such a person was ideal for later generations that wanted the honor of an eponymous ancestor.

The Amarna Age, a noteworthy era in Egyptian cultural history, was a primary, if unwitting, contributor to the development of Israel. Amenhotep IV (Akhenaten) promulgated a radically new concept of divine worship to a universal God, Aten, the sun disc. He pursued this vision over the seventeen years of his reign, despite the opposition of an entrenched priesthood. Like so many great ideas in history, it was largely ignored when first presented, having addressed a lethargic peasantry wholly dominated by a host of animal-headed gods. Akhenaten's insights were canceled and his memory effaced within twenty years after his death. The traditional religious beliefs of Egypt, like a relentless tide, swept aside his unique contribution but not before some disciples had taken its full measure, nurturing its ideas in the protected realm of memory. A few generations later the corm began to flower, finding a new life in Moses and a group of Semitic outcasts in Egypt.

The persona of Moses is axiomatic to the history of Israel, just as the new, ethical obligations that characterized its religion had to begin somewhere. The only known antecedent to Israelite monotheism occurred in Egypt during the Amarna Age.

The bicultural origins of Moses, as a Hebrew in Egyptian clothing, have been emphasized with an obsessive passion. The Torah has pointedly reinforced his Hebrew ancestry for fear that the Egyptian provenance would come to predominate. Indeed, the evidence that we have points inexorably to Moses as a high-born ethnic Egyptian, perhaps royal, and very likely a postulant of monotheistic Atenism, which had steadily receded from official favor after Akhenaten's death. Realizing that the concept had been muffled in Egypt, Moses attempted to graft it onto the consciousness of a small group of Semites whose marginal status presented him with that opportunity. He hoped that they might preserve and nurture it on their own soil if only they could be moved away from Egypt. Pharaoh cooperated for reasons of his own, allowing Moses to leave the country freely with the people he championed.

Moses showed an appropriate understanding of the difficulties that he would face in shepherding a rude band of foreigners across several hundred miles of untamed wilderness while teaching them to foreswear their more atavistic urges and to adopt the self-denial that would support an evolutionary social compact. He selected the Levites as armed guards for internal as well as external security. These men, supposedly of the "tribe" of Levi, had an earlier history of belligerency and likely were serving in the army of pharaoh, given their access to the newly introduced sword. So many of them had Egyptian names and associations that they could have been either native Egyptians or Egyptianized Semites.

At the same time, Moses acquiesced to the traditional religious sensibilities of the people by appointing Aaron and his sons to continue in their previous cultic roles. To ensure the ascendancy of his own monotheism over an established Amoritic pantheon, Moses gradually eased the Levites into a sacerdotal function alongside the Aaronites. The Levites were to be a countervailing force against the people's native religion and a positive influence toward modifying their spiritual orientation. Prior to that, the many confrontations between the two groups had been contained by shrewd diplomacy, the overwhelming power of the Levites, and not least the frequent invocation of God. But the gap between the abstract divinity of Moses and the native idolatry of the Hebrews was too wide to bridge until they met the Midianites in Sinai. These people and their traditions offered Moses a key that would link all their disparate practices into a broad coalition.

The nomadic Midianites roamed widely over the area of northwest Arabia, southern Canaan, and the Sinai peninsula. It is quite likely that they recognized a kinship with some of the Exodus Semites who had migrated to Egypt in previous generations. The Midianites worshipped Yahveh, a supposedly fierce and bloodthirsty god whose name was previously unknown to Moses. The biblical description of this deity indicates that he derived his power from a volcanic setting. If the Exodus people could identify with and accept Yahveh, this god could be declared the one and only God and integrated with the fundamentals of the Mosaic religion. The adoption of a common deity would make the people more tractable to Moses' rigid demands. Perhaps he intuitively recognized that ethical principles, especially those requiring self-denial, would reside more comfortably within a tangible, familiar divinity until the two were no longer separable. It was less than crucial whether God's name would be Aten, Elohim, or Yahveh.

Moses, possessed by a mission to elevate religion to a transcendent moral level, was determined to accomplish it within some Semites who happened to be in Egypt at the time. But the world often destroys the visionary as it honors the vision. The Exodus group spent the next two years in the wilderness of Sinai and southern Canaan, presumably learning to appreciate the benefits of an encompassing morality in which the rules applied equally to everyone. It was not easy; the people often reverted to their pagan habits, as in the notorious episode of the golden calf. The Aaronites and their allies began to show independence by fomenting insurrection. Although the Levites maintained a fierce loyalty to Moses, ensuring a temporary stability, the continuous "murmuring" and "rebelling" indicate a persistent dissatisfaction with his leadership. Resentment of his alien origin grew as the people gained confidence in themselves and in their emerging native leaders. Perhaps his obsession with imprinting the demands of an exacting God on a resentful people was too intimidating, making a backlash inevitable. Moses was not to live much longer.

The Exodus of tradition can be fairly dated to the latter part of the Thirteenth Century. Within a few generations all the cardinal elements for the establishment of Israel were in place in Canaan: the Ten Commandments with their just and egalitarian rules for human behavior, a cadre of committed believers, and groups of kindred persons eager to embrace the new ideals. But the mythic quality of the Moses biography and the cant of the miracle episodes indicate that strategic alterations had been made in the interests of a viable creed.

It is curious that previous commentators did not look for signs of a natural paroxysm that would have buried Moses and ended the conflict even sooner. Scripture all but begs us to see this happening. Yet it was only in 1922 that the subject was timidly broached by a German scholar who read into Hosea 13:1 the murder of Moses by the Hebrews. Sigmund Freud confirmed this suggestion by applying the tenets of psychoanalytic theory; the jealousy implicit in the Oedipal conflict was acted out by the Hebrews against the man with all the power—the symbolic father, Moses.

There is presumptive evidence that the demise of Moses involved unpalatable and subsequently repressed memories. If the people who owed their well-being to Moses killed him, they would try to assuage their guilt by denying and even repressing the episode. A strong case for this happening can be made from the suddenness with which Moses, his deeds, and his sons disappeared from the later literature of Israel. Freud's classic concept holds that what has been repressed frequently returns to consciousness in changed but acceptable form. This is exemplified in the Torah's near apotheosis of Moses while he lived and in a death story that finds God punishing him for an almost risible lapse of obedience. But the point remains that the foremost leader of Israel suffered a mysterious death and afterward disappeared ignominiously from the consciousness of the nation—a response contrary to a people's usual memory of its founding hero.

We are not the first generation to ponder the many discrepancies in Scripture; scholars have tried to explain the meaning of ambiguous passages for thousands of years. But because most could not distance themselves sufficiently from their emotional attachments, the commentaries tended to confirm, and even augment, the original textual ambiguities. Those scholars allowed their loyalty to the perceived inerrancy of the Word to dictate exculpatory conclusions rather than to probe for direct, rational explanations. Our contemporary skills in text criticism and the understanding of human nature now provide the opportunity to read the text with more clarity, especially about Moses and his relationship to the people he led.

The Book of Joshua ostensibly completes the story of the arrival and settlement in the Promised Land by the Exodus group. With the certainty that they numbered only in the hundreds, or a few thousand at most, it is very unlikely that these people could have successfully confronted the powerful military potential of the Canaanite city-states. Joshua's resounding military victories over the natives are now generally discounted by scholars, in turn raising the question of how else Israel could have become a dominant force in history from such humble beginnings, all within a few hundred years.

The answer obviously involves other peoples already in the land and surrounding areas. Canaan was host to several large groups seeking security outside the organized city-states, then in the throes of internecine strife. The Hab/piru, those part-time mercenaries who expropriated living space in the hills; peasants displaced from the lowlands by social and economic warfare; and seminomads disrupted by climatic conditions and seeking more stability in agricultural work were all caught up in events they could not control. It must have been obvious to each of them that their traditional gods were singularly useless in bettering their precarious existence.

Into this maelstrom wandered the ragged band of newcomers from Egypt, having spent two years in the wilderness, learning to live by a more exacting moral code. Their Mosaic religion, with its demonstrably beneficent God whose miracles and justice were available for only a promise of fidelity, proved to be most attractive to these other victims of fate. The brilliant spark of light, carried out of Egypt by Moses and transplanted to the Exodus group, became the focus for the disestablished of Canaan. That they were already distantly related to the newcomers settling in their midst made the adoption of their monotheism somewhat easier.

It was the consummate time for all groups claiming the "promised" land to come together in a loose confederation of mutual purpose. It happened, albeit slowly and imperfectly, when they accepted the Covenant with an abstract God of justice. They became Israelites by deliberate conversion, fueling an evolutionary spurt in humankind's worldview.

The world got lucky when Moses met Israel.

Asia:
The Primordium

3

The small corner of the world where our quest for the origins of Israel must begin is the Near East during the Middle and Late Bronze Ages (circa 2200–1200 B.C.E.). A span of one millennium in pointing to a date might appear irresolute if it were not for the almost total absence of more precise indicators. The theoretical date at which an evolutionary process is thought to begin must first be bracketed within the extremes of probability. Only when specific associations are made can a narrower date range be considered. At best the chronology of early biblical events must be considered with a latitude of decades, even centuries.

The first extrinsic mention of Israel occurred when an Egyptian pharaoh inscribed his military successes in pacifying various places along the eastern Mediterranean coastline. The stele of Merneptah made mention of an "Israel" around 1200 B.C.E. This reference can therefore be considered as a *terminus a quo*, the earliest point of awareness, although there is no indication how long before this Israel might have been in existence. Also, the stele supplies little information about the form or structure of Israel other than a name. An institution incubates for a variable period until reaching the critical mass at which it can be distinguished from its matrix. A consensus of scholars suggests that the history of Israel began when the twelve-tribe body, living in cultic unity, was recognized. This moment probably came later, during the Twelfth Century, and the Israel of Merneptah was thus a "proto-Israel," already of indefinite duration.

But who were the people before they joined into the tribes that characterized Israel? Where did they come from and when? In what ways were they distinguished from their neighbors, and what brought them together? Questions such as these direct our attention to western Asia early in the Second Millennium.

Conditions in the Ancient Near East

Sumerian records of 5000 years ago attest to the fact that a reasonable degree of civilization was already present in the southwestern part of Asia at the beginning of the Bronze Ages. The area extending from the Persian Gulf in the east to the Mediterranean coast in the west has been called the Fertile Crescent. It encompassed the entire valley of the Tigris and Euphrates Rivers as they emptied into the Persian Gulf. Both rivers arise in the Anatolian Plateau and flow southeastward, at first separating widely in the plains of Mesopotamia and then moving toward each other as they near the sea. The amply watered lower valleys are flat and extremely fertile. The gulf itself in earliest times extended about 130 miles deeper into the land mass than it does at present, and the two rivers emptied into it separately. By the Middle Bronze Age (2200–1500 B.C.E.) large Semitic elements of Akkadians and Babylonians were living there. Some smaller rivers to the west of the headwaters flowed southwesterly into the Mediterranean Sea, also yielding highly productive land along that coast.

The Fertile Crescent was named by James Breasted in 1916 because it was uniquely conducive to the development of agricultural, and hence sedentary, societies.[1] It can be traced arcing northwestward from the Persian Gulf, bypassing the arid Arabian Peninsula in the south and gradually turning westerly and then south along the Mediterranean coast. The Fertile Crescent is functionally contiguous with the Nile River delta farther to the west.

The horns of the crescent are about 1000 miles apart, and its width varies considerably. The narrowest part of the arable land is at the western horn, where Israel came to be located. In the middle, where the crescent broadens to about 300 miles, its northern edge nestles into the foothills of Asia Minor. The land narrows progressively into the eastern horn, following the two great Mesopotamian rivers to the gulf.

By the beginning of the Second Millennium trade routes in this region were well established from one end to the other, with the known permanent roads concentrated lengthwise through the Syro-Palestine corridor. The "Way of the Sea," the later Roman *Via Maris*, ran along the coastal plain, whereas the "King's Highway," the later Roman *Via Nova*, traversed the plateau just east of the Jordan River. Over these roads came the people who were to become Israel, as well as traders, merchants, and armies.

The Fertile Crescent varies markedly in climate, topography, and fertility. It is not a uniformly productive land of rich soil and plentiful rainfall. Along the outer periphery of the area are mountainous ranges: the Zagros on the east, the Taurus and the Anatolian headlands to the north, and the Lebanon and Anti-Lebanon ranges within the western horn. Cradled by the peripheral mountains, the land slopes downward to highlands and plateaus, gradually becoming plains and valleys through which run the life-giving waters. The endless Arabian Desert lies south of the crescent. The steep mountains could not support grain crops, but the upper plains, although only moderately fertile with rocky, unstable soil, would nevertheless sprout lush vegetation after the spring rains. Seminomadic peoples moved into this region for the purpose of grazing and expanding their flocks. In southern Mesopotamia the annual overflow of the rivers laid down massive amounts of alluvial soil that fostered crop growth. Demographic stability came with successful agriculture, and the first recorded western civilization, the Sumerian, developed here.

The climate along the concave southern edge of the Fertile Crescent is distinctly arid, the soil less fertile, and the population more nomadic. The Early and Middle Bronze Ages (3000–1500) saw frequent incursions by peripheral peoples. Later migrations within the crescent involved West Semites, known as *amurru*, or Amorites (Westerners), from central and eastern Syria. They constituted the major element of Akkad, an indistinct political entity of central Mesopotamia north of Sumer. There were also depredations from the south by fierce Arabian tribesmen, most of whom either did not remain or otherwise disappeared within the land. From the northern and eastern mountain areas came non-Semitic peoples, such as the Urartu, Hurrians, Hittites, and Kassites. Population shifts seemed to be mainly within the fertile Mesopotamian lowlands during the period of the Middle Bronze and Iron Ages (2200–900). Migrations increased in a predominantly westward direction toward the Mediterranean Sea. Peoples of various ethnic backgrounds were on the move, seeking to sustain and improve their lives.

Nomadism was generally incompatible with ownership of land. Self-sufficiency became the highest virtue because mobility did not afford easy replenishment of supplies. As a group traveled, it had to carry ample food staples for a given period and to assure itself of watering places and grazing lands along the route. And not least, a group had to have sufficient armed men for the protection of personnel and property against brigandage.

These interrelated requirements clearly defined the optimal size of any migratory group. The minimum number of able-bodied men who could discourage attacks against the group, and conversely could ensure success in depredations against other groups, was the factor of success. A group that traveled with too many people was vulnerable if food could not be procured along the way. Too few people, unable to defend themselves against predators, lowered the chance for sustained independence. A group was bound together primarily by family relationships, but in the harshness of the desert environment some ethnic and cultural differences were tolerated in the interest of group survival.

One characteristic of nomads was their sense of solidarity and collectivity. Security considerations bred a tribal chauvinism that placed the well-being of the group equal to or above that of the individual. Property rights and ownership were mainly communal, with only personal possessions exempted.[2] Hospitality to strangers and a zealous egalitarianism were obligatory in that unremitting climate, and group leadership usually devolved to elders whose experience with the past was seen to augur well for the group's future. The most charismatic elder became the undisputed leader, and the tribal organization was stabilized around him. However, the position was not hereditary, and the leader's authority was often limited; he was essentially *primus inter pares*. Without pressing the analogy too far, the present-day Bedouins of the Arabian Peninsula represent a close approximation of the social structure of the patriarchal clans of Genesis, which become our first reference point for the people of Israel.

True nomadism did not exist until the middle of the Second Millennium, when the camel became domesticated. This animal was uniquely adapted to desert existence, capable of traveling long distances without food or water and subsisting on fibrous vegetation growing on the desert steppes. Before camels the pack animal of choice was the jackass or donkey, and the patriarchs are still considered by some to have been "donkey-caravaneers."[3] These animals needed more water and a level of nutrition not readily found in the desert proper but more likely at its periphery. Such groups were technically seminomads in that they required more frequent stops near cultivated areas to replenish their own and their animals' needs.

A single species of domesticated animal, such as sheep, goats, cattle, or asses, might be the focus of a specific group, although there were also mixed herds. During each year, some changes of location were necessary. When grasses and other plants were lush, usually in the spring, the entire group, or a part of it, would lead the animals to graze in the hills, returning to their former locations when there was no more edible growth. Occasionally they sought out new areas more receptive to them and their animals. They purchased and sold necessities there and even engaged in some seasonal agricultural activity themselves before repeating the cycle. By arrangements with the landowners, they grazed their animals on the stubble of a harvested field, thus dressing and fertilizing it in return for the fodder.

People who were involved with pastoral nomadism usually came to this occupation because there was insufficient tillable land to support the whole group.[4] An example is found in the Joseph story, in which a portion of the community—in this case his brothers—had taken the flocks to a distant, hilly region for grazing while Jacob and his retainers stayed in the lowlands (Gen. 37:12–17). However, pastoral nomads were not necessarily landless. They often engaged in some agricultural work on land of their own or that of others or were part of a community that did.[5]

It could not have been long before the seminomads realized that a sedentary or rooted existence held fewer hazards than did their seasonal migrations and began to settle, making permanent contact and natural alliances with others. Thus many groups with particular ethnic differences within a common heritage could live side by side over a vast area of the ancient Near East. Cultural homogenization frequently took place by conscious adaptation, political necessity, and intermarriage. It has been pointed out that the major channel of cultural transmission was the colony, or enclave.[6] That these were common and normative within an ethnically diverse area such as Canaan is suggested by the presence of Hittites in Gen. 23 and Hivites (Hurrians) in Gen. 34. Both peoples were originally non-Semites but came to dominate large Semitic populations. Their specific ethnicity has little relevance beyond historical interest, since they all ultimately merged with others and lost their original identities. Given the natural accommodation of peoples living in mutual proximity over long periods of time, the identification and tracking of any specific group becomes a very tenuous process.

Exactly who were the Semites who populated Syro-Palestine, and who were the major migratory peoples? It is generally accepted that they all originated within the desert of Arabia in prehistory and later fanned out northward into the Fertile Crescent. The end of the Third Millennium finds them in Mesopotamia and Syro-Palestine. Their language, despite regional nuances, stemmed from a common origin. All Semitic dialects had a basic consonantal system and prominent glottic and uvular phonation that made them different from other languages of the time.[7] The earliest known dialect is Akkadian, which was also the language of the Babylonians and Assyrians, all Mesopotamian Semites. Other distinct dialects have been recognized: Canaanite (which includes Hebrew), Aramaic (from northern and eastern Syria and later becoming the *lingua franca* of Israel), Arabic, and Ethiopic.[8] The Semitic character at the core of the Near East was never in jeopardy, despite the sporadic incursions by non-Semites.

The first translation of cuneiform writing occurred less than 200 years ago, exposing the world to a new understanding of the early social, political, and economic conditions that obtained within the ancient Near East. Many texts from recently discovered sites have become available for study and comparison: Cappadocian (Turkey, Nineteenth Century), Mari (Eastern Syria, Eighteenth Century), Babylonian (Southern Iraq, Nineteenth to Sixteenth Centuries), Nuzi (Eastern Iraq, Fifteenth Century), Ras Shamra/Ugarit (Syrian coastline, Fourteenth Century), and the Amarna letters (Egypt, Fourteenth Century). In pursuit of the early origins of Israel, we are uncommonly fortunate to have access to these records, many of which describe a way of life in startling parallel to biblical narratives. Israel obviously had authentic origins within the geographic setting of the greater Near East.

An awareness of Nuzi life came less than 100 years ago with the discovery of that ancient city close to modern Kirkuk (Iraq) and many thousands of individual clay tablets written mainly in the Akkadian dialect. The Hurrians came there, achieved dominance, and ultimately left their stamp on the city's Semitic culture. Their legal codes and family customs have remarkable correspondence to those involving the patriarchs of Israel. The relationship is only inferential, but Ephraim Speiser concludes that the traditions from which the biblical customs derived were coincidental with Nuzi or Hurrian patterns.[9] He therefore claims strong support for dating the patriarchs to the Hurrian period. But others hold that the Nuzi documents describe specific and uniquely personal contracts and should not be considered identical with patriarchal customs.[10] It will be seen in a later chapter that the process of dating the patriarchs by their customs is both complex and uncertain.

The continual movement of Near Eastern peoples into the river valleys strained the resources of existing population centers. There was little surcease to the aggressiveness of incoming peoples and host vacillation between resistance and accommodation; the overall effect was to hasten the process of cultural assimilation. The population that originally sprang from the Arabian Desert was Semitic, but many who ruled the subsequent empires of the region were not.

The Indo-European Hittites probably came from the Danube basin and extended into the Caucasus. They could have entered Asia Minor from the northeast or from the west, via the Bosporus.[11] Over the course of several hundred years of merging with indigenous Anatolians, they became a powerful empire in the middle of the Second Millennium, muscling into northern Mesopotamia and Canaan. They are clearly mentioned several times in Scripture. Their empire began to disintegrate at the end of the Thirteenth Century, when they were invaded by the Sea People from the western shores of the Mediterranean Sea and its islands. The Philistines, so prominent as antagonists of early Israel, are considered to have been part of the same invasion.

The Hurrians were another non-Semitic people, sweeping into northern Mesopotamia from the Caspian Sea area, specifically around Lake Urmia, as early as the Third Millennium.[12] Probably related to the Urartu (later Armenians), they ruled over a predominantly Semitic population with whom they merged. Expert horsemen, the Hurrians were much-feared warriors, and their empire, called Mitanni after an ancient chieftain, reached its peak around the middle of the Second Millennium. The Old Testament refers to them as "Horites" and "Hivites."

The Elamites were yet another non-Semitic people, originating in the Zagros Mountains (the western part of modern Iran). These people dominated southern Mesopotamia for a short time early in the Second Millennium but remained as a secondary power in the region for more than 1000 years before yielding to the Persians. Gen. 14 contains the only biblical reference to Elam, but it lacks historical relevance because King Chedorlaomer, against whom Abraham fought and won, is not otherwise known. Extant documents list forty kings of Elam in the period 2100–1100, but Chedorlaomer is not among them.[13] However, the possibility exists that he had another name that was unknown to the biblical writers.

Literary Influences

Much of what can be inferred about an ancient people's culture comes from the literature that they created. In this we are fortunate that the civilizations of the Near East left behind extensive literary evidence, early germinal tales, contracts and business records, legal codes, diplomatic discourse, and even a primitive historiography via King-lists and Omen-lists. This is also true of Israel, although the earliest evidence is found only in the Torah, which reached its essentially final form about 1000-plus years after the older Near Eastern documents.

In Genesis the story of humankind was extended back to the beginning of the world. Creation legend, obligatory for an unschooled audience, was grafted as a head onto the body of a continuing epic history. Few modern scholars seriously consider the first eleven chapters of Genesis as valid history. Yet the rest of the Torah, with its remarkably descriptive details, obliges us to seek within it the skeletal remains of real persons and real events. It can never be a history that fulfills all criteria of modern scholarship, but perhaps we may at least be able to sweep away some of the simplifications and obfuscations that have trivialized the picture over time.

The first eleven chapters of Genesis have very close connections to older Near Eastern texts. Alexander Heidel compared the details and order of the creation process in Genesis, commonly referred to in Hebrew as *B'reshith* ("In the beginning . . .") with the Babylonian version, *Enuma elish* ("When on high . . .").[14] The chart below highlights the salient features of both texts.

BABYLONIAN CREATION MYTH	GENESIS
Divine spirit and cosmic matter coexist and are coeternal.	Divine spirit creates cosmic matter and exists independently of it.
Primeval chaos; Tiamat (the mother goddess) is enveloped in darkness.	The earth is a desolate waste, with darkness covering the deep.
Light emanates from the gods.	Light is created.
The firmament is created.	
Dry land is created.	
The luminaries are created.	
Man is created.	
The gods rest and celebrate.	God rests and sanctifies the seventh day.

Many of the creation motifs in Genesis were influenced by Sumerian literature. Although the Sumerians disappeared long before the earliest estimate of Israel's arrival on the scene, they affected all the ancient Near Eastern cultures, including Canaanite and Aramean. They anticipated the Garden of Eden by a story of divine paradise on earth, reserved for the use of gods, although a single mortal did gain access. They had a goddess, Nin-ti, who was created to heal the god Enki's rib, one of his "sick organs" that was associated with his giving birth. *Nin-*

ti in Sumerian can mean both "the lady of the rib" and "to make live." In the Genesis tale woman is made from Adam's rib, and the name Eve means "she who makes live." Even though the word for *rib* in Hebrew has nothing in common with "who makes live," the association of a rib and birth has to be more than coincidental.[15]

Even with significant differences in the creation stories, they are strikingly similar. Three explanations for the close relationship between them have been offered. First, *Enuma elish* dates back at least to the period of 1900–1600, and the biblical tradition, existing for many centuries before it was recorded, could possibly have been contemporaneous with it. Second, the Babylonian language and script were used all over the Near East, and therefore their creation and deluge stories were very likely known to the Israelites. It was common at that time to adopt foreign ideas without acknowledgment. Third, both versions may have sprung from a common source, although none has as yet been identified.[16]

There is another notable parallel in Babylonian and biblical tales. The Gilgamesh epic contains an extended description of a deluge that is mimicked in Genesis (6:13–8:22). As with the creation myth, the two tales have so many obvious similarities that a close relationship is beyond doubt. The major differences seem to be in the theological details.

In Genesis God's acts are purposeful and directed to the improvement of humanity, whereas the Babylonian deities seem frivolous and unconcerned with the sequelae of their acts. To clarify the complex intersecting points in the two flood tales, I have prepared a chart on page 28 from Heidel, similar to the previous one on the creation myth.[17]

It is evident that the mythic cosmogony presented in the first eleven chapters of Genesis is not unique to any time or place. The generation myths that arose in the Israelite tradition, as well as in other cultures, satisfied the yearning of all human beings to comprehend the world and their place in it. Some persons even then must have harbored doubts about the validity of the cre-

GILGAMESH	GENESIS
Deluge decreed by an assembly of gods.	Deluge decided on by a single god.
Reason uncertain; ordered by the great gods. Unspecified sin of man mentioned.	Reason: the moral depravity of the human race.
Destruction decreed for all, but Utnapishtim given immortality after the deluge was over.	Pious Noah and his family spared to repopulate the earth.
Utnapistim told by god Ea only to destroy his house and to build a boat.	Noah received direct communication from God about cause and future.
Boat to be seven stories high, cube-shaped, 200 feet to a side (intrinsically unstable).	The ark to be 3 stories high, rectangular: 450 feet long, 75 feet wide, and 45 feet high.
On board were Utnapishtim, all his gold and silver, as well as all his relations, game and beasts of the field, and craftsmen.	On board were Noah, his wife, their three sons, their wives, and one male and female of every living thing (alternate inventory in Gen.7:2, 3).
Rain and mighty winds, thunder, and lightning, with breaking of dikes and reservoirs.	Torrential rains and eruption of subterranean waters.
Deluge lasted seven days and seven nights.	Deluge lasted forty days and forty nights, but the flood persisted for another 150 days.
Boat landed on Mount Nisir, probably in Armenia.	Boat landed on Mount Ararat, probably in Armenia.
Seven days after the boat landed, Utnapishtim sent out a dove. It did not return.	Forty days after other mountains were seen, Noah sent out a raven. It did not return.
After an unspecified time, a swallow was released and came back.	Seven days later, a dove was let out, and it returned.
Later a raven was sent out, and it stayed away.	Another dove was released, and it returned with an olive leaf.
	In seven days Noah released a third dove. It stayed away.
Utnapishtim left the boat at his own time and "sent forth (everything) to the four winds."	Two months after the waters had dried up, God told Noah to go forth.

ation stories. Yet in the absence of an alternative understanding, these tales offered some internal coherence to their lives.

The fashion in contemporary historiography was to ennoble an issue by beginning at the moment of creation, and the Israelites followed the same pattern. Given that the literature

H	TORAH
#53-36: If a freeman was too lazy to make the dike for his field strong enough and it broke causing damage to his neighbor's fields he must make good in various ways the damage caused.	Exod. 22:4–5: When a man lets his livestock loose to graze in another's land and so allows a field or a vineyard to be impaired he must make restitution. If a fire starts and stacked standing or growing grain is consumed he who started the fire must make restitution.
(It should be noted that flooding was an ever-present danger in the agricultural milieu of Mesopotamia, whereas fire and unconstrained animal grazing were the ultimate agents of loss in the drier, pastoral Canaan.)	
#200-1: If a freeman knocks out a tooth of one of his rank, they shall knock out his tooth. If he knocks out a commoner's tooth, he shall pay one-third mina of silver.	Lev. #24:19f: If anyone maims his fellow, as he has done so shall it be done to him: fracture for fracture, eye for eye, tooth for tooth.
#250-1: If an ox, in the normal course of events, gores a free-man to death, there is no claim. But if the ox was a known gorer, and the owner did nothing to restrain the ox, and he gored a freeman, he must pay one-half mina of silver. If it was a slave that was gored, he must pay one-third mina of silver.	Exod. #21:28–32: When an ox gores a man, woman, or child to death, the ox shall be killed but its flesh not eaten. The owner is not to be punished. If the ox has gored before, and its warned owner failed to take precautions, and it gores someone to death, then the owner shall also be put to death. However, he may redeem his life by paying whatever ransom is laid upon him. If the ox gores a slave, the owner must pay 30 shekels of silver to the master, and the ox shall be killed.

from Mesopotamia is dated from early in the Second Millennium, whereas the biblical traditions appear several hundred years later, there is little likelihood that the sequence of influence could have been reversed.

Additional evidence linking Israel with Mesopotamia is contained in the legal codes of both. The Code of Hammurabi, containing 282 numbered laws, represented an epochal standardization of the rules of justice. They were promulgated by edict in the second year of his reign (probably at the beginning of the Eighteenth Century), mainly for internal administration.[18] The major portion of the laws deal with mercantile matters. The Torah, in its last four books—Exodus, Leviticus, Numbers, and Deuteronomy—also contains laws for civil justice. These, however, are admixed liberally with a moral code, creating an ambiance in which all laws appear to be God's laws and not made by humans. Although the moral level of Israel's laws generally express a greater humaneness, and certainly a more balanced egalitarian quality than do those of other contemporary nations, the remarkable similarities in the area of personal injury again betray the influence of earlier Mesopotamia.

The Hammurabi laws, designated on page 29 by (H #), have been taken from James Pritchard[19] but abridged. The corresponding Torah verses are likewise abridged.

The parallelism between the literatures of Mesopotamia and Israel has a logical explanation; the patriarchs had been part of the Mesopotamian culture. They would naturally have carried the familiar tales and conventional laws to new settlements.

The Canaanites

A people generally referred to as Canaanites occupied much of the western horn of the Fertile Crescent from the Third Millennium on. They were Semites of that amorphous group of Amorites who first migrated to the area. Before moving to the Mediterranean coast, they occupied the central Syrian steppes and were known to the Sumerians by 2600 B.C.E.[20] It is not certain whether the original settlers arrived via Mesopotamia or migrated from parts of the Arabian peninsula directly to the Syro-Palestine area. But they were an important element in the downfall of the Third Dynasty of Ur (circa 2000 B.C.E.) and in the final disappearance of the Sumerians. Exposed to the continual pressure of many ethnic strains, particularly the Hittites in Asia Minor and the Hurrians from the mountainous regions to the northeast, the Canaanites developed a unique ability to receive, accommodate, and then phagocytize the intruders.

Most of the small Canaanite kingdoms, actually city-states, disappeared around 1200 B.C.E. with the advent of the Sea People from the west and the Arameans from the east. Thereafter the term Amorite, although still used extensively, lost its specificity. The Assyrians of the Eighth Century used Amorite and Hittite synonymously. In the Persian period (after the Sixth Century) Amorite referred to the people of northern Arabia.[21] In the parallel passages of Num. 14:39–45 and Deut. 1:41–46, Canaanites and Amorites are interchanged. Also, in 1 Samuel there is considerable overlap between Amorites and Philistines.

The soil of the region's lowlands was so fertile that Canaan was always an exporter of food. International commerce was attracted by the excellent seaports, and Canaanite cities became transshipment centers for goods between distant Mediterranean lands and Mesopotamia, Asia Minor, and Egypt. Lying athwart the major routes of trade, possessing a monopoly in a highly prized purple dye made from local mollusks, and benefiting from an agricultural abundance, Canaan was most attractive to migratory peoples seeking better opportunity, as well as a highly prized addition to the imperial designs of aggressive neighbors. The open coastal plain, running the entire length of the seaboard, and the longitudinal inland valleys opened Canaan to incursions from several directions. Yet the people never bonded like others in this region. Perhaps their entrepreneurial instincts taught them that economic strength was the only way to ensure survival under temporary foreign governance. Given their adaptive capacity, they ultimately survived Hittites from the north, Hurrians and Arameans from the east, Sea Peoples from the Aegean and Mediterranean Seas, and Egyptians from the south. In the process the Canaanite cities developed an intense intermural rivalry.

It has been thought that the early Canaanites learned the art of building impregnable walls around their cities from the Hyksos, who supposedly came from the northeast, perhaps from the shores of the Caspian Sea. The Hyksos were new to Canaan in the first part of the Second Millennium and were probably related to the Hurrians. They introduced horses and chariot warfare, which required the service of a professional warrior class. This may have fostered a feudalism with privileges and inheritable fiefs, which stratified Canaanite society.[22] Isolated enclaves, each protected by a massive wall and ruled by a petty tyrant, gave Canaan its profusion of city-states. Little concern was given to those outside the walls, even in their own hinterlands. The historical influence of the Hyksos as Canaanites will be considered in context with their involvement in Egypt.

The Second Millennium saw so much population mobility that specific origins are difficult to place. The rooted elements continued to experience pressure from restless and unsettled groups of people, mostly Semites, who coveted land for themselves. There also was a continuous intrusion by some of these same groups into northeast Egypt, predominantly in the delta region. During the Thirteenth Century, and most likely in the latter half, some of them left Egypt and returned to the Canaanite lands in one or more versions of the Exodus. Although they still carried traditions in common with related groups that never left Canaan, more significantly they bore traces of a unique Egyptian experience. When the new spiritual concepts carried by the Exodus people were made available to the Canaanite masses, yearning for economic and political liberation after generations of fratricidal war, the birth of Israel became inevitable.

Notes

1. J. H. Breasted, *Ancient Times: A History of the Early World* (Boston: Ginn, 1916), pp. 100-107.
2. S. Moscati, *Ancient Semitic Civilizations* (London: Elek Books, 1957), p. 38.
3. W. F. Albright, "Abram the Hebrew: A New Archeological Interpretation," *Bulletin of the American Schools of Oriental Research* 163(1963):36–54.
4. G. E. Mendenhall, "The Hebrew Conquest of Palestine," *Biblical Archeology* 25(1962):69.
5. N. K. Gottwald, *The Tribes of Yahweh* (New York: Orbis Books, 1979), p. 438.
6. C. H. Gordon, *Before the Bible* (New York: Harper and Row, 1962), p. 26.
7. S. Moscati, op. cit., p. 25.
8. Ibid., p. 29f.
9. E. A. Speiser, *Genesis*, The Anchor Bible Series (Garden City, NY: Doubleday, 1986), pp. xl-xliii.
10. T. L. Thompson, *The Historicity of the Patriarchal Narratives* (New York: Walter de Gruyter, 1974), p. 322f.
11. J. G. Macqueen, *The Hittites* (Boulder: Westview Press, 1975), p. 25f.
12. I. M. Diakonoff, "Evidence of the Ethnic Division of the Hurrians," in *Studies on the Civilization and Culture Nuzi and the Hurrians*, ed. M. A. Morrison and D. I. Owen, (Winona Lake: Eisenbrauns, 1981), pp. 77–89.
13. I. Hunt, *The World of the Patriarchs* (Englewood Cliffs, NJ: Prentice-Hall, 1967), p. 25.
14. A. Heidel, *The Babylonian Genesis*, 2d ed. (Chicago: University of Chicago Press, 1951), p. 129.
15. S. N. Kramer, *From the Tablets of Sumer* (Indian Hills, CO: The Falcon's Wing Press, 1956), p. 172.
16. A. Heidel, op. cit., p. 133f.
17. A. Heidel, *The Gilgamesh Epic*, 2d ed. (Chicago: University.of Chicago Press, 1949), pp. 224–269.
18. J. Oates, *Babylon* (London: Thames and Hudson, 1986), p. 62.
19. J. B. Pritchard, *Ancient Near Eastern Texts*, 3rd ed. (Princeton, NJ: Princeton University Press, 1969), pp. 168–176.
20. H. Haldar, *Who Were the Amorites?* (Leiden: E. J. Brill, 1971), p. 4.
21. J. Van Seters, "The Terms 'Amorite' and 'Hittite' in the Old Testament," *Vetus Testamentum* (1972) 22: 64–81.
23. J. Gray, *The Canaanites* (London: Thames and Hudson, 1961), p. 35.

Background and   4
Cultural Development

During the first half of the Second Millennium, no Israelites can be identified in the Near East: only distant, potential antecedents. By the mid-Tenth Century, however, Israel had become an established kingdom. To understand the transformation of vaguely defined proto-Israelites into recognizable Israelites, we must first look at the most obvious source, the Hebrew Bible, particularly the Torah portion. But this proprietary source raises an immediate problem: How much can we rely on a literary work that was written primarily to support a creed and only tangentially as history?

Genesis begins the definition of Israel by developing a theme of special individuals who are called on to transmit a reciprocal relationship with God to their descendants. Clearly the attributes that bound Israel together were more important to the author(s) than an accurate résumé of the route by which it reached substance. The traditions contain much that is recognizable as universal human behavior, but the criteria for objective history, as we understand it today, are lacking. What we have instead is a stock of creedal precepts, wrapped in a layered saga of accomplishments and basted with narcissistic legends—essentially a literary baklava, easily swallowed and nourishing to the infant ego of Israel. Yet few scholars would deny that a trove of historical seeds are hidden within the bulky pod.

The first unequivocal indication that the Torah sprang from human sources rather than the traditional belief that God simply dictated it to Moses came in 1753. A French physician, Jean Astruc, noting persistent differences in style and perspective, suggested that Moses had at least two sources available when he wrote it. In one document the name of God was Elohim; in the other it was Yahveh.[1] It is remarkable that the intrinsic differences were not detected earlier, given the concentrated attention by Jewish and Christian scholars over the previous 2000-plus years. The storytellers and scribes who were most proximate to the onset of the ambiguous traditions must have entertained some reservations even as they embraced and transmitted them. Perhaps open skepticism would have been dangerous in a time when mere survival demanded all-inclusive group loyalty. When the Enlightenment permitted biblical criticism to burgeon as a learned discipline, several sources of tradition became apparent. Today we can readily accept the idea that no matter when the narratives were fixed, they used authentic memories in becoming protected traditions. Not only have sources with unique perspectives been identified, but also the textual differences have become signatures for each. It is thought that the geographic orientation and ancestral loyalty were factors in the source documents, some expressing a compulsion to enhance and protect cultic purity. Whoever the writer(s) were, and their identities are unknown, they nevertheless inscribed the traditions they received in distinct and recognizable styles.

Biblical Sources

The first four books of the Torah—namely Genesis, Exodus, Leviticus, and Numbers—contain three early sources, designated as J, E, and P. The recognition that the Bible had several unique sources gave rise to the Documentary Hypothesis theory. Although the various documents may not have been contemporaneous with one another, there is general agreement that the one labeled J is the oldest. Biblical research of the nineteenth and early twentieth centuries was dominated by German scholars, and their spelling of Jahweh gave the J source its name. The writing style is characterized by a terse, dramatic narration, with characters generally portrayed in spare, balanced prose. It was a master storyteller who could find cosmic significance in ordinary human events, and it was always assumed that the writer was a man—that is, until Harold Bloom suggested that she might have been a woman.[2] Unfortunately such speculation does little to narrow the search, but the thought was long overdue.

The J source is conveniently associated with the tribe or territory of Judah and tentatively dated to the Tenth Century. This source is distinctive by naming Reuel as Moses' father-in-law and Horeb as the mountain where the people gathered to receive the Law from God. The United Monarchy, under David and Solomon, catapulted the Israelites onto a stage where culture came with its own mythology, warranting the destiny of its people. Responding to the need for an epic history with appropriately heroic ancestors, the J document came to serve national pride. The tribe of Judah supplied the Davidic line, and it is not unreasonable that most of the court scribes were drawn from the same tribe.

After the division of the country into the Dual Monarchy at the end of the Tenth Century, another version of the extant traditions was recorded. The two kingdoms were split along tribal lines, becoming rivals for God's sanction. This new document, designated E, was associated with the northern kingdom of Israel and is a duplicate source but espousing another perspective of the same material. The E source represents God as Elohim, the name used before Yahveh was introduced, and champions the tradition of the tribes with the Egyptian experience. It is interesting to note that Elohim is the plural form of the Canaanite god El and may refer to a very early period in pre-Israelite history when there were multiple gods. Also characteristic of this document is the name Jethro for Moses' father-in-law and Sinai for the mountain of revelation. Ephraim, one of Joseph's sons, was the dominant tribe in the northern kingdom, so E can also be linked mnemonically to that tribe. The literary style of E differs from J, tending to elucidate events rather than merely to relay them. In another perspective the Yahvist accentuates the epic quality of the history, whereas the Elohist seeks to balance the nationalism of J by emphasizing covenantal responsibility and prophetic experiences. Because E is so fragmentary in the Bible, we cannot be certain whether it was a completely separate document, drawn from common traditions, or whether it was a modification of the earlier J.

Where J and E had geographically clear tribal origins, later traditions of the priesthood gave rise to the P document. Its date was post-Exilic, that is, in the late Sixth and early Fifth Centuries, but it used traditional sources known from earlier times. P was more likely the work of a small group within the hereditary class of priests, whereas J and E are each thought to have been written by one, or at most a few, persons. The concern of the P writers was mainly with ritual and legal matters. The Book of Leviticus, along with the latter part of Exodus and the beginning of Numbers, contain God's exposition of the rules that will govern the community and is wholly P in origin. Characteristically there is a great emphasis on a meticulously recorded genealogy, with many seemingly endless lists of families and the ages of their leaders. P refers to God as *El Shaddai* (God Almighty), and theosophy is an essential concern, one notably absent in the other documentary sources.

Even as David welded Israel into a single nation, a troublesome parochialism persisted within the component tribes. J and E probably existed together as competing versions of the original traditions for about 200 years, each in its own tribal bloc. However, when the northern kingdom was overrun by the Assyrians in 722 B.C.E., Judah remained sovereign, and the J tradition understandably became dominant. J and E were later combined into a single narrative, with the J document the one relied on, and E folded into it even at the cost of the inconsistencies we recognize today. It is likely that when the redactors found a general consistency in the two documents, the E version was discarded. But where the accounts differed, both were honored by inclusion, indicating that the traditions transcended mere political orientation. Differences that were allowed to remain in the canon do not indicate how extensive they might have been in the original documents. Today's scholars recognize the redacted tradition, labeled JE, as distinct from J or E. The JE document probably was completed before the end of the Seventh Century.

A fourth major source of distinct tradition, D, is found from Deuteronomy through 2 Kings. The D writer(s) developed a sermonic style that stressed the importance of God's covenant with the people, the necessity for adhering to the given Law, and a strong commitment to social responsibility. This documentary source, also referred to as Deuteronomistic History, was written during the period of the northern kingdom. After the kingdom of Israel had been conquered, the D document found its way into the southern kingdom of Judah, where it survived in tension with the redacted JE tradition. The source of the D narratives, detailing the dates and events of the kings and their reigns, may have been drawn from documents called "Chronicles of the Kings of Judah" and "Chronicles of the Kings of Israel." These documents have not yet been found, although such documentation of a ruler's reign has ample precedent in ancient Near East literature. King-lists of both Mesopotamia and Egypt are sources for much of the data we have about events that happened in those respective regions. D seems to approach events more objectively than the other sources do, but its validity must nonetheless be qualified.

Deuteronomistic History has a special affinity for the exhortation so characteristic of the Prophetic writings. In 622 B.C.E., during the reign of King Josiah, a copy of the book of Deuteronomy, supposedly written in Moses' own hand, was discovered in the Temple. The reforms promulgated by Josiah likely came from this alleged discovery, perhaps an early example in the use of media in manipulating public opinion. Yet the fact that a southern monarch would adopt and advocate the tradition of a defunct rival kingdom indicates a deep respect for its idealistic thrust.

A fascinating alternative to the Documentary Hypothesis appeared in 1936, when P. J. Wiseman noted an irregular but repetitive pattern in Genesis.[3] The key was the recurring formulaic phrase "These are the generations of . . ." The generations seemed to delineate the history of family segments in chronological order, naming in turn Adam (5:1), Noah (6:9), the sons of Noah (10:1), Shem (11:10), Terah (11:27), Ishmael (25:12), Isaac (25:19), Esau (36:1, 9), and Jacob (37:2).

The first reference is in 2:4: "These are the generations of the heavens and the earth." Generally the mantra is sandwiched between genealogical lists, family data, and events. Comparing the narratives contained in ancient Babylonian tablets, Wiseman postulated that the repeated formula was authentic to those times, each announcing an installment of history. Also, the person named in the phrase was the writer, or owner, of the tablet on which the information was inscribed. This would imply that the writer had been privy to the details of each segment. The corollary implication is that no ordinary person living in succeeding generations could have accurately reconstructed the history in Genesis without records.

Germane to Wiseman's thesis is that Genesis was written, probably on clay, more or less simultaneously with the events it describes rather than passed on as an oral tradition. He notes, again from Babylonian texts, that when material could not all be impressed on a single tablet, the last few words were repeated as the first words on the subsequent tablet ("catch-lines"). Also, they would sometimes connect the text of multiple tablets by using the first few words of the first tablet as the last words of the other tablets ("titles"). He stresses that Babylonian words and a literary style that would have been known to the Hebrew ancestors who lived there was used only in the first eleven chapters of Genesis. In contrast, he points out, the last fourteen chapters, dealing with Joseph, contain appropriate Egyptian words and names. The implication is that real persons had real experiences and left tangible records.

Unfortunately this theory has little to recommend it over the Documentary Hypothesis. It avers that a real Adam lived, had dialogues with God, and wrote about it on clay tablets. Adam's descendants also recorded, or had written for them, the seminal events of their lives. Wiseman's position seems to be grounded in the need to prove that the whole of Genesis, and by implication the Torah, is documented history, with Moses as its sole designated compiler.

To accept that all the tablets providing verbatim material were carefully preserved and passed on through succeeding generations for Moses' use in writing Genesis, then to disappear without trace, strains credulity. But perhaps we are being too hasty in assuming that clay tablets could not have traveled continuously around the Near East from Adam to Moses for a few thousand years without any loss or breakage! Certainly the existence of such tablets would establish an unimpeachable source, but to accept this theory without the figurative "habeas corpus" needlessly undermines the painstaking research of so many dedicated scholars.

Can fact and fiction be separated in the Torah? The answer has to be yes, although the process can never be complete, and the results will be inconclusive to many. But this remarkable conflation of history and ethic will not be disturbed by the quest to validate its narrative history. If the ancient writers felt compelled for reasons of their own to plait together religious and historical units, we should not flinch from seeking to separate those strands. That which is authentically creedal will not be tarnished by the exposure of another component to the light of critical analysis.

The first event of what purports to be history occurs in Gen. 11:26, where the birth of Abram, later to become Abraham, is recorded. Prior to that point, God had completed the creation of the world, made man and woman, and then revised the quality of life by means of a flood. Genesis 11, in pursuing the generations of man, reaches Abram, who represents the twentieth generation after Adam. The metaphysical aspect of the creation of the world and the origin of the human race, including a specified lineage, is complete by then. The early tales in the first eleven chapters can be understood only as an etiological myth underlying a self-conscious national epic.

By the time Abraham was born, the world was 1946 years old, according to Genesis. However, the first ten human generations, including Adam, had an average life span of more than 875 years, and the generational interval was 105 years. Thus Noah, of the tenth generation, might still have been alive with Abraham, although Genesis understandably does not make this association. In 11:12 the age span of the later ancestors falls progressively to a still unlikely few hundred years, while the generational interval assumes a much more natural average of thirty years. It is not difficult to understand why historical criticism rarely concerns itself with this part of Genesis. Perhaps the original writers did not expect that the material would be seen as human history but rather as an impressive prolegomenon for a time when humankind believed that legends could be real.

A Covenantal Legacy

Israel's first three progenitors—Abraham, Isaac, and Jacob— were called from the common mass of humankind to begin a special link to God. Abraham secured the promise that his descendants would become "a great nation" (Gen. 12:20). When Abraham had settled in Canaan, God further promised that land to him and his spawn forever (Gen. 17:8). It was part of a covenant wherein they would obey God's law and be circumcised "throughout the ages." Even the male slaves of his household were included (Gen. 17:13f). The idea of a covenant with God must have originated with suzerainty treaties, in which the relationship between a king and his vassals was prescribed in vivid detail.[4] The same promise was repeated to Isaac and again to

Jacob. One important innovation of this new creed was its implication for a classless society. Free men, strangers, slaves, and
women were all granted the opportunity for membership in the
community of God, even though social inequalities persisted.

But were the patriarchs real men who lived at some previous
time, or were they merely literary skeletons on which to hang
muscular tales? A strong current in contemporary scholarship
holds them to be cult figures in the service of religion. But few
scholars are intrepid enough to declare them totally fictitious.
Likewise none, short of fundamentalists, would certify their reality. In either case they symbolize community ideals that were
later codified by Moses. Writers from academic disciplines seem
to have less compunction in placing the patriarchs within a literary genre that allows for eventual reality, whereas those who
carry a theological background are loathe to relinquish the protective staff of biblical tradition. Fortunately it is not necessary
for us to choose sides in every academic debate.

Stories of the patriarchs set the history of Israel on its course
but in an undated world. Where most authorities grant them a
degree of reality, the approximation of a time frame is essential
for an appropriate perspective. The date of the patriarchal era
bears directly on the view of them as either human beings, albeit
with heroic overtones, or literary figures, molded to fill gaps in
the evolution of a concept. The narratives in Genesis often show
currency with records from the ancient Near East, but effective
use of all sources demands a disciplined reason along with a
highly speculative intuition.

A surge of literary creativity took place during the reigns of
David and Solomon (1000–930). New genres were developed in
poetry, psalms, and historiography, all bearing the manifest
imprint of Mesopotamian and Egyptian literature. The Sumerians of the Third Millennium had such advanced cosmology and
theology that "their doctrines became the basic creed and dogma
of much of the Ancient Near East."[5] The literature of the Sumerians could not influence the Israelites directly, because they had
disappeared long before Israel existed as an entity. However,

Sumerian culture profoundly influenced the Babylonians, Assyrians, Hittites, Hurrians, Canaanites, and Arameans, who in turn influenced the Israelites.[6]

Throughout most of the common era (C.E.) it has been accepted that the patriarchs were real and that the narratives in Genesis represented history. Until two centuries ago, there was no satisfactory alternative to religious dogma; biblical history had been declared self-evident. The Enlightenment fostered an attitude whereby the search for elemental realities led to new views of old truths. Toward the end of the nineteenth century, biblical criticism as an academic movement found a loud voice. It was especially strong in Germany, where the Hebrew Scriptures were viewed primarily as a literary form of the ancient Near East and the patriarchs as models of a biographical genre.

Coincident with this intellectual approach came the archeological discoveries of the late nineteenth and early twentieth centuries. Aspects of Near Eastern life were seen as almost identical with descriptions in Genesis. The excitement of the 1902 discovery of the Code of Hammurabi, with its parallels in the laws of the Torah, augmented the trend to secular biblical scholarship. The code, which was thought to date from early in the First Babylonian Empire (2000–1600), set rules and regulations that spread throughout the entire region and lasted for well over a thousand years. There was a renewed tendency to see the patriarchs as real persons within a specific time period. Convinced that the new data described them in everything but name, many writers suggested 2000–1500 as the appropriate period for them. However, subsequent research moved the dates of Hammurabi's reign forward, compelling modifications in patriarchal dates. The debates over this issue, based on conflicting documentation, were joined in scholarly journals. Although the artifacts of Mesopotamia could be dated within reasonably narrow time frames, it had to be acknowledged that similar laws and customs in the Bible certified not that the patriarchs lived during those periods but only that their traditions were commonly derived.

Some scholars sought to find the patriarchs in the period of the Third Dynasty of Ur (circa 2000 B.C.E.), because their names were considered to be of West Semitic origin. However, where the same names can be found in other Semitic dialects and among later peoples, their allocation to that specific period becomes less persuasive. Also, to postulate that early date for them is to assume that the later writers could carry infinite details of specific persons in their memories for several hundred years. Such minutiae inevitably fade after a few generations unless they have been imbued with special meaning. It would not be remiss at this point to remind ourselves how little we know about our own great-grandparents, even in this literate age. And that is only three generations ago!

There is no credible evidence beyond the Torah to suggest that a unique religion existed among the Hebrews prior to Moses or the Thirteenth Century. However, in using earthy, readily recognized human tales, the Torah adds credence to the idea that the three named forefathers were real persons. The traditions about the patriarchs served the purposes of an evolving covenantal religion, but if these had not been reasonably complete before they were inscribed, improvisation within the purview of living witnesses would have undermined their determinant roles in the new faith. Perhaps that is why their stories contain so much evidence of human frailty and imperfection; divine behavior in real human beings would have little credibility in a religious tract that purported to be valid history.

In recent years the tendency has been to place the patriarchs much later, in one instance into the time of the Exile (early Sixth Century), because of the many anachronisms that exist in Genesis. [7] When contradictions occur in a documentary source, the later detail is often given greater credence. One might be tempted to assume that modern writers are closer to the truth, having at their disposal more and better data, as well as the advantage of previous scholarship. However, the known cyclicity of historians' trends makes that assumption precarious.

A recent article states, "It is much more within reason that the way of life and the ethnic and socio-political picture reflected in the patriarchal accounts generally correspond to the end of the period of the Judges and the beginning of the monarchy."[8] Evidence could also place them within the period of 2000–1250.[9] Within the earliest levels of cities mentioned in Genesis, recent archeological findings that could be only of the Late Bronze or early Iron Age (1500–900) have convinced another author that they were First Millennial figures.[10] Consensus today holds that because the patriarchal traditions were fixed around the beginning of the First Millennium, creating a *terminus ad quem*, they must have lived earlier.

The Arameans as a political entity are unknown much before the Twelfth Century, and their presence in Genesis is considered to be conclusive by the "late" school of dating. Obviously the biblical scribes of the Tenth Century, fresh with the Aramean experience, might have legitimately used these descendants of the more distant West Semites to identify the patriarchs. In Deut. 26:5 the prayer that every Israelite was to pronounce with his sacrificial offering began with, "A wandering Aramean was my father." In Gen.28:6–10 both the Arameans and the Ishmaelites are contemporary peoples, with Ishmael being the son of Abraham by Hagar, a concubine. Jacob is sent to find a wife in Paddan-Aram, which was Aramean territory. Esau, on the other hand, is seen as the progenitor of the Edomites, who were contemporary neighbors to the east, along with Ammonites and Moabites at the time of writing. Details of contemporary life were clearly retrofitted to describe earlier persons and events.

In dating the patriarchs, we must assume that the traditions about them existed within common knowledge prior to their inscription. The founding heroes of the nation had to precede their descendants, or the life story of each would be recognized as an expedient artifice. Where many proto-Israelites had already been living in various regions of Canaan, all with their own functioning tribal traditions, the scribes could later introduce them into the communal narratives because they were part of the lore.

Certainly the span of several generations is within the capability of human memory, and different perspectives would soften the anachronisms created by later biblical writers. It is therefore most likely that the patriarchs lived earlier, prior to the Exodus. They could then be ensconced within the Fourteenth Century, a date that can be readily harmonized with most extrabiblical data.

It seems all but certain that the patriarchs established the historical roots linking the promised destiny of Israel to its emergence on the international scene under David and Solomon in the Tenth Century. The biblical writers, serving an imperialistic monarchy, sought to justify current glory by invoking an epic past. This practice mimicked the pattern of historical writing throughout the ancient Near East.

Notes

1. E. O'Doherty, "The Conjectures of Jean Astruc, 1753," *Catholic Biblical Quarterly* XV(1953):300–304.
2. H. Bloom, *The Book of J* (New York: Grove Weidenfeld, 1990), p. 9.
3. P. J. Wiseman, *New Discoveries in Babylonia about Genesis* 1936. Now offered as *Ancient Records and the Structure of Genesis* (New York: Thomas Nelson, 1985).
4. G. E. Mendenhall, ""Covenant Forms in Israelite Tradition," *Biblical Archeologist* 17(1954):50–76.
5. S. N. Kramer, *From the Tablets of Sumer* (Indian Hills, CO: Falcon's Wing Press, 1956), p. 71.
6. Ibid., p. 169.
7. J. Van Seters, *Abraham in History and Tradition* (New Haven: Yale University Press, 1975), p. 310.
8. B. Mazar, "The Historical Background of the Book of Genesis," *Journal of Near Eastern Studies* 28(1969):73–83
9. Ibid., p. 76f.
10. T. L. Thompson, *The Historicity of the Patriarchal Narratives* (New York: Walter de Gruyter, 1974), p. 325f.

The Patriarchs: 5
Abraham, Isaac, Jacob

Few scholars, if not fundamentalist, seriously believe that Abraham, Isaac, and Jacob were grandfather, father, and son, respectively. It is even unlikely that these men were closely related to one another or to the twelve eponymous sons, as the neat family sequence in Genesis would have us believe. The patriarchs most likely were individual clan leaders in various parts of Canaan, perhaps living within a few generations of one another. Their relative importance rests on the subsequent achievements of their tribal descendants, which also may have dictated the ultimate family sequence. It is reasonably certain that most of the people who became Israel were already living in Canaan before the period of Judges (1200–1000). The contribution of traditions seems to have been made on the basis of each tribe's relative strength and the time of its entrance into the confederation of early Israel. The duration of the Patriarchal Age can only be conjectured, because we don't know how much time elapsed between the principals.

In Gen. 11:31 Terah, Abraham's father, takes his family and leaves the city of *Ur Kasdim* (Ur of the Chaldees/Chaldeans), settling in Haran to the northwest. Although these people were not seen in the region until early in the First Millennium, it does not ensure that the patriarchs belong to this later period. It is more likely that the writer added *kasdim* simply to localize a very distant place not otherwise well known to the Israelites of 1000 B.C.E.

Terah's family settled in Haran, having traveled about 600 miles northwestward along the Euphrates River and passing through the population centers of Babylon and Mari. All along the route, but certainly in Haran, Abraham would have been exposed to Babylonian and Hurrian cultures. Later he left for Canaan, continuing the westward migration. Although there has been ample evidence of Amorite movements to the east, it is not improbable that smaller groups could have moved west without attracting the attention of historians. The question about the provenance of the patriarchs, whether they were Mesopotamian or Amorite, must remain moot, given the conflicting details in Genesis. One author believes that a historical relationship between the patriarchs and the early West Semites is untenable but nevertheless writes that "this material, particularly from Mari, can play an extremely valuable role in biblical studies, as an analogue, if not to the patriarchal period, to the settlement of Israel in Palestine; for it is our most complete source for understanding the process of sedentarization."[1]

The Torah contains the names of many peoples having an indistinct relationship to the twelve tribes. Some are variously described as enemies of Israel, but there is strong indication that sooner or later, they merged with them. Among these peoples are the Kennizzites, Perizzites, Calebites, Othnielites, Jerachmeelites, Jebusites, and Kenites, who may also be the Midianites, so prominent in the Mosaic traditions. Residing in the south and associated with Judah, they perhaps represented a counterweight to the ten northern tribes.

As tribal leaders of tent-dwelling seminomadic shepherds living on the periphery of Canaan, the patriarchs came to embody a yearning for that land. God's promise of permanent possession, given to them while they occupied temporary sanctuaries within it, served to associate the patriarchs with specific regions. An imagined compact was thus born between themselves and God. This cultic relationship is stressed in the statement, "Even the original tradition of the patriarchs was not, however, much concerned with their human personalities, but rather with the divine promises that had been made to them."[2] The close generational kinship assigned to the three patriarchs is patently a conflation of disparate elements. Their descendants, seeing the occupation of the land as a fulfillment of that promise, began a cult that worshipped "the God of our fathers."[3] The itinerary of each patriarch defined the area that was to be sacred to him. A sanctuary developed into a primary association: Hebron for Abraham, Beersheba for Isaac, and Bethel and Shechem for Jacob. Abraham and Isaac built altars in the south, whereas Jacob built altars in the central highlands. The Torah presents altars and pillars as symbols of Divine residence, but in a political context it is very likely that they also served as territorial claim markers. The cross-association of the patriarchs with one another's sanctuaries came later in the evolution of a unitary Israel, when a merger of the ancestors into a single family became urgent.

The phrase "God of our fathers" contains a major clue to the relationship among them. Although it could imply ageless continuity of a single, common God, it is more likely a later device to blur their original distinctions. The likelihood that each patriarch was the leader of a separate unit and had his own personal god is compelling.[4] In Gen. 28:13 *elohai avraham* names the god of Abraham. In 31:42 the god of Isaac is called *pachad yitzhak*, which translates to "Isaac's fear." Jacob's god in 49:24 is *avir ya'akov*, "mighty one of Jacob." These uniquely nuanced deities make it possible to believe that in the very early formation of Israel, especially among those peoples who had not been to Egypt, a polytheism existed not dissimilar to that of their neighbors, the Canaanites. Also, the fact that each god had a different name suggests that they were not viewed as the same deity.

Joseph is another figure who exerts a fundamental influence on the formation of Israel, although he is not a patriarch in biblical usage, having neither received a promise nor participated in the direct covenant with God. The extensive treatment accorded him in Genesis as the rescuer of the entire family nevertheless posits a quasi-patriarchal status. His story, with its Egyptian locus, has been likened to a novelette[5] inserted within the traditions of Jacob.

Genesis unequivocally holds Joseph high above the other eleven brothers in importance. Levi and Joseph are dropped from their eponymous roles as tribal heads, but Joseph's sons, Manasseh and Ephraim, are given the status of Jacob's own sons, continuing the twelve-tribe confederation. The replacement of Levi will become clear in chapter 14, on the Levites, but the Torah offers no hint for Joseph's exclusion. His sons were referred to as "the house of Joseph"; this oblique reference is all that was left of his preeminent rank. His persona will be explored later, in the more logical context of Israel's Egyptian connection. We shall see that once persons bearing a fateful association with Egypt have served their purpose in advancing the story of Israel, they are mysteriously hustled offstage. This is especially true of Moses. Those tribes whose later numbers and power dominated central Canaan were the ones most closely associated with Egypt, Joseph's heroic past, and the Mosaic traditions.

An alternative reality is hidden in the ambiguities and inconsistencies of Genesis. The knowledge that every tradition was purposefully included suggests that the scribes themselves were unsure about which one described the situation most accurately. Therefore all information had to be presented, even at the risk of mutual contradiction. The Bible here becomes a classic patient for the psychoanalytic technique often referred to as "listening with the third ear."[6] Truth is often hidden in the figurative archaisms and ambiguous emendations of the text's words and style.

Two of the three patriarchs undergo inexplicable name changes. Abraham's original name, Abram, is changed in Gen. 17:5 when God concludes the covenant with him. Jacob also undergoes a name change, to Israel, in Gen. 32:29. One scholar found significance in the abandonment of the names just before an impending change in each man's status to that of covenanter.[7] In the latter episode Jacob is attacked and placed in mortal danger by God in the guise of an angel; the two wrestle all night to a draw. Given this indecisive outcome, we would have to assume that the divinity's heart was not really in that fight. At daybreak the angel can disengage only by a sneak attack on Jacob's "thigh," a euphemism for a proximate and vulnerable male anatomical landmark. God then tells him, "Your name shall no longer be Jacob, but Israel," which with variations can mean "he who struggled with God" or "may El (God) persevere." Speiser understands this episode as preparing Jacob for his destiny; he thereafter becomes an honorable man "invoking a higher concept of morality."[8] As we shall see, this had to be a welcome change from his earlier character!

Ancient cultures provide ample precedent that names were often based on personal characteristics. Abraham and Israel become new men, belonging to a new history and owned by a new, restricted clientele. Why Isaac is excluded from these formulaic events is uncertain, but it might be related to the demographics of later Israel, where his descendants were not as numerous or as important as those of the other two patriarchs.

In Gen. 12:1–9 Abraham begins the migration from Haran to the city of Shechem in Canaan and then south to the Negev Desert region. We have already suggested that such movements of small clans throughout the Fertile Crescent in the Second Millennium were probably very common. There is no reason to doubt that an Abraham with his family and retainers made such a trip and that the remembrance of it remained as an early tradition. An influential scholar in the middle of this century opined that Abraham was a "donkey caravaneer" and by implication also a merchant-trader.[9]

Much of Abraham's biography exposes a materialistic vein. It is difficult to understand why God chose him for a covenantal relationship when his first moral lapse appears almost as soon as we meet him (12:10–20). It certainly comes long before his implied nobility as the first of the founding fathers of Israel.

Abraham in Egypt

Abraham and his party have gone down to Egypt because of a famine in Canaan. Sarai, his wife (her name becomes Sarah in 17:15, although the reason for it is obscure), is "a beautiful woman." Abraham says to her, "If the Egyptians see you, and think, 'She is his wife', they will kill me and let you live. Please say that you are my sister, that it may go well with me because of you, and that I may remain alive thanks to you" (12:12–13). Events unfolded just as he had foreseen; Sarah was taken by pharaoh, and he was allowed to live. But in addition, "And because of her, it went well with Abraham; he acquired sheep, oxen, asses, male and female slaves, she-asses, and camels" (12:16). He was obviously well rewarded in this exchange. When pharaoh and his household were later afflicted "with mighty plagues on account of Sarah," he sent for Abraham and said, "What is this you have done to me! Why did you not tell me that she was your wife? Why did you say, 'She is my sister,' so that I took her as my wife? Now, here is your wife; take her and begone!" (12:18–19). We are not told how he discovered their true relationship, but it is quite obvious that pharaoh was affronted and wanted to get rid of them as soon as he could. They were escorted to the border by pharaoh's men, with Abraham retaining "all he possessed" (12:20). Is it not strange that pharaoh's anger against Abraham is so muted? We can never know whether the deal he made was short term or long term, but surely it did not include "plagues."

If this were an isolated episode, perhaps the product of a storyteller's imagination, proving how clairvoyant or clever Abraham was, it might be easily dismissed. But the same episode, with minor variations, is again reported in Gen. 20, where Abimelech, king of Gerar, in southern Canaan, takes Sarah because Abraham assured him that "she is my sister" (20:2). However, God forewarns Abimelech in a dream that she is married. His sense of honor offended, he supposedly rejects her. Abimelech calls together his servants the next morning and tells them of the night's happening, seeking justification and acquittal for himself. Then he summons Abraham and berates him for his duplicity, saying, "You have done to me things that ought not to be done" (20:9). Abraham explains the relationship by stating that Sarah is truly his sister, daughter of his father, though not of his mother. This results in gifts of sheep, oxen, and male and female slaves to Abraham (20:14). And to Sarah, Abimelech says, "I herewith give your brother a thousand pieces of silver; this will serve you as vindication before all who are with you, and you are cleared before everyone" (20:16). That he persists in referring to Abraham as her "brother," when by that time he knows their primary relationship, is problematic. The gifts to Abraham, including silver, would precisely fulfill the custom of paying a bride-price to the bride's brother. But is this the only possible explanation? Abimelech should have been spared the "plagues" of pharaoh because of his reported abstinence, but Genesis goes on to state, "Abraham then prayed to God, and God healed Abimelech and his wife and his slave girls, so that they bore children; for the Lord had closed fast every womb of the household of Abimelech because of Sarah, the wife of Abraham" (20:17–18).

Later in Genesis (26:6–11) an abortive third episode occurs, this time involving Isaac. He tells the retainers of the same Abimelech that Rebekah is his sister, but the ruse is uncovered before any liberty had been taken with her. In this episode Isaac is not rewarded; nor is there any mention of "plagues." The first and third versions come from the J source, whereas the second one, so remarkably similar to the first, stems from E. Why was this essentially single episode subjected to a threefold, slightly varied repetition?

The implication inherent in these parallel episodes has been profoundly disturbing to biblical scholars. Speiser does not consider the wife-as-sister representation unusual for the period, but he questions rhetorically why the J and E writers were at such pains to include these ancient customs and legal arrangements when at a remove of hundreds of years, they probably could not fully understand the meaning. He suggests that they had no choice, since a long-held tradition had to be recorded whether or not it made sense.[10]

Hurrian custom allowed a man to marry a woman and also to legally adopt her as his sister. The idea behind the dual relationship was that in a fratriarchy a brother had more authority than a husband. Marriage in such a society was of a type called *beenah* (understanding), whereby the husband joined the wife's clan but always owed first loyalty to his original tribe. The wife's oldest brother was therefore the head of the extended family, stabilizing its organization. Where the husband was free to leave whenever his own people called him back or at his own whim, paternity could always be called into question. The principle of matrilinearity was thus established, and inheritance followed the same pattern. Perhaps this was the strongest reason for the adoption of a wife as sister, which seems to have been practiced mainly in the upper classes.[11] A man could adopt a woman for the purpose of marrying her himself or giving her in marriage to his son. If Sarah were such an adoptive daughter, she could also have been her husband's sister in a legal sense.[12] Accordingly the episodes were consonant with history, and technically there was no dissimulation to pharaoh or Abimelech.

Citing the biblical stories, some believe that Abraham and Isaac married women of superior social station, although this point of view may owe more to hubris than to genealogy. When Sarah is first introduced in Genesis (11:29), there is no mention of her parentage. In the E version Abraham identifies her as Terah's daughter, his sister by a different mother (20:12). Up to this point there is no indication that Sarah or Rebekah bore a higher status than either Abraham or Isaac.

Speiser raises and defends the question of morality by stating, "Such an affirmation of the wife's favored position was, hence, an implicit guarantee of the purity of her children," which issue he feels was needed to establish the superior strain of the patriarchal descendants.[13] It is unlikely that either pharaoh or Abimelech would have been much impressed with the women's social status, given the purpose for which they were taken.

To those familiar with the three chapters in Genesis (12, 20, 26), it should be obvious that the real moral issue remains unaddressed. Speiser may have proved that either Sarah or Rebekah could have been a wife/sister, but it is irrelevant because the clear implication remains that these patriarchs hastened their wives into the beds of other men without hesitation. A husband was always perceived as an obstacle to a woman's availability for sexual purposes, but offering her as a sister could only remove that obstacle and make her all the more vulnerable as he protects himself. Abimelech's rebuke that Abraham did "things that ought not to be done" seems to confirm that Sarah had been sold or leased. If readers prefer to think that his remark referred only to the deceptive wife/sister issue, the next paragraph may be shocking.

A feature common to both episodes may seem inconsequential at first glance, but it is critical to a clearer understanding of the entire episode. In Gen. 12:17 the "plague" afflicting pharaoh and his household "on account of Sarah" has a distinct medical connotation. The passage in 20:18, "For the Lord had closed fast every womb of the household of Abimelech because of Sarah," reflects a precise description of the medical consequence of chronic sexually transmitted disease in the female.[14] One has to marvel at the prescience of those ancient scribes who, without the benefit of modern public health research, were able to correlate infertility, plague, and Sarah. By placing the salient features of these narratives in sequence, namely, that the two rulers had sexual relations with Sarah and also with their wives and other household women, that Sarah may have carried a sexually transmitted disease, and that her husband was well remunerated for temporarily absenting himself while all this was going on, Abraham's occupation as a merchant or trader assumes a much darker dimension.

The J and E writers could not have been unaware of the real meaning of these episodes. Still, their inclusion of them, "warts and all," indicates a refreshing affinity for truth. The three episodes could have been different tribal versions of a single one, although the extension of the action to Isaac and Rebekah would be inexplicable unless his followers felt the need to achieve a perverse parity with Abraham. The more logical explanation for the deliberate inclusion of this indiscreet tale is best summed up in the statement, "By approaching the patriarchal episodes as inviolable, by faithfully reproducing details whose meaning had grown obscure, the narrator bears testimony to the prior canonical, or quasi-canonical, standing of such material."[15]

This exegesis, describing unvarnished human behavior, should in no way diminish the transcendental power of other patriarchal stories, where they rise to higher ethical planes. Genesis presents a universal, if sometimes unflattering, historical portrait that every generation can recognize. However, before judging the actions of an ancient people, we must remember that morality is culture-coded and time-variable. Multiple wives, concubinage, and the "master's right," the later *droit du seigneur*, were normative customs at various periods in the history of civilization, albeit accepted with considerable reluctance by its victims.

Another custom exemplified in the Bible but no longer acceptable is contained in Gen. 16 and 30. Infertility in women was a particularly harsh stigma even though immaturity at marriage and relative malnutrition may have caused its incidence to be far above today's level. Children, male and female, had value beyond the natural psychic reward; they were an additional category to be reckoned in family assets. Nuzi family law details the obligation of a childless wife to procure a concubine for her husband, who could then produce sons, although she retained authority over the offspring of that union.

In the patriarchal stories infertile wives offered their husbands other women of the household to be bearers of their children, a custom known to be practiced by the Hurrians. Sarah, who was childless at seventy-five years of age, gave her Egyptian maidservant, Hagar, to Abraham, saying, "Consort with my maid; perhaps I shall have a son through her" (16:2). In a similar episode Rachel, smarting from the shame of childlessness in contrast to Leah's fecundity, says to Jacob, "Here is my maid

Bilchah. Consort with her that she may bear on my knees and that through her I too may have children" (30:3). When Leah experienced a hiatus in her child-bearing function, she also gave Jacob her maid, Zilpah. All three wives therefore acted in conformity with Hurrian law.[16] The ancient practice of placing a newborn on the mother's knees stemmed from the squatting position that was used in parturition and later came to have proprietary significance.

Building the Central Family

The stories that make up the bulk of Genesis are directed mainly to the foundation of a unique relationship between God and the patriarchal descendants. To achieve even a tentative unity, the various peoples had to be brought into a clear, genealogical relationship. The P source served to incorporate family listings that directly or indirectly include people who become related to Israel and could be drawn into a unified pool of descent. Competition among the three forefathers for tribal primacy was solved by linking them as grandfather, father, and son. Once the line was established as the bona fide and ancestral authority of Israel, the profusion of narrative tales, however legendary, lent flesh and blood to the bony limbs of the new, expanded pedigree. "God of our fathers" could then become the one and only "Lord, our God."

Jacob, as the grandson of Abraham and the father of twelve sons, has been awarded over half the space in Genesis, whereas Abraham and Isaac together occupy less than one-quarter of it. This emphasis reflects the power and importance of each patriarch and his descendants at the time in which the common traditions were being accepted.

The genealogical lists that appear from Genesis through Numbers clearly perform a unifying function. Biblical writers labored compulsively to convey familial strands toward the now integrated ancestral line of patriarchs and even past them to

Adam and Eve at the beginning of the world. At the same time, their efforts could account for the exclusion of similarly ethnic, neighboring peoples. Their interest was not in historical accuracy per se but rather in the power of converging traditions. The chronologic and demographic details served to cement relationships of different peoples. Lists are characteristic of the priestly writers; most authorities credit them with such meticulous record keeping that all the names mentioned reflect real persons and groups, however peripheral they might have been.

In the Torah women, especially the wives and concubines, play prominent roles as compared to women in the literature of other contemporary peoples. Sarah in Gen. 18:12 is unafraid to display a little mordant wit when she overhears that she will become a mother at ninety years of age. Again in 21:10 she is able to prevail on Abraham to cast out Hagar, her love rival, and Ishmael, his first-born son. Rebekah travels to a distant land without hesitation for a husband (24:58). Her later role in awarding Isaac's blessing to Jacob is intrinsically disturbing, but leaves little doubt about her dominance in the family. Rachel outwits her father, Laban, when he challenges the fleeing Jacob (31:25–35). Lot's daughters, in arranging for their own pregnancies (19:32–38), and Judah's daughter-in-law, Tamar, who by her own effort rectifies a levirate omission (38:14–19), continue the emphasis on feminine initiative. Although this literary prominence could indicate the effects of a matriarchal society, it helps to explain Israel's uniqueness within the male-centered Near Eastern culture of the time. The ethical egalitarianism of later Judaism might have prompted the scribes to include women in heroic events. Perhaps the descriptions of these forthright and steely women subtly acknowledge the intrinsic power of their sex.

God's promise to Abraham that "I will make of you a great nation" (12:2) is the essence of the Covenant and happens twenty-five years after the flight from Ur. Certainly he had sufficient time to develop a proprietary interest in acquiring his own land, but because Sarah had borne no children, he had no heir to it. The story continues when Sarah offers him her Egyptian maid, Hagar, as a surrogate for breeding purposes. Hagar might well have been part of pharaoh's gift of "male and female slaves" in 12:16. Ishmael was born of this union. Later God allowed Sarah to give birth to Isaac (17:17), but Ishmael, as Abraham's first-born, ordinarily would have inherited his father's estate. Sarah protected her own son's interest by forcing her husband to discharge Hagar and to disinherit Ishmael. In that way she ensured that Isaac became sole heir in fulfillment of God's promise. After her death Abraham, then 137 years old, took another wife, Keturah, and sired six more sons by her (25:1–4). Much of Gen. 25 consists of family lists, beginning with Keturah's six sons and including the line of Ishmael. Of the twenty-eight named descendants of Keturah, only those of Midian and Kedar are mentioned in later biblical episodes. Jacob's descendants, in contrast, are in the hundreds and extend over six generations in the first two books of the Torah. Lot, who was Abraham's nephew, became the ancestor of the Moabites and the Ammonites by an inadvertant coupling with his two daughters (19:37–38). That these unsavory traditions were included in the Torah is further evidence of the scribes' dogged determination to record all received traditions, hallowed or not.

Of Abraham's many sons Isaac is the one who inherits his father's promise and in turn passes it on to his own second son, Jacob, rather than to his first-born, Esau. The son who willingly gave up his birthright and then had his father's blessing snatched from him by Jacob became the ancestor of the Edomites. He was intimately involved with non-Israelites by his marriages to two Hittite women and a daughter of Ishmael (26:34, 28:9).

The story of Isaac's unplanned blessing of Jacob, with its overt deception, is not likely to have been falsified. Many less reprehensible scenarios were available to the imagination. Earlier Esau had exchanged his birthright for "pottage" (stew) that Jacob had made (25:29–34). The patent inequality of the exchange is usually ascribed to Esau's gluttony and lack of judgment rather than to Jacob's avarice. Yet after Jacob cheated him again, this time of the critical paternal blessing (27:1–29), we are allowed to see in feral Esau a sensitive human response: pathos rather than murderous revenge (27:30–34).

Rebekah is the unmistakable instigator of the purloined blessing, having overheard Isaac's plan to award it to Esau after having eaten the game that Esau went to hunt. Jacob raises no objection to his mother's plan, providing the first example of an irresolute and pusillanimous character—hardly the stuff of nobility. This behavior is seen again and again in his relationship to Laban (Gen. 29–31), his reconciliation with Esau (Gen. 32), and the notorious deception at Shechem (Gen. 34). Ordinarily it would be unthinkable for Rebekah to interfere in such a critical prerogative of her husband unless the intent of the tradition was to sanitize Jacob's involvement in the sordid plot.

Rebekah, anticipating Esau's impending return with game, hurriedly prepares a favorite dish of goat meat for Isaac. But before Jacob serves it to him, she covers his hands and neck with the pelts, lest the smooth-skinned Jacob be discovered usurping the place of the hirsute Esau. Isaac, old and blind, asks which son it is who serves him, and Jacob answers, "I am Esau, your firstborn" (27:19). Suspicious that too little time had elapsed for the killing and the preparation of the meal, Isaac asks how it all was achieved so quickly, and Jacob answers, "Because the Lord your God granted me good fortune" (27:20). But Isaac is still suspicious, because the voice is Jacob's. He calls him closer so that he can feel his skin, now covered with goat hair. That, together with the animal smell and a second assurance from the son standing in front of him that he is indeed Esau, finally convinces Isaac to give him the blessing. No exegetical legerdemain can obscure the outrageous lie implied in the plain words of the text.

The testamentary process described in chapter 27, shorn of the deceit, would certainly be recognized as customary by the people of that time. Isaac's opening statement to Esau, "Behold now, I am old, I know not the day of my death" (27:2), is a variant of the formula for pronouncing a final declaration of property distribution: an oral last will and testament. Such a deathbed declaration was legally binding in Nuzi society.[17] A father was allowed to divert an inheritance from a first-born son, but this was never done capriciously. Primacy of birthright was more a matter of a father's discretion than of chronological priority.[18] In that era of polygamy an understandable distinction was made between sons of different mothers. Abraham's legacy to Isaac (17:19) instead of to the older Ishmael can be seen in this context. Isaac's blessing to Jacob, although falsely obtained, is seen as the fulfillment of God's promise, and his refusal to withdraw the blessing when he realized his mistake symbolizes the inviolability of a last testament.

The effort to wrest the inheritance from an older sibling with the connivance of their shared mother is most unusual in the epic history of a people. Certainly when mothers classically have been involved in the rescue of their sons, as in the case of Moses or Jesus, the motivation was to overcome injustice. Rebekah and Jacob simply commit a blatant violation of trust. That this episode was retained to become creedal rather than having been doctored by succeeding, prestige-oriented generations, is another indication of the reverence inspired by venerable traditions. Some might argue that this is merely a folk legend demonstrating the power of fate or how prized was an ancestor's ability to outmaneuver an adversary. Perhaps it was considered commonplace at the time, as it is in some quarters today, that if the operative legal code is not violated, there is no crime, despite obvious moral turpitude. Notwithstanding such possibilities, it is difficult to believe that the inherent taboo on intrafamily deception was not recognized then. Jeremiah may have been thinking of this issue when he says, "Beware, every man of his friend! Trust not even a brother! For every brother takes advantage" (Jer. 9:3). However, this particular episode is best understood in explaining the later dominance of the Israelites over the Edomites. Its historicity within the chronicle of Israel is therefore irrelevant.

Another deathbed blessing is offered in Gen. 49:1–27, where Jacob assigns the future in varying proportions to his sons. In this instance Jacob's final blessing is merely a contrived prophecy reflecting the relative political condition of each eponymous tribe during the later settlement in Canaan.

Isaac's anger at Jacob is very short-lived in the J version. Beginning with chapter 28 the roiled family is suddenly calm and self-possessed. The anger that we would expect in Isaac because he was deprived of the right to choose his heir is gone. He sends for Jacob and instructs him not to marry a Canaanite woman (in contrast to the foreign wives that Esau took) but to go to Laban, Rebekah's brother in Paddan-Aram, and choose a wife from that family. In 28:4 Isaac also passes the Abrahamic covenant to Jacob.

The Documentary Hypothesis is helpful here in explaining Isaac's sudden change of attitude from offended to solicitous. Obviously there were two separate traditions about this episode, each with different perspectives and neither aware of the other's existence. The J writer, with knowledge of the birthright and blessing ploys, presents it in the usual terse, matter-of-fact style. P, on the other hand, is unaware of any fraud, or perhaps discounts it, and continues Isaac in his role as a concerned and solicitous father. The different motivations for Jacob's trip to Paddan-Aram also indicate a dual source. In the J version Esau's anger at having been cheated threatens Jacob's life, and Rebekah urges him to flee to the home of Laban, where he will be given refuge (27:42f). The P source (28:1f), alternatively, sees Jacob's trip as merely for the procurement of an appropriate wife to ensure genealogical purity.[19]

Jacob Becomes Israel

Jacob is hardly a model of virtue, despite his inheritance of the patriarchal mantle. However, he meets his moral match in the person of his uncle, Laban. Jacob falls in love with Laban's beautiful younger daughter, Rachel, and agrees to serve him seven years for her hand. When he awakens on the morning after the wedding, he is dismayed to find that the now unveiled bride is not Rachel but her less desirable sister, Leah. Laban's explanation for the switch is that local custom did not permit the marriage of a younger daughter before an older one (29:26). He then offers Rachel to him but in exchange extracts another seven years of labor.

At the end of the fourteen years of service for his two wives, Jacob wishes to go back home. He proposes that Laban pick out of his flocks all the less desirable animals, dark-colored sheep, speckled or spotted goats and that he will accept these in lieu of wages (30:32). He offers to stay on longer to care for all the flocks if Laban will accede to this arrangement. The latter agrees but craftily sends the marked animals far away so that Jacob would get none of them. However, Jacob is not without tricks of his own. In 30:37–42 he uses magical ways to produce marked but sturdier animals, which he keeps while Laban gets the weaker ones: "So the man (Jacob) grew exceedingly prosperous, and came to own large flocks, maidservants and menservants, camels and asses" (30:43). Although the Torah never stands in judgment of moral ambiguity in the patriarchs, any reasonable person would be hard pressed to decide which of the two, Jacob or Laban, is less guilty of fraud.

Genesis 31 is laced throughout with human emotion and is well worth reading for its narrative sweep as well as for its dramatic tension. After twenty years of service, Jacob finally finds the courage to gather his two wives, all his children, livestock, and possessions and to flee Paddan-Aram. He has become aware of the hostility of Laban's family, and God also urged him to leave (31:1–3). Laban overtakes Jacob's caravan in Gilead, a place-name that probably did not exist until many years later: It was to become the designated land of the descendants of Gad after they returned from Egypt. At first Laban acts as the outraged victim of Jacob's ingratitude (31:26–28), pointing out that although it is in his power to harm all of them, his only demand is that the household gods stolen from him be returned. Jacob protests his innocence and naively invites his father-in-law to search for them among his possessions. When Laban does not find them, he is visibly frustrated. Jacob, now self-righteous, takes to the verbal offensive, berating him for his perfidy and evil intentions. Laban answers in his own defense, "The daughters are my daughters, the children are my children, and the flocks are my flocks; all that you see is mine" (31:43). Laban's claim that he owns all that Jacob has amassed would again seem to be based on Nuzi law texts, which hold that a slave's possessions belong to his master. Jacob retorts that the inadvertent loss of animals mentioned in 31:39 should have been borne by the owner, Laban, which law was part of the Code of Hammurabi.[20] Although the narrative does not present Jacob as a slave, it could be argued analogically that his labor of twenty years, in defined service periods of seven years, constituted one accepted form of slavery in that era.

Laban's obsession with the recovery of his household gods is also historically sound. Their importance in primitive religions is widely acknowledged. Typically small figurines, *teraphim*, were fashioned in some recognizable human form, representing deities that could most benefit the family. In Hurrian society a daughter who possessed the household gods shared in the distribution of her father's property, because they implied the right of inheritance. Laban therefore showed appropriate concern about the disappearance of his figurines, because it restricted his freedom in distributing his property. However, neither man was aware that Rachel had stolen them (31:19) or that at the very moment of frantic search, they were hidden in the camel cushion on which she was sitting. To prevent her father from searching in that place, she apologizes, "Let not my lord be angry that I cannot rise up before thee; for the manner of women is upon me" (31:35). The J writer merely reports her words, although we suspect that the menstrual condition she pleads is false. Knowing that she did steal the icons, we can assume that she is eager to obstruct her father's search at any cost. Another reason to doubt that Rachel was telling the truth is that on the same trip to Bethlehem, she gave birth to Benjamin (35:16–18).

One explanation for Rachel's seizure and defense of the teraphim is that she knew it would be very unlikely that Laban would favor them with their due inheritance, given his rage at losing Jacob's services. In that circumstance she acted to ensure their claim to Laban's property by taking physical possession of the figurines. This was especially important because the natural heirs, his sons, are not mentioned until 30:35, confusing the inheritance claim that his first-born daughters would have. In Hurrian law daughters inherited only if there were no sons.[21]

Possession of household gods is emblematic of the role of paterfamilias as much as it implies title to inheritance. Rachel's action can also be seen as an attempt to ensure leadership for her husband. The episode is hardly certifiable history, but given the importance of the symbols and the psychological state of the participants, the drama creates a realism that supports its social historicity. It is unlikely that such ancestral dishonesty, without a modicum of creedal importance, would have been improvised for inclusion in a national epic unless it wore at least a veneer of reality.

Another example of the Near Eastern milieu in which the patriarchs lived is the treaty concluded between Jacob and Laban (31:44–54). They raise a stone pillar and build a mound of stones that are to be witness "that I am not to cross to you past this mound, and that you are not to cross to me past this mound and this pillar, with hostile intent" (31:52). In 31:53 they swear respectively by the God of Abraham and the god of Nahor (Laban's ancestor) to uphold the pact. Such invocation of each party's god as witness to the pact has its origin in the parity treaty forms of Second Millennium Mesopotamia.[22] On other occasions even mutually acknowledged foreign deities were used. This family meeting can also be viewed as a dramatic representation of an ancient border dispute, stone markers and all.

En route back to Canaan, Jacob again is shown to be clever, devious, and unprincipled. When told by his messenger that Esau is coming to meet him with 400 men (32:7), Jacob's fear for his life is palpable. He divides all his possessions into two widely spaced camps, thinking, "If Esau comes to the one camp and attacks it, the other camp may yet escape" (32:9). The next morning he sends a lavish gift of animals to Esau, dividing them up into several droves, each separate in line, and each following at an extended distance behind the others. The servants in charge of each group of animals are instructed to answer Esau's expected inquiry about their ownership with the identical statement, "[They are] your servant Jacob's; they are a gift sent to my lord Esau; and Jacob himself is right behind us" (32:17–19). He reasoned that Esau would be dazzled by the lavish gifts that kept coming to him at intervals and would then be in a mood to spare his life when they finally met. Jacob's presentation succeeds, and in the following chapter Esau makes his peace with him.

Shechem

In Gen. 34 Shechem, in the central highlands region, becomes the scene for yet another example of moral ambivalence. Jacob is not the instigator here, although he is not yet the righteous father of Israel he will later become. After he and his family reached Shechem, where Hivites (Hurrians) had settled, Dinah, his daughter by Leah, is raped by the prince of the land, also named Shechem. The latter repents his lustful act after he realizes that he loves her and asks his father, Hamor, to obtain Dinah for him as a wife. Jacob and Hamor are about to conclude the necessary arrangements when Jacob's sons come in and express outrage at the proposal. Hamor pleads that if they all were to intermarry, Jacob's people will become as his own. This brings a disingenuous response from the sons, "Only on this condition will we agree with you; that you will become like us in that every male among you is circumcised" (34:15). All the men of Shechem submitted to circumcision, and on the third day, when "they were in pain," Simeon and Levi "took each his sword, came upon the city unmolested, and slew all the males" (34:25). Then the other sons came and looted everything, including the wives and children of the slain men. Jacob weakly remonstrates with his sons after the fact, saying, "You have brought trouble on me, making me odious among the inhabitants of the land" (34:30). The Shechemites, however, were not innocent victims; their acquiescence to circumcision was based on the expectation that they would acquire "their [Jacob's] cattle and substance and all their beasts" (34:23).

If the settlement in Canaan were truly a military conquest, as described in the Book of Joshua, Gen. 34 could easily fit into that paradigm. However, as we shall see later, the conquest model carries little support outside the pages of the Bible. Another proffered explanation is that Jacob's family, denied legal status and socially ostracized, could redress Shechem's insult only by taking the law into their own hands.[23] The episode may also indicate that in the process of sedenterization, the Israelites had to reach out to the native Canaanites for marriage. Certainly the evidence within the Bible from Exodus through 2 Kings overwhelmingly portrays an ongoing social and cultural relationship between Israel and its neighbors. The J writer again has exposed a family skeleton that resonates with some probable event in Israel's obscure past.

Gen. 34 can also be taken for evidence that Shechem had been the territory of the tribes of Levi and Simeon in an earlier history. Jacob's deathbed prophecy about them—"I will divide them in Jacob, scatter them in Israel" (49:5–7)—symbolizes their punishment because of the episode. The Simeonites were probably ejected from the area and later joined with Judah in the southern desert. The Levites, also being without a patrimony of land, are later awarded the priesthood of Israel, a most ambiguous punishment. Chapter 12, on the Levites, will present a more logical explanation for their elevation to priestly status.

* * *

The episode at Shechem involving Jacob and his sons and the one in Gen. 14 about Abraham and his men may be typical of the political activity in Canaan during the latter half of the Fourteenth Century. At that time an extensive and rootless mass of people within Canaan, the Hab/piru, were involved in the continual friction among the city-states. As stateless persons they had to contend with all the aggressiveness of Canaanite power in addition to the natural hazards that attended sedenterization. Perhaps their crude behavior was due to an awareness that they had to live by their wits in a world offering them no lawful security. Their stories are realistic and instructive, proving that the human behavior we explain by modern psychology had analogs even then and that the patriarchal ancestors could well have been real persons.

Later tradition tried to portray them as men of probity, even nobility, living marginally in turbulent times. The world might never have known of their existence but for the unique, theosophic spark that caught fire in the midst of their descendants. The Patriarchal Age may have introduced the first proto-Israelites, with Genesis recording a lifestyle and personal proclivities quite at variance with what might have been desired by later religionists. The "God of the fathers" is portrayed as a personal, approachable deity who protects and favors His people in a simple relationship. His blessings and promises are assured, not conditional, as they will be for later Israel.[24] It remains uncertain how much ethical content was contained in the patriarchal cult, but a dramatic change will occur when it encounters the coming Mosaic contribution, specifically in the Decalogue.

Notes

1. T. L. Thompson, *The Historicity of the Patriarchal Narratives* (New York: Walter de Gruyter, 1974), p. 88.
2. M. Noth, *The History of Israel* (New York: Harper and Row, 1960), p. 123.
3. Ibid.
4. J. Bright, *A History of Israel* 2d ed. (Philadelphia: Westminster Press, 1972), p. 97.
5. D. B. Redford, *A Study of the Biblical Story of Joseph* (Leiden: E. J. Brill, 1970), p. 27.
6. T. Reik, *Listening with the Third Ear* (New York: Farrar, Straus, 1954), passim.

7. E. A. Speiser, *Genesis, The Anchor Bible Series* (Garden City, NY: Doubleday, 1986), p. 256.

8. Ibid., p. 255 n. 26; p. 257.

9. W. F. Albright, "Abram the Hebrew: A New Archeological Interpretation." *Bulletin of the American Schools of Oriental Research* 163(1963):36-54, p. 44ff.

10. Speiser, op. cit., p. xli.

11. Ibid., p. 92.

12. E. A. Speiser, *Oriental and Biblical Studies* (Philadelphia: University of Pennsylvania Press, 1967), p. 78.

13. Ibid., p. 80ff.

14. N. G. Kase, A. B. Weingold, and D. M. Gershenson, *Principles and Practice of Clinical Gynecology*, 2d ed. (New York: Churchill Livingstone, 1990), p. 589.

15. E. A. Speiser, "The Biblical Idea of History in Its Common Near Eastern Setting," *Israel Exploration Journal* 7(1957):201–216

16. Speiser, *Genesis*, p. 120f.

17. E. A. Speiser, "I know Not the Day of My Death," *Journal of Biblical Literature* 74(1955):252–256

18. Ibid., p. 256.

19. Speiser, *Genesis*, p. 213ff.

20. Ibid., p. 247, note 39.

21. A. E. Draffkorn, "Ilani/Elohim," *Journal of Biblical Literature* 76(1957):216–224

22. J. Lewy, "Habiru and Hebrews," *Hebrew Union College Annual* 14(1939):587–623

23. S. Yeivin, *The Israelite Conquest of Canaan* (Istanbul: Nederlands Historisch-Archeologisch Instituut in Het Nabije Oosten, 1971), p. 281.

24. C. Westermann, *Genesis*, trans. D. Green (Grand Rapids: Eerdmans, 1987), p. 254.

The Hyksos: Semites in Egypt

6

It can be said without challenge that Israel's earliest footprints are embedded in the Near East. The preceding chapters outline the migratory patterns of various Semites as they moved inexorably toward Canaan around the middle of the Second Millennium. These aboriginal Israelites slowly evolved into the people who would adopt the unique belief in a single, just, egalitarian, and implacable God. The patriarchal narratives alternate between lofty dedication and vision to abject opportunism, but they always speak with a human voice. Drawn by fortuitous circumstances to the underpopulated hills and xeric sands of Canaan, these various clusters of Semites were in position for the call of history.

Unfortunately ancient Israel had few outside observers and even fewer internal monitors. When we are first able to distinguish the amorphous group from its neighboring peoples at the end of the Thirteenth Century, it was already a conglomeration of West Semites and Mesopotamians who were resident within the Syro-Palestine area. Another group, much smaller in size but perhaps part of the original mass at one time, joined them by way of Egypt. This Egyptian contingent was led by Moses, who imposed the concept of ethical monotheism on this mixture of mainly Semitic peoples. How, when, and under what circumstances they came to be in Egypt are shrouded in uncertainty.

Early Egyptian documents give no indication of a uniquely monotheistic group of Semites either living within the land or leaving it. Most textual sources refer only to "Asiatics." However, the gap between Asiatics and the emigrants described in Exodus does not appear to be irreconcilable.

The later scribes of Israel attached great importance to the Egyptian connection by enhancing the determinative suffering of the people who sojourned there. The Torah recounts how Israel came and stayed in Egypt for a period of 400 years. Gen. 46:27 states that when Jacob arrived in Egypt, his household numbered seventy persons, including Joseph and his family, who were already there. When the group finally marched out in the Exodus, they were 600,000 men strong (Exod. 12:37). After little more than a year en route, a census of all Israelite men twenty years or older was taken, and 603,550 were counted (Num. 2:46).

These numbers are patently exaggerated, given the normal process of generation and attrition. If they had any significance at the time of writing, it was only to symbolize the group's fecundity within Egypt and to establish their power to overcome all obstacles. The question that must be examined now is who these people in Egypt were and how they came to cluster as the group that contributed its unique doctrines to later Israel.

* * *

Throughout history the Nile River valley has been one of the most fertile regions on earth. One characteristic of the yearly flooding was the deposit downriver of massive amounts of fresh alluvial soil that supported a luxuriant growth of food crops. Irrigation, highly developed even in the Old Kingdom (2600–2200), used river water throughout the rest of the year.[1] In ancient times, when agriculture was not intensive, the fertility of the land was never depleted. Agricultural communities flourished on its banks wherever the topography was favorable, despite the Nile's annual inundation. The biggest problem was in the low-lying delta, where the overwhelming hydraulic forces of the annual flood caused a continual reformation of the land mass, which inhibited the development of widespread permanent agricultural settlements, especially in the northernmost islands. Fishing and other water-oriented activities were more common. The finger-like delta islands were oriented north and south in parallel, inhibiting communications in all directions. There were no bridges, and river crossings were made by crude ferries.[2] Thus despite the delta's legendary fertility, the region was sparsely settled until the beginning of the Second Millennium.

Records from the XIIth Dynasty (2000 B.C.E.) tell about transient migrations of Bedouin-like Asiatics into Egypt, where forage, food, and water were plentiful. These Asiatics were known to the Egyptians as *Shasu*. Without a dense native population to resist their encroachment, they must have found the lushness of the eastern delta paradise in comparison to their own arid deserts and steppes. It is a wonder that these visitors ever returned to their original land. Or did they? The "squatter" problem was severe enough that the Pharaoh Amenemhet I (1990–1960) finally built "walls of the ruler" along the Suez isthmus to keep them out. Despite these efforts, groups from Asia continued to infiltrate the delta islands.[3]

The First Intermediate Period of Egyptian dynastic history (2200–2000) is usually offered as the earliest time when Asiatics can be documented in that country.[4] This era becomes the stage for Abraham in Gen. 12 and for Joseph in Gen. 37, tales that certainly could be true within the known migrations of nomadic peoples into the delta area. It is their descendants who were led out by Moses in the Exodus.

The Torah, by allocating 430 years to the period of sojourn in Egypt (Exod. 12:40), emphasizes its determinative importance. This number becomes less compelling, however, when we consider how unrealistic it would be for a people to maintain a fervid yearning for a land they had not seen for twelve generations. The sojourn of four-plus centuries has no supporting evidence, but it is unlikely to be a number totally without rationale. Despite many calculations to justify the number of years, none are clearly convincing. Before we discard that figure, let us remember that Asiatics, a number of whom were surely Semitic, were known in Egypt around 2000 B.C.E., or 800 years before the Exodus. There is further evidence that people from Canaan ruled northern Egypt for about 150 years beginning around 1700 B.C.E. Since the Exodus took place in the Thirteenth Century, it is not impossible that the beginning of the traditional four-century sojourn in Egypt has been referenced to those conquering Canaanites, who became known as Hyksos. However, a definite connection of the Hyksos with the Exodus group would have to be established.

Originally the Hyksos were thought to be Hurrians who conquered northern Canaan and then marched into Egypt. This concept is now open to serious question. The Hyksos' ruling elements did come to Canaan from the far northeast where other Indo-European peoples arose. Analysis of proper names in the extant name lists reveal that whereas the military elite tended to have Hurrian or Indo-European names, the peasant names were predominantly Semitic.[5,6] The latter were most likely Amorites from Syro-Palestine. The assumption that the Hyksos, as Aryans, could conquer Egypt because they had mastered the military use of horse and chariot has also been challenged. This particular attack vehicle was used by the Hyksos only near the end of their rule.[7]

The Amorites of Canaan had been in commercial contact with Egypt since the Middle Bronze Age (2200–1500). Canaanite amphorae and household pottery have been found in the vicinity of the later Hyksos capital, Avaris.[8] Although it seems that most Semites/Asiatics came to Egypt freely, there is evidence that they also came as prisoners of war from military expeditions by the pharaohs of the Middle Kingdom (2000–1700). It is not certain whether their status was that of servant or slave, but many were part of the trade patterns between the two regions, and some of them may have remained as voluntary indentured servants.

As their number increased, so did their integration into Egyptian society. Each adult was listed with both an original name and an Egyptian one. Children had only Egyptian names, which might imply that a subtle assimilation was taking hold, especially for those born in Egypt. One record lists eighty persons, many with Semitic names, who served in a single Theban household. Egyptian texts of the period refer to these people from Canaan as *aamu*. The Aamu were considered permanent residents, many employed as caravaneers and guards in the transportation of turquoise and copper from the mines in Sinai.[9] This occupational involvement implies that they possessed a singular knowledge of natural hazards in the intervening terrain, such as encroaching tides and marshy land covering the treacherous isthmus of Suez.

The Aamu soon appeared as temple functionaries, as well as in other positions of honor and responsibility. Most of them assimilated in all respects, although they still bore the ethnic term Aamu.[10] An ebb in Egyptian power during the XIIIth Dynasty presented the Amorites and other Semites living in Syro-Palestine with an opportunity for further expansion into the eastern delta region, later named Goshen in Hebrew sources.[11]

The weaker pharaohs might have viewed the underpopulated delta on the doorstep of Asia as somewhat peripheral to their more pressing concerns. But stronger ones, such as Amenemhet I and Senwosret III (1875–1840), strengthened the fortifications along the eastern frontier and effected basic administrative changes. During this period, Egypt was divided into three departments. The northern one, including Memphis and the vast delta, had its center in the area of Qantir-Khatana. There had been close cultural ties between the area of Qantir-Khatana and Byblos on the coast of northern Canaan. A temple inscription called this area "the mouth of the two ways," indicating a terminus for both the road to Canaan and the road to the Sinai mines.[12] The other two departments were along the Nile to the south, with Thebes as the great center of one, and the other included Nubia, farther to the south.

Toward the end of the Middle Kingdom, political weakness in a sequence of rulers, as well as an increasing influx of people from Syro-Palestine, resulted in what has been called the Hyksos "invasion." This movement was not predominantly a military one but rather an infiltration into the delta region by individuals or small, self-sufficient clans. Political upheavals in Byblos at the end of the Eighteenth Century stimulated an exodus from there to the Nile delta, where their own people were already established.[13] The newer population came with its own leadership and perhaps with some of the strengths in newer military technology that had been developed in Asia. Although government in Canaan was by "an overwhelming number of kinglets," there is no indication that these rulers mounted a military invasion of Egypt.[14] The Egyptian term for them was "rulers of foreign countries," and it had been commonly used to describe Asian groups since the XIIth Dynasty.

Our first knowledge of the Hyksos challenge comes mainly from Manetho, a Third Century Egyptian priest at Heliopolis. The events he described had taken place at least 1400 years earlier, and we can only conjecture whether his sources were documents that were subsequently lost or merely folklore that somehow survived to his own time.

We have already seen how evanescent history can be after long periods of oral tradition without the constraint of documentary witness. In addition to Manetho's testimony, there are several pharaonic references about the Hyksos, dating from the XVIIIth Dynasty. But these are also of questionable historicity, because the aggrieved and humiliated pharaohs could not be objective about the truncation of their empire. They usually recorded events in a particularly self-aggrandizing literary form.

According to Manetho, "Their race as a whole was called Hyksos, that is 'king-shepherds': for hyk in the sacred language means 'king', and sos in common speech is 'shepherd' or 'shepherds': hence the compound word 'Hyksos'."[15] Living in Ptolemaic Egypt and writing in Greek, he gave immortality to that term, which is at best ambiguous and at worst misleading. The term seems to have a pejorative undertone, indicating considerable ill-will between the later Egyptians and this foreign rule. The other translation, "ruler(s) of foreign lands," is also compat-

ible with an Amorite provenance.[16] Pharaonic inscriptions by
Kamose in the Sixteenth Century and by Hatshepsut in the Fifteenth Century refer to the Hyksos as "Asiatics."

But let Manetho himself speak: "Tutimaeus. In his reign, for
what cause I know not, a blast of God smote us; and unexpectedly, from the regions of the East, invaders of obscure race
marched in confidence of victory against our land. By main force
they easily seized it without striking a blow; and having over-
powered the rulers of the land, they then burned our cities ruth-
lessly, razed to the ground the temples of the gods, and treated all
the natives with a cruel hostility, massacring some and leading
into slavery the wives and children of others."[17] Tutimaeus is
thought to be the pharaoh who was in power when the Hyksos
first arrived. The name probably refers to Dudu-mose, a late
XIIIth Dynasty pharaoh.

Many writers, using Manetho's description as their main reference, conceived of an external aggression. Certainly a conquest
by predatory Amorite neighbors would not be unknown in the
overall history of the ancient Near East. Also, because the mili-
tarily advanced Hurrians had extended their control into eastern
Syria at this time, it is assumed that they were heavily involved in
this further encroachment into the Nile delta.

The Hyksos hegemony began around 1700 B.C.E., when evidence shows that they ruled all of Egypt, including the Sudan
and Lower Nubia.[18] They lost most of the southern territories
later. The native pharaohs of the XVIIth Dynasty, who ruled
Upper Egypt from Karnak (Thebes), were largely ineffective.
They were forced to pay tribute to the Hyksos, but the relationship was not outwardly hostile.[19] The respect that the Canaanite
princes showed for native traditions contributed much to their
success in winning support from the indigenous population.
They allowed the administrative offices in their region to continue to function with Egyptian personnel. They also adopted
the prominent regional gods, including Seth and Re. Some kings
even added Re to their own names.[20]

A peculiar change in the process of pharaonic succession had occurred in the XIIIth Dynasty (1780–1650), when the rulers began to be elected to office. As the major administrative capital was then in Qantir-Khatana, it is not surprising that some elected pharaohs of that dynasty had Semitic names.[21] The assumption of power by the Hyksos can be viewed as a culmination of their gradual increase in numbers in the delta region or by an "internal coup d'état" by local leaders.[22]

At first they ruled from the old capital at Memphis but later moved farther north into the delta area, where they built the city of Avaris on the Qantir-Khatana site. The reason for this relocation is uncertain, but one explanation might be military expediency, given the proximity of Memphis to the simmering frontier with the Egyptians. A city closer to the Mediterranean Sea would also establish better communication with kindred states in Canaan. Avaris was about 70 miles downstream from Memphis, and at the time it was a site that could anchor a sea trade. Now, as modern Tell el-Dab'a, it is almost landlocked. This is but another of the significant topographical changes that altered the delta region over time.

The Amoritic city-states of Canaan had a rigid feudal organization. It is not unreasonable that as they became more secure and successful in the new land, their hierarchies expanded. When their princes declared themselves to be the rulers of the delta, they met little resistance from any quarter. The natives generally cooperated to partake of the trade-induced prosperity.[23]

The success of the Asiatics in the delta is clearly described in "The Admonitions of Ipuwer," a historical allegory supposedly about life during the Middle Kingdom. It was written during the Second Intermediate Period (1650–1530), which coincides with the time of the Hyksos. Some of its appropriate lines are, "Foreigners have become people [Egyptians] everywhere" (1:9), "a foreign tribe from abroad has come to Egypt" (3:1), "there are no Egyptians anywhere" (3:2), and "The foreigners are now skilled in the work of the Delta" (4:8).[24] Unfortunately this suggested model of accession to power by population pressure has not always been widely accepted. One characterization of the arrival of the Hyksos is, "a sudden dash by a Syro-Palestinian king at the head of a compact army on the Egyptian Delta."[25]

By the Thirteenth Century, when the Exodus was gathering momentum, the Semites of the eastern delta were at least three centuries removed from the Hyksos. It has been acknowledged that "numerous Asiatics were present in Egypt during the Thirteenth Century . . . but their presence in Egypt is irrelevant to the character of the Hyksos coup, and they should not be included under the term 'Hyksos'."[26] Whatever differences existed between the Hebrews and the earlier Amorites/Hyksos were more time-related than due to divergence of origin.

The Egyptian reconquest was supposedly initiated by Kamose, the last pharaoh of the XVIIth Dynasty (1650–1550). Judging by the words of a recently discovered stele that he erected at Karnak, one would think that he was about to sweep Egypt clean of the Hyksos. "You have been forced away in the company of your army. Your speech is mean when you make me a [mere] 'prince,' whereas you are a 'ruler,' as if to beg for yourself the execution-block to which you will fall. Your back has been seen, O wretch! My army is after you. The women of Avaris will not conceive; their hearts will not open within their bodies when my army's battle-cry is heard."[27] It is another example of the hyperbole so characteristic of the post facto view of history expressed by many pharaohs. Whatever success Kamose might have had, it nevertheless fell to Ahmose (1550–1525), the first pharaoh of the New Kingdom, to rid Egypt of the Hyksos kings at the beginning of his reign. The Egyptians had become strong enough to disrupt the Hyksos' commercial activities in the south, exposing them to pressures from their rejuvenated forces.[28] Manetho wrote that they were defeated by "Misphragmuthosis" and "Thummosis" (probably Thutmose III and Thutmose IV, respectively) and that "240,000 persons" had to return to their former lands in "Syria." Further "they built a city in the land now called Judaea . . . and gave it the name of Jerusalem" to accommodate all the people who escaped from Egypt.[29]

There are several obvious problems with Manetho's version of this episode. In the first place, the two last-named kings lived more than 100 years after the Hyksos departed. Second, evidence is lacking that Jerusalem was ever anything more than a minor town until it became David's capital some 500 years later. Manetho ascribed the motivation for building the city of Jerusalem to fear of the Assyrians, who were then occupying Syria.[30] This is a flagrant anachronism. The earliest presence of Assyria in the eastern Mediterranean could not have occurred prior to the Twelfth Century, or about 400 years after the fact.

We know no more about what happened to the Hyksos who had to leave Egypt than we know about those who might have remained. There is no evidence that the Hyksos dynasty's defeat, which was essentially in the nature of a civil war, resulted in the expulsion of the population. The Semites probably continued to live in the delta as they had before.[31] The term Hyksos, although given to them by the Egyptians, seems to have disappeared from the vocabulary rapidly and completely.

Khamudi (1540–1530), the last Hyksos king, may very well have left Egypt by a negotiated settlement rather than the crushing defeat promised by Kamose's stele. "On these terms the Shepherds, with their possessions and households complete . . . left Egypt."[32] Manetho's statement would seem to affirm that it was a retreat, not a rout. Another text dealing with the Hyksos withdrawal suggests, "It was caused by the majesty of this god that his voice was heard. . . . The sky makes precipitation." This intrigued a contemporary scholar, who theorizes that the "voice" was a volcano. An item in a separate papyrus states that the Mediterranean Sea at one time came close to Avaris, perhaps describing a tidal wave. Because the Island of Thera in the Aegean Sea experienced a massive volcanic eruption around this time (actually about 100 years later), he further assumed that the "precipitation" might have been tephra (volcanic ash). Leaning on these interpretations, his interesting conclusion is that Khamudi, taking it as a sign of divine displeasure, struck a deal and left quietly.[33]

However the issue was settled, Hyksos rule lasted about 150 years. There is evidence to suggest that at least toward the end of the period, the Hyksos kings tried to adapt to Egyptian ways by copying their titulary, as well as their architecture and statuary. Still, some authors believe that they never really succeeded in becoming acceptably Egyptianized to the natives, and because they ruled severely, as Manetho implied, they were never forgiven. As soon as they were pushed out of Egypt, a great effort was undertaken to efface the monuments they left behind.[34] There can be no question that the Hyksos ruling class disappeared from the northern territories during the middle of the Sixteenth Century. Nor can anyone contest that the triumphant pharaohs tried to alter posterity's perception of their role in the process.

* * *

John Van Seters characterizes the Hyksos era as the product of natural political impulses by various peoples who tried to occupy the same space. A strong element of Amoritic culture persisted in the delta region long after they were ejected. This is evidenced by the continuation of Semitic deities that entered the Egyptian pantheon in the New Kingdom and by continued use of Semitic place-names throughout the delta region.[35] Thus an early and long-standing presence of Semites who lived more or less peacefully in Egypt for several hundred years can be established. It has been suggested that the Exodus story may be a variant on a dimly remembered earlier experience: Semites who entered Egypt voluntarily, became numerous and powerful, and after several generations had to retire to their place of origin.[36]

The position is widely held that the patriarchal family entered Egypt during the Hyksos period, using the logic of an assured welcome by a beleaguered Semitic regime. However, setting the patriarchal age at this early date creates exceptional difficulties with the evaluation of other chronological data bearing on Israel. Certainly the Hyksos period lends a measure of reality to the Joseph story, namely, that he arrived as part of a Midianite trade caravan, was given an Egyptian name in addition to his own, and then rose to a position second only to the pharaoh. This is not to suggest that Joseph's arrival coincided with the Hyksos rule, only that the acceptance of Asiatics into the socioeconomic life of Egypt was not uncommon. As we shall see, the Joseph story belongs to the New Kingdom.

Notes

1. K. W. Butzer, *Early Hydraulic Civilization in Egypt* (Chicago: Univ. of Chicago Press, 1976), p. 12.
2. J. Van Seters, *The Hyksos* (New Haven: Yale Univ. Press, 1966), p. 140.
3. S. Herrmann, *Israel in Egypt* (Naperville, IL: Allenson, 1970), p. 10.
4. J. Van Seters, op. cit., p. 17.
5. T. Säve-Söderbergh, "The Hyksos Rule in Egypt," *Journal of Egyptian Archeology* 37(1951):53–71.
6. A. E. Glock, "Early Israel as the Kingdom of Yahweh," *Concordia Theological Monthly*, 41(1970):558–605.
7. T. Säve-Söderbergh, op. cit., p. 59.
8. M. Bietak, "Canaanites in the Eastern Delta," in *Egypt, Israel, Sinai*, ed. A. F. Rainey (Tel Aviv: Tel Aviv Univ., 1987).
9. J. Van Seters, op. cit., p. 88f.
10. Ibid., p. 90.
11. A. Kempinski, "Some Observations on the Hyksos (XVth) Dynasty and Its Canaanite Origins," in *Pharaonic Egypt*, ed. S. Israelit-Groll (Jerusalem: Magnes Press, 1984), pp. 129–137.
12. J. Van Seters, op. cit., p. 93.
13. M. Bietak, op. cit., p. 52.
14. T. Säve-Söderbergh, op. cit., p. 55ff.
15. W. G. Waddell, *Manetho* (Cambridge: Harvard Univ. Press, 1940), p. 85.
16. D. B. Redford, "The Hyksos Invasion in History and Tradition," *Orientalia* 39 fasc.1(1970):1–51.
17. W. G. Waddell, op. cit., p. 79.
18. T. Säve-Söderbergh, op. cit., p. 55.
19. Ibid., p. 67.
20. Ibid., p. 64f.
21. J. Van Seters, op. cit., p. 95.
22. Ibid., p. 103.
23. T. Säve-Söderbergh, op. cit., p. 61.

24. J. B. Pritchard, *Ancient Near Eastern Texts*, 3rd ed. (Princeton: Princeton Univ. Press, 1969), p. 441f.
25. D. B. Redford, op. cit., p. 17.
26. Ibid.
27. J. B. Pritchard, op. cit., p. 90.
28. M. Bietak, op. cit., p. 55.
29. W. G. Waddell, op. cit., p. 89.
30. Ibid.
31. J. Van Seters, op. cit., p. 194.
32. W. G. Waddell, op.cit., p. 89.
33. H. Goedicke, "The End of the Hyksos in Egypt," in *Egyptological Studies in Honor of Richard A.Parker*, ed. L. H. Lesko (Providence: Brown Univ. Press, 1986), pp. 37–48.
34. D. B. Redford, op. cit., p. 7f.
35. J. Van Seters, op. cit., p. 189f.
36. D. B. Redford, "An Egyptological Perspective on the Exodus," in *Egypt, Israel, Sinai*, ed. A.F. Rainey (Tel Aviv: Tel Aviv Univ., 1987), pp. 137–161.

The Hab/piru: Hebrews?

7

T he Semitic lodestar seems to have been the southwest corner of the Fertile Crescent, which beckoned nomadic peoples with its temperate climate and well-watered land. Charismatic leaders of extended families began to lay claim to real estate that they saw as workable and defensible. The three patriarchs of Israel who chose Canaan were such men, and their originality lay in an egocentric belief that God promised the land to them. They even succeeded in transmitting this creedal inheritance to their descendants. Although no data extrinsic to the Torah confirm the existence of these primogenitors, reason insists that such prototypes existed in reality at some time and place. If they represent the earliest stirrings of Israel, we must enter Fourteenth Century Canaan.

It was a land in turmoil, fragmented by many isolated and independent principalities. Each city-state harbored a rigidly feudal society within its walls, with the rulers treating their own poorer classes indifferently. Jealousies and irrational hatreds festered among and within the domains of each. Life for the peasants who tilled the peripheral fields became more burdensome the farther they lived from the city. Everybody seemed to ignore the incoming nomadic peoples, who hovered in the surrounding hills, until the intrusion impacted their daily routines.

Egypt's political control over the region, dating from early in the XVIIIth Dynasty, had weakened perceptibly after peaking a century earlier. A power vacuum beckoned to all who watched and waited. Large and small groups of displaced persons roamed the underutilized hinterlands beyond the city walls, seeking sustenance by seizing land and booty. Mercenary soldiery and banditry became a unified occupation for these have-nots. Ethnically and organizationally diverse, they presented formidable problems to the established princes. Their motivation was the desire of all who were disenfranchised to profit in a period of opportunity, here afforded by Egypt's preoccupation with internal matters. It was at this time that the people called Hab/piru came to the attention of the world in the place where Israel would develop.

A fortuitous discovery in Egypt yielded the first clues about this turmoil in Fourteenth Century Canaan. Some clay tablets, written in cuneiform, were uncovered a century ago at El-Amarna on the eastern shore of the Nile River, halfway between Memphis and Thebes (Karnak). The ancient ruins where they were found proved to be the site of a long-forgotten city built by the Pharaoh Akhenaten sometime after 1350 B.C.E. At that time Egypt's age-old traditional religious patterns were undergoing a dramatic revision by the pharaoh. His preoccupation with these matters left little time for foreign affairs, forcing his loyal vassals in Asia to fend for themselves against the mounting pressure of restive warlords and self-serving Hab/piru. This religious revolution in Egypt and the chaotic situation in Canaan together gave a name to the latter half of the Fourteenth Century—the Amarna Age.

The local peasants who found the tablets intuitively recognized their importance and tried to sell them, but scholars and dealers at first were skeptical of their authenticity. Without apparent commercial value for the tablets the locals began to pulverize them for fertilizer, and the world stood to suffer an irretrievable loss.[1] Belatedly some of the tablets were recognized for what they were, an extensive diplomatic correspondence directed to the pharaohs of the Amarna Age from their vassals in Syro-Palestine. A hurried scientific expedition then recovered hundreds of tablets, which reported ominous incursions and looting by groups of people known to the Egyptians as SA.GAZ. This term is considered synonymous with Hab/piru.

The Canaanite princes, recognizing that Egypt's imperial ambitions had waned, used that opportunity to increase their own authority by attacking those city-states still loyal to the Egyptian throne. The Hab/piru were people who had no land within the area and therefore were available for hire, augmenting the forces of the cities. The Hab/piru were so numerous in Canaan at the time that they appeared to hold the balance of power.

* * *

To understand the origins of Israel, we must clearly define the interlocking relationship of patriarchs, Hab/piru, Hebrew (*ibri*), and the Amarna Age. The philological aspect of the name Hab/piru has given rise to a strong inference that the word Hebrew derives from this source. Certainly the biblical depiction of the patriarchs as chieftains of aggressive groups of landless strangers insinuating or fighting their way into various areas of Canaan is consonant with what is known of Hab/piru behavior. Abraham's activities in Gen. 14, where he fights the Canaanite kings with his 318 men, or Jacob's involvement in Shechem in Gen. 34, would also seem to justify such an assumption.

In 1955 Moshe Greenberg published the still definitive dissertation on these people, neatly shorthanding the name into Hab/piru,[2] which seems to catch the tentative nature of the many transliterations most appropriately. His spelling is used throughout this book to identify this important class of people who lived throughout the Near East and specifically in Canaan.

The earliest reference to the word Hab/piru or to its corollary term, SA.GAZ, dates from the Third Dynasty of Ur (2100–2000). At that time the lower Mesopotamian valley was undergoing a Semitization by the increase of Akkadian influence, as well as a significant infiltration by Amorites from the Syrian and Anatolian highlands. Both names, Hab/piru and SA.GAZ, were used for depicting certain individuals or groups. The frequency of reference to them in Sumerian and Egyptian sources indicates that they were a widespread phenomenon in the Near East during much of the Second Millennium. Why two philologically different words for the same object were used is uncertain. However, SA.GAZ is from the Sumerian root *saggasu*, meaning murderer or killer, whereas Hab/piru was an Akkadian term from the root *habbatu*, meaning to wander or roam. Another translation of the latter term is "robber, bandit, raider."³ Hab/piru probably represents a gloss of the earlier SA.GAZ, to further define aspects of this common population element from passive servant to soldier or bandit.

In 1930 Benno Landesberger suggested that the Hab/piru were "not a people but a class of the population, the class of the destitute and the uprooted, the criminal and the fugitive, people who had severed all connections with their families and usually with their countries of origin."⁴ More recently the term has been defined as a "social ethnonym" to highlight a common social origin rather than an ethnic relationship.⁵ However, there is evidence that by the Ramesside Age in Egypt (1300-1200), Hab/piru had picked up an ethnic connotation in the use of the term Hebrew. Egyptian sources speak of the Hab/piru working stone, probably in the building of royal monuments, and Exodus tells of the Hebrews who are making bricks for the same purpose.⁶ The suspicion that both names recognize one people is unavoidable.

A broader perspective of the Hab/piru became available with the sequential discovery of ancient records, beginning with the Amarna letters through Hittite and Nuzi sources to the Ras Shamra (Ugarit) and Mari data. The Amarna letters revealed that roving bands of freebooters, either in the employ of local Canaanite princes or for their own benefit, were stirring up the political landscape. It has already been noted that this activity can be found in many of the narratives in Genesis. Hittite archival discoveries revealed that the Hab/piru were known to Rim-Sin in Sumer and to Hammurabi in Babylon several hundred years before the Amarna references, a full thousand years before Israel was an identifiable unit. These older Hab/piru were not shown as buccaneers but rather as people who "received state rations, manned royal garrisons, and had their gods invoked in state treaties. . . ."[7] On the other hand, some records report them attacking and looting towns on their own, including the region of Haran, which was Abraham's second residence on his way to Canaan. This behavioral duality was similarly emphasized in the Amarna correspondence.[8] The Nuzi data fostered the view that they were mainly individuals or small groups of persons characterized by "an inferior, dependent status; they are mostly depicted as binding themselves into slavery, although the conditions of their servitude distinguish them from ordinary slaves."[9] The Hab/piru, as the foreign servants of Nuzi, were considered to be of two classes. In one the slave served for a limited period of years, after which he was free to leave; in the other he was permanently indentured. The rules for Hebrew slaves set forth in Exod. 21:2ff and Deut. 15:12ff use the same two classes.[10] Even Jacob's service to Laban can be seen in this light. Obviously there are differences as well as similarities in the details, but a close relationship between the Hab/piru of record and the Hebrew patriarchs is compelling.

The kingdom of Mari during the Nineteenth and Eighteenth Centuries also offers witness to the early patterns of Hab/piru development. Mari was situated midway along the Euphrates River in northwestern Mesopotamia, and its lifestyle has been extensively reconstructed from data recently uncovered there. Mari had a mainly Semitic population, although it was ethnically Hurrian. The country represented a dimorphic society in which one element, sedentary and urban, lived in agricultural towns and villages. This element was part of a rigid social organization in which the overall political control emanated from the hierarchy centered in the capital city of Mari. The other major societal element was pastoral nomadic.

The pastoral nomads were organized in tribal groups that had both sedentary and seminomadic characteristics. The leader was freely chosen, but his role was mainly as the spokesman for the tribe and the liaison with local authorities. The pastoral nomads generally deferred to urban authority but without complete submission. Incidentally, it is still not certain whether pastoral nomadism, or seminomadism, represented an intermediate stage in the sedenterization process or merely a specialization within the sedentary group, whereby people could move away when more land for pasturage was needed. The group would withdraw with its tribal organization intact when faced with economic hardship or oppressive decrees. In leaving they often combined with others to form a splinter group strong enough to ensure a viable future. This separation from the sedentary portion of society, whether temporary or permanent, has been called "retribalization."[11] Often individuals or families also left their urban or tribal societies. These people also came to be called Hab/piru.[12]

In order to survive after they had severed their natural economic relationships with the host society, they had two basic choices. One was to accept work as servants within the villages, with the same disabilities as our own migratory farm workers might experience. If they chose servitude, they could maintain their smaller size and a more independent role. The other activity consisted of plundering towns and villages to replenish their supplies and livestock. Their predatory activity needed manpower, usually obtained by merging with similar groups, and served to develop a notable fighting skill. The earliest of these aggressive, marauding "social dropouts" were identified in the upper reaches of the Habur valley north of Mari. A question might well be asked whether these people were not simply given the name of the geographic region where they were first identified and only later given professional implications.

At Nuzi most of the at-large population had Hurrian names, but Semitic names made up at least two-thirds of the Hab/piru lists.[13] Ethnic purity seems to have been less relevant in Mesopotamia, and Assyrian data frequently describe foreigners who were being added to the population and treated as natives.[14] It is significant to note that in periods of political instability, the term Hab/piru could connote variously a savage, a destroyer, a murderer, or a plunderer. Less harshly the meaning might be a disturber, a wanderer, a migrant, a person on the move, or someone on a pay list and receiving public support.[15]

The Hab/piru have been found in the northern Jezreel Valley, considered to be the territory of the tribe of Issachar, which means hired man. Seti I (1305–1290), the second pharaoh of the XIXth Dynasty, fought the Hab/piru in Galilee around the end of the Fourteenth Century, at the same time that the tribe of Asher is thought to have been living in the area.[16] This evidence suggests that significant numbers of Hab/piru were living in widespread urban or rural centers shortly before the Israelite tribal structure developed.

The Amarna letters give the impression that the Hab/piru of Syro-Palestine in the Fourteenth Century were solely mercenaries who hired themselves out to local chieftains. Although the letters often referred to the entire force of dissident Canaanite leaders as Hab/piru, the term technically applied only to the mercenaries. Such references indicate a relatively large number of hired auxiliary soldiers as compared to native fighters. That these soldiers were paid additionally in booty or land is mentioned in letters from Er-Heba, the governor of Jerusalem. One letter tells how Labaya, one of the marauding chieftains, gave the city of Shechem to his Hab/piru soldiers. Greenberg feels that this probably means only that he quartered them in that city.[17] However, with a minimal change in perspective we might well see in Gen. 34 how Jacob and his sons, as Hab/piru, were acquiring the same Shechem.

When the power of Egypt over Syro-Palestine showed signs of weakness, as happened within a single generation after the death of the great conqueror Thutmose III (1480–1425), the resultant instability appeared to be the usual political and economic maneuverings of petty kings. The Hab/piru, feared as much as wooed, suddenly found themselves in great demand to augment the armies of the local rulers in their battles with each other. Because of their large numbers, the Hab/piru could easily tip the balance of power by changing sides. They were most often the attacking force but with a strong tendency to plunder for their own benefit. Perhaps this laxity of discipline was merely a natural by-product of the pervasive anarchy. Also, chronic insecurity in the disenfranchised often seeks extra compensation in a time of obvious opportunity.

The fact that the Hab/piru were centered in the hill country of Syro-Palestine is of critical importance in understanding their modus operandi. Topology, which in its broadest sense enlists factors of physical environment to assess history, provides some of the rationale for their choice. The hill country, with its rugged cliffs, steep gorges, and heavy forestation, was less tightly controlled by the forces of state because it was inaccessible to the military ordnance of the time. Also, the potential for both successful ambush and evasive guerrilla action that lurked everywhere did not favor the attacking army.[18] Bands of Hab/piru could occupy these areas continuously for generations without fear of facing the full might of Canaanite armor. In the course of time many disenfranchised people found refuge and perhaps purpose in joining these bands. They chose this harsh but independent life over the relatively secure indenture of servitude or soldiery-for-hire.[19]

The Hab/piru of the Second Millennium were people mainly outside the accepted social structure, often at the fringes of the law. There is no evidence that they were desert nomads or Bedouin-like. Although their settlements were recorded only in Boghazkoy, the Hittite capital, and Ugarit in northwestern Syria, Greenberg states that, "it may be safely assumed that wherever they were employed in large numbers—at Larsa, Alalah, Nuzi, or Syro-Palestine—they were settled in their own quarters."[20] Their apparent mobility and aggressive rootlessness indicate that general acceptance by the natives was cautious and then only when their presence was advantageous to the hosts. The ethnic diversity among the Hab/piru, within a Semitic predominance, resulted from a tolerance and hospitality to other vagrant persons. Perhaps the traditional Israelite concern for the stranger has older roots than the biblical admonition "Remember that you were a slave in the land of Egypt"(Deut. 5:15).

More than 300 years after the Amarna Age, the activities of David before he became Israel's king are still compatible with the aggressive aspect of the Hab/piru. As a fugitive from King Saul, he managed to attract 400 hundred men under him "in any kind of distress or in debt or with a grievance"(1 Sam. 22:2). He became an ally of the Philistine king of Gath, who gave him the town of Ziklag for his men and their families. From that base David ravaged the countryside for his own benefit. He also offered to fight for Achish, another Philistine ruler, against King Saul, but the offer was rejected because of suspicions about his primary loyalty. That such an ignoble tradition about Israel's greatest king could reach a fixed form, perhaps within the span of his own lifetime, represents another example of historical obstinacy in Torah traditions. Other men in Scripture also could have been Hab/piru. Abimelech in Judg. 9 is very much the buccaneer, gathering about him men of dubious loyalty and fighting the establishment; Ga'al and his band in turn challenged Abimelech.

Among established societies a surprising aspect of Hab/piru status, in light of their generally inferior position, is the prominence given to some members. In northern Syria at the end of the Fifteenth Century, the grandfather of a king, Tettis, was Hab/piru. Another Hab/piru was described by a Babylonian king around 1150 B.C.E. as the ruler of Assyria. Also, one who was in the service of a Babylonian king around 1050 B.C.E. received valuable gifts of real estate. In Egypt and Nuzi Hab/piru served in professional capacities, as well as in slavery.[21] These examples merely indicate that with a certain confluence of ability and personal motivation, even a Hab/piru could rise above the limitations of his birth status. The story of Joseph in Egypt may represent an example of this: the recognition and promotion of a particularly capable person who is then able to offer benefits to others of his class. If the patriarchs were indeed Hab/piru and their pattern of opportunism more than coincidental, the general historicity of the Torah receives further confirmation.

Another intriguing point about this marginal people is the invocation of their gods as divine witnesses to various treaties, especially between the Hittites and the Mitannis. International treaties routinely solicited the power of each country's deities in the interests of enforcement, but the Hab/piru were not representative of any specific country. The inclusion of their gods certainly implies recognition of the group as a legitimate and perhaps important element in Hittite and Assyrian society.[22, 23] That a people considered inferior could be so honored through its gods inevitably raises the question whether the gods of the Hab/piru already had some mysterious potency as compared to the gods of dominant Near Eastern societies. One might also wonder whether the relative alienation of the Hab/piru from the mainstream peoples contributed to cultic differences that elicited grudging respect. Unfortunately very little is known about their religious practices, but given their ethnic diversity, it is unlikely that they practiced a creedal unity. Perhaps this changed when they began to believe that God promised them land.

Some scholars have been loathe to accept the equivalence of Hab/piru with Hebrew. The Hab/piru did not display the precise criteria of tribal organization but rather those of a loose, relatively amorphous underclass, although the differences are admittedly slight. Their lack of property-holding rights created a dependency that in peacetime saw them submitting to voluntary servitude and seasonal occupations. Only in periods of political disturbance did they assume the more aggressive roles of mercenaries or looters.[24]

Conquest patterns also have been cited as evidence of contrast. The Hab/piru would loot and burn the cities but were indifferent to the populace.[25] Israelite tribes, on the other hand, were supposed to keep the conquered cities intact while killing the indigenous population. This supposed strategy, coming from God, is at best questionable. We shall see in chapter 14 of this book that the "invading" Israelites under Joshua were remarkably few in number and avoided open confrontation. In fact, the conquest of the Promised Land by the Israelites is still an unresolved issue.

Norman K. Gottwald has drawn a scholarly and compelling picture of the Hab/piru-Hebrew correlation from the Amarna period to the beginnings of the Israelite monarchy.[26] Approached from a sociopolitical perspective, the Hap/piru can be seen as outsiders to the feudal organization of the Canaanite city-states, representing either a threat or a benefit, depending on their host's economic interests. The Canaanite kings, fiercely competitive among themselves, saw personal profit in the fighting ability of the Hab/piru. The perennial outsiders had developed useful martial skills in fighting as small units during the few hundred years from Nuzi to Ugarit. The quarreling city-states used them as easily against each other as against the Egyptians. There seem to have been enough of them throughout Canaan to supply every ruler who wanted additional manpower. They were consignment warriors except when they pursued hostile adventures for their own benefit.

The Hab/piru were held at arm's length socially from the urban Canaanites for whom they ostensibly fought. Seeking more tangible rewards, they occupied and perhaps expropriated lands peripheral to the city-states, especially in the more easily consolidated hill country. This geographic reality allowed groups of Hab/piru to be in contact with one another, reinforcing their identity and cooperation. This cellular arrangement effectively isolated the individual city-states, which then found themselves functionally on the defensive, surrounded by hostile and self-serving Hab/piru. In their isolation from one another both politically and economically, it is not too difficult to comprehend the urgency that we read in the Amarna letters of the local Canaanite princes. The specter of siege at the hands of the very people they had previously hired to fight for them leaps from every tablet.

* * *

Greenberg considers the term Hab/piru as an appellative for "a population element composed of diverse ethnic elements, having in common only a generally inferior social status." They did not demonstrate tribal loyalties or mass movements. Further, there is no evidence that they invaded the land; nor did they resemble "the purposeful bodies of Israelite tribes."[27]

The word for Hebrew in the Bible is *ibri* (or *ivri*), and the etymology of the term must be considered in any equation of Hebrew with Hab/piru. This consonantal similarity led to the logical presumption that *ibri* could be equated with Hab/piru. But Greenberg holds that the biblical use of the root term *ibri* is a gentilic denoting implicit descent from Eber, Noah's great-great-grandson. Greenberg points out that the corresponding use of *mitzrim* (Egyptians) and *ibrim* (Hebrews) in Gen. 43:32 indicates the ethnic content of the words. He also cites many uses in the Bible of *ibri* as a gentilic, assuming that *ibri* and Eber are coequal terms.[28] On the other hand, he does allow that the patriarchs, as leaders of a seminomadic, land-hungry people, technically may have been Hab/piru.[29]

M. P. Gray, in a penetrating analysis, raises questions about the eponymous honor conferred on Eber. Given the importance of Shem (Noah's oldest son) as the ultimate ancestor, she asks why they would not be better called "*hash'mi*" if a gentilic were desired.[30] The well-documented appellative meaning of the root term *ibri* came into wide use as a synonym for Israel only during the intertestamental period (200 B.C.E.–100 C.E.). The Semitic root *br* can mean "to cross a boundary" and could therefore be associated with the concept of wandering, as in Hab/piru.[31] She postulates that by then the pejorative use of the term had been long forgotten. *Avram ha-ivri* (Abraham the Hebrew) was used as early as Gen. 14:13, when the gentilic form suggested itself, and Eber was adopted.[32] The term *ibri* is in continual use in the Old Testament but only once by an Israelite to define himself. That reference is found in Gen. 40:15, where Joseph explains that he was "stolen away out of the land of the Hebrews [*m'eretz ha'ibrim*]." It is especially noteworthy that he would use this term when it is absent from any New Kingdom document that names the land.[33] It has been stated that "there is no longer room for any legitimate doubt as to the correctness of the contention that, on principle, the Hab/piru of Akkadian sources correspond to the *ibrim* of the Old Testament, and that, accordingly, *ibri* was an appellative denoting a member of a particular class of the population before it became a gentilic denoting an Israelite or a Jew."[34]

It must be argued here that despite the resemblance of Eber to *ibri*, the middling ancestor himself reveals no singularity in the genealogical tree to warrant an eponym. His name is mentioned in Gen. 10:24, 25; 11:14–16 and 1 Chron. 1:18,19, 25 but only within the ancestor lists beginning with Shem. Eber is also mentioned in Gen. 10:21, still within the ancestor list, but with the addition of "And unto Shem, the father of all the children of Eber, . . . were children born." Again, in Balaam's oracle (Num. 24:24) he states, "Ships come from the quarter of Kittim [thought to represent either Crete or Greece]; They subject Asshur [probably a textual error for "Asher"], subject Eber." In the two latter references Eber is obviously used as an ancestral name. The tribe of Asher, occupying the northern coastal plane of Canaan abutting the Phoenicians in Tyre, would surely be vulnerable to sea attacks, but the textual relationship to Eber, who was not a tribe, is uncertain. In the absence of other clues the reason for Eber's eponymic prominence is puzzling.

Could the Hab/piru have been the original source of the Hebrews of biblical tradition? As with most questions raised in this book, data are so sparse and encumbered with potential interpretive distortions that reason and logic must again be our guide. The consensus of scholars after a century of discovery and analysis seems to favor the coincidence of the two terms. There are significant demurrers from this position, even though most issues regarding the Hab/piru are attended by general agreement that they represented a large percentage of people living in the Fertile Crescent throughout the Second Millennium and in Canaan in the Fourteenth Century. There were elements of a docile, servile, classless people among them—almost "untouchables"—whereas others were mercenaries or part of bandit groups that created economic and political havoc in settled areas. Because they seemed to attract and accept other downtrodden and displaced persons, they tended to occupy the lower echelons of society. It appears that in most cases they were both foreigner and native, living in border areas and in towns.

* * *

We must temporarily leave the Hab/piru fighting for their place in the land, although it should be obvious that we will have to deal with them again in the assembling of Israel. That the patriarchs could have been Hab/piru migrating into Canaan for a better life is hardly contestable. A similar conclusion is found in the statement, "It is probable that a part of these 'Apiru are none other than Hebrew tribes that became united with the passage of time in the covenant of the Israelite tribes."[35]

How they evolved from a pervasive but despised social class existing throughout the Near East into an ethical people, a "light to all peoples," needs further exploration. For this we must turn to Israel's Egyptian experience.

Notes

1. F. J. Giles, *Ikhnaton* (Rutherford, NJ: Farleigh Dickenson University Press, 1970), p. 148.
2. M. Greenberg, *The Hab/piru* (New Haven: American Oriental Society, 1955).
3. M. B. Rowton, "Dimorphic Structure and the Problem of the Apiru-Ibrim," *Journal of Near Eastern Studies* 35(1976):13–20.
4. M. B. Rowton, "The Topological Factor in the Hapiru Problem," *Assyriological Studies* 16(1965):375–387.
5. V. H. Matthews, *Pastoral Nomadism in the Mari Kingdom*, (Cambridge: American Schools of Oriental Research, 1978), p. 159ff.
6. M. B. Rowton, "Dimorphic," p. 19.
7. M. Greenberg, op. cit., p. 6.

8. Ibid., p. 63.

9. Ibid., p. 8.

10. J. Lewy, "A New Parallel Between Habiru and Hebrews," *Hebrew Union College Annual* 15(1940):47-58.

11. N. K. Gottwald, "Domain Assumptions and Societal Models in the Study of Pre-Monarchic Israel," *Vetus Testamentum Suppl.* 28(1974):89-100.

12. V. H. Matthews, op. cit., p. 159.

13. M. Greenberg, op. cit., p. 68.

14. H. W. F. Saggs, *The Might That Was Assyria* (London: Sidgwick and Jackson, 1984), p. 126.

15. M. Greenberg, op. cit., p. 89.

16. Y. Aharoni, *The Land of the Bible* (Philadelphia: Westminster Press, 1979), p. 192.

17. M. Greenberg, op. cit., p. 74.

18. M. B. Rowton, "Topological," p. 382.

19. Ibid., p. 385.

20. M. Greenberg, op. cit., p. 86.

21. Lewy, op. cit., p. 618f.

22. M. Greenberg, op. cit., p. 77.

23. J. Lewy, op. cit., p. 614.

24. Ibid., p. 88.

25. Ibid., p. 95.

26. N. K. Gottwald, *The Tribes of Yahweh* (New York: Orbis Books, 1979), pp. 401–480, passim.

27. M. Greenberg, op. cit., p. 95.

28. Ibid., p. 92.

29. Ibid., p. 93.

30. M. P. Gray, "The Habiru-Hebrew Problem in the Light of the Source Material Available at Present," *Hebrew Union College Annual* 29(1958):135–202, 175.

31. Ibid., p. 171.

32. Ibid., p. 194.

33. D. B. Redford, *A Study of the Biblical Story of Joseph* (Leiden: E. J. Brill, 1970), p.201.

34. J. Lewy, op. cit., p. 609.

35. Y. Aharoni, op. cit., p. 191.

Amarna: The First Monotheism

8

Egypt plays an essential role in the history of Israel, although Scripture goes to great length to marginalize its importance. Abraham visits Egypt early in Genesis, and Jacob dies there, with his whole family in attendance, at the end of Genesis. Moses' Egyptian association is extensively defined in Exodus, that remarkable voyage of an embryonic Israel. With a Semitic presence of long duration clearly established in Egypt, it is obligatory to examine the Amarna Age, which preceded the Exodus by no more than two or three generations.

The New Kingdom, during which the Amarna Age occurred, began with the XVIIIth Dynasty and was a remarkable period in all important civic aspects, including religion. This line of kings, lasting for 250 years, from 1550 to 1300 B.C.E., can be distinguished by two functional periods: an early imperialism (1550–1400), during which a remarkable resurgence of Egypt's political fortunes took place; and a later slow involution (1400–1300). Ahmose (1550–1525) cleared the delta of Hyksos rule, restoring a unified kingdom. During the reigns of Thutmose III (1480–1425) and his son, Amenhotep II (1425–1400), both of whom repeatedly drove deep into western Asia, the Egyptian empire reached a new zenith. Its suzerainty extended from the uppermost reaches of the Nile River to the banks of the

Euphrates River. The involutional period was characterized by several weak, short-lived rulers who tended to avoid foreign adventures. During this quiescent period, an important religious experiment was attempted, which gave rise to its special appellation, the Amarna Age.

The New Kingdom saw Egypt reverse its domestic isolation of the past by aggressively moving into Asia. The route between the eastern Nile delta and Canaan through northern Sinai became critical to its success. The Way of Horus, as it was known in Egyptian documents, ran along the shoreline of the Mediterranean Sea and was secured by forts that served as supply and customs stations. Movement into or out of Egypt without detection was thus rendered almost impossible. But the ultimate development of this road as a military highway occurred under Seti I (1305–1290).[1]

Thutmose III instituted the practice of taking the princes of conquered states back to Egypt as hostages. The younger ones were reared and educated as part of the royal retinue; when the need arose for new rulers in the vassal states, these princes, now thoroughly Egyptianized, were sent back to take charge. The practice proved to be an efficient form of political insurance; the bereft father became a compliant vassal, and the young prince learned to think Egyptian.

In their multiple campaigns into Asia the early pharaohs of the New Kingdom captured many Semites. Thutmose III brought at least 7000 prisoners back to Egypt, according to the Karnak annals, and Amenhotep II mentions 100,000.[2] All captives of war were the sole property of the pharaoh. The more comely of the captive women were usually awarded to officers as their personal slaves, many ultimately becoming concubines or even wives.

A large number of war captives were given to the service of the gods all over Egypt. There is a reference to colonies of "Syrians" who lived beside the temples and in other sacred places within the cities.[3] The vast tracts of delta land that were left ownerless when the Hyksos were defeated also belonged to the pharaoh. Much of this land was dedicated to the regional gods, thus depriving any potential pretender of a power base. The priesthood of the particular deity administered the given land, using the slaves that were also provided. The priests became the essential purveyors of government, and with the revenues of land and slaves they also became politically dominant. As we shall see, a powerful priesthood could easily become a threat to pharaoh, as well as an ally.

Although the number of captured foreigners was not insignificant, another large group of people were also entering Egypt. The cultures of western Asia encountered by the Egyptians were sufficiently advanced to offer them new skills and obvious trade benefits. The quest for goods seemed to dissipate the anger that followed the Hyksos interregnum. Mercantile records reveal how brisk the sea commerce had become between Canaanite Byblos and the Nile delta. Land caravans in large numbers crossed the narrow isthmus of Suez, always a trade route in the past. These merchants and other people with skills to offer, many of whom came to Egypt by their own volition, added to the Semitic presence there. Canaanite dialects were commonly heard, and "to do business speaking the [foreign]-tongue" meant to haggle.[4] The Hab/piru were also increasing in Egypt, along with displaced elements of Semitic groups and indigenous semi-nomads fleeing across the isthmus into the delta region.

Besides the Amarna letters, which detail the activities of the Hab/piru within the Egyptian possessions in western Asia, other texts describe similar groups of people who were in Egypt proper. They were referred to as ʻpr.w and were almost identical to the SA.GAZ (or Hab/piru) of cuneiform script.[5] These people were an element of Syro-Palestinian population who were captives or imported laborers after Thutmose III and Amenhotep II completed their Asian campaigns. The rapid expansion of the empire demanded more labor. They worked in the wine industry under Thutmose and Hatshepsut (1475–1460), his strong-willed queen and half-sister. Ramesses II (1290–1225) of the XIXth Dynasty later had them hauling stone for building projects. The latter fact parallels the description in Exod. 1:11 in which the

Hebrews "built garrison cities for Pharaoh," suggesting that both groups essentially could have been one and the same. The listing of 'pr.w in the order of various prisoner lists is noteworthy in that they follow "princes of Retenu [Canaan]" and "brothers of princes" but precede the captured native population of Palestine and Syria. The same relative position of the Hab/piru in Hittite lists has caused Greenberg to wonder whether they had a similar, highly valued connection to both ruling classes.[6] One can speculate that the Hab/piru, as a mercenary component of all militaristic societies, were awarded a modicum of status.

The *Shasu* were another nonnative element recognized in Egyptian texts of the Amarna period and later. They were people whose place of origin ranged from southern Canaan to northern Arabia and from the Dead Sea area to the Suez trough. The term Shasu might be generally synonymous with Bedouin, although the association may be strained. This equation merely attempts to define a poorly documented ancient people in terms of a contemporary one. The Shasu are pictured primarily as a militant and warlike force in Egyptian territories, as well as in their own region. Their political structure was egalitarian and based on kinship and family.

As we have seen, philological methods of defining ancient terms frequently result in divergent meanings. In the case of Shasu there are two meanings: "to roam," from an Egyptian root, and "to plunder," from the Semitic one.[7] It must be more than sheer coincidence that the two words are almost identical with those describing Hab/piru. As in the dual use of SA.GAZ and Hab/piru, the term Shasu may be another gloss defining differences in groups coming from Asia.

By the end of the Fifteenth Century many of the Semites had risen to high offices in the priesthood, the palace hierarchy, and the foreign service. These persons were frequently given Egyptian names, often compounded with the king's name.[8] However, this increasing assimilation was by no means pervasive among the Semites. The Shasu remained unwelcome, probably because their nomadism was seen to deplete national assets without contributing proportionate benefits.

As Egypt became a world power by its conquests, Mitannian and Babylonian princesses were imported to become the wives and mothers of pharaohs. Amenhotep III (1390–1350) was only half Egyptian; his mother was a Mitannian princess who took the name Mutemuya.[9] However, royal marriages were not reciprocal; an Egyptian princess was never allowed to become the wife of a foreign king. It is obvious that this international matrimonial market, both royal and common, coincided with an increasing tolerance for foreign influences within Egypt.

* * *

Akhenaten's reign (1350–1335) in the latter years of the XVIIIth Dynasty heralded a major change in Egyptian religious practice. A new and radical monotheism was adopted in this period, giving the Amarna Age its special character. But it had a very limited and short duration, effectively discredited shortly after Akhenaten's death. Certainly with the experience and perspective of an additional 3300 years, we could have told them that great philosophical movements can be only broached but rarely set within a single generation. However, an idea once propounded does not disappear completely, even if it is subsequently dismissed. The Amarna Age is therefore a unique milestone in the evolution of religious philosophy. Although it opened on an Egyptian stage, its effect on Western civilization was mediated through Israel. The monotheistic belief that could not take root in its native soil lay dormant for almost a century before it reappeared as the central tenet of a mushrooming twelve-tribe entity in Asia. Egypt in the Amarna Age merits priority in the development of monotheism, although Israel is traditionally associated with its origin. The process by which the beacon was passed from one to the other is critical to understanding the Israelite phenomenon.

The area commonly called El-Amarna turned out to be the site of the capital of Egypt during most of Akhenaten's reign. The city that he built and named Akhetaten, the horizon, or seat, of Aten, contained an enormous temple, palace, government buildings, and many tombs. It had every facility needed for a self-contained royal city. The uncovered cache of letters to the pharaoh apparently had been part of governmental archives and supplied the modern world with dramatic insights about Canaan at the time of the patriarchs. Those letters yielded information about the disestablished class of people who became, or at least unwittingly lent identity to, the Hebrews of history.

In a more restricted sense the Amarna Age can be considered as only the years of Akhenaten's rule, during which religious changes had official sanction. More liberally it includes the reign of his father until the repeal of Aten's divinity, a period of seventy years (1390–1320). The longer time span is more realistic, because the concept of monotheism probably required more than a single generation to complete the cycle from inception to demise. Cresting during Akhenaten's reign, it still had to follow a natural parabolic curve, regardless of its relatively brief tenure. A change in human ideation of this magnitude would be inconceivable without an introductory development or a reactionary decline. But most important is the fact that this concept of a single, universal god *had never occurred previously anywhere else in the world!*

This brief period in Egyptian history also witnessed a vertiginous ferment in the social and artistic life of the country. Documentary evidence indicates that these changes were not widely accepted during the Amarna Age. Monotheism may have started earlier and ended later than the dates cited here, but the essential force that moved and characterized the climax of this period can be found only in the person of its iconoclastic king, Akhenaten.

During the latter half of his reign, he instituted a radical change in the ancient and static religion of Egypt. The efficacy of all other gods was denied by the deification of Aten, the sun-disc, representing the sun's omniscience. This dramatic displacement will be associated forever with Akhenaten (spirit, or glory, of Aten), the name he adopted to underscore his commitment to the god. His given name was Amenhotep IV. Egyptian records show that the process was not as abrupt as heretofore believed but rather began in the reign of his father, Amenhotep III, and perhaps even before that. Some authorities think that Aten was a divinity from the beginning of the New Kingdom.[10] But Akhenaten should not be viewed as an isolated aberration in an otherwise torpid royal history.

To comprehend the immense intellectual importance of the Amarna Age to Western civilization and to Israel, we must pursue, like a fugal duet, two separate but intersecting lines of inquiry. First is the question of what relationship Akhenaten's monotheism bears to that of early Israel; second is whether there was sufficient involvement by some Semites already in Egypt to become the proto-Israelites of Exodus. It is likely that Joseph, the eponymous ancestor of those Egyptian Semites who later left Egypt in the Exodus, lived at the beginning of this period.

Amenhotep III is the pivotal figure in this dynasty. The pharaohs before him were aggressively expansionist, whereas those that succeeded him, except for the last one, Horemhab, were relatively timid and more domestically oriented. It is thought that the early years of his reign may have been shared in a co-regency with his father, Thutmose IV (1400–1390), and later with his son, Akhenaten. We know that Amenhotep's mother was a Mitannian princess, and therefore it would not be illogical to assume that his childhood education included a strong influence from Semitic cultures, mediated through the many Asiatic retainers and princes who were his teachers and playmates.

Amenhotep's age on accession to the throne of Egypt is uncertain, but given the relatively short reign of his father, the absence of a known regency period, and the fact that he arranged his own love marriage during his second regnal year, it is reasonable to assume that he was a young adult. His independence of mind and self-assurance can be gauged by a most dramatic act: He married a commoner, breaching an ancient royal tradition. Throughout Egyptian history pharaohs married their sisters, or even their daughters, to ensure that a male heir would have the unassailable right of succession. This right was passed through the female line, even though the power to rule was given to the male.

His reign is noteworthy at the beginning for its pursuit of Egypt's imperial interests and later for a gradually increasing indolence. When he first became king, the turmoil in Syro-Palestine, which usually tested a new pharaoh's militancy, occurred on schedule. He adopted the response of earlier rulers and marched into western Asia to subdue the fractious vassals. This act preempted the smoldering revolts and resulted in a long, relatively peaceful reign. He never went to war again but instead turned to more personal pleasures, hunting and erecting monuments. His massive building program provided a stage for new art forms.

Amenhotep's marriage to a commoner was accepted, although the legitimacy of his immediate family remained under a cloud. In a XIXth Dynasty King-list Amenhotep III was immediately succeeded by Horemhab, effectively eliminating the kingships of Akhenaten, Smenkhkare (1335–1333), Tutankhamen (1333–1323), and Aye (1323–1320), respectively.[11] A gap of thirty-five years in Egyptian history was thus spitefully declared. However, the legitimacy question may not have been the primary issue; it also represented a rejection of the Aten cult. Certainly Horemhab's own royal credentials were not beyond question, but he vigorously expunged the remains of Atenism.

Amenhotep designated the commoner Tiy as his "Great Wife." This royal title was usually given to the mother of the next ruler, most often the pharaoh's favorite. Whoever else the pharaoh may have married necessarily occupied a secondary role, essentially becoming another member of the harem. He remained close and faithful to Tiy, in an Oriental way, for almost forty years, although he did marry a Mitannian princess ten years later for diplomatic reasons. Yet Tiy's name and that of her parents appeared directly beneath his own on the scarabs commemorating the event.[12] Her influence in his world becomes more significant when we realize how unusual it was for a pharaoh to use his wife's name, let alone that of her nonroyal parents, on any of his own inscriptions. But her name was very commonly included along with his, and his penchant to honor her has given the world a better picture of Queen Tiy than of almost any other royal wife in Egyptian history. We may question his insouciant sense of protocol, but we cannot fail to be moved by his steadfast loyalty to the woman he loved.

Notwithstanding that Tiy was a remarkable woman, our interest is directed primarily to her parentage and to her son, Akhenaten. At issue is the relationship that her ancestry might have had to the Semitic groups that would leave Egypt later and also the effect that her son's monotheism had on that group and the subsequent Israelite religion.

The Mysterious Grand Vizier

In 1905 an American, T. M. Davis, discovered a hitherto unknown tomb in the Valley of Kings in Thebes, the resting place of pharaohs. This royal burial site was a narrow, serpiginous depression between limestone cliffs on the western bank of the Nile River opposite the city of Thebes. The tomb in question was decorated simply and contained two mummies in excellent preservation, along with a great deal of funerary furniture. The mummies, a middle-aged man and woman, were clearly not royalty.

The man's name was Yuya and the woman was his wife, Tuya. They were the parents of Queen Tiy. His sarcophagus and all the other major funerary possessions were inscribed with portions of his extensive titulary: "the holy father of the Lord of the Two Lands," "Prince, bearer of the seal of the King of Lower Egypt," "Master of the Horse," "Deputy of His Majesty in the Chariotry," "Overseer of the Cattle of Min," "Overseer of the Cattle of Amun," "Confidant of the King," "Mouth of the King of Upper Egypt," "Ears of the King of Lower Egypt," and "One made great by the Lord who does things." The question that springs to mind is why Yuya was so exceedingly honored. He was obviously more than just a father-in-law to Amenhotep.

One examiner described him as a tall man with a determined jaw and a great hooked nose like that of a Syrian.[13] He wrote, "One feels on looking at his well-preserved features, that there may be found the originator of the great religious movement which his daughter and grandson carried into execution."[14] He was referring, of course, to Joseph. A British anatomist working at the Cairo Museum noted that Yuya's head shape was unusual among pure Egyptians but could not state with certainty that he was a foreigner. Since the discovery of the tomb, scholars have continued to debate whether Yuya's face is that of a Semite.[15] The results of such a debate can remain only inconclusive at best, because Semites had been living in Egypt for at least several hundred years by that time, intermarriage eventually altering distinctive head shapes and nose shapes so that they would no longer be indicative of racial origins, if indeed they ever were.

However, a topical piece of evidence appears to support the Asiatic origin of Yuya. In 1913 a small bowl that apparently had been overlooked eight years earlier was found in the tomb. The bowl contained the hieroglyphic inscription "King's wife Tuyu [Tuya], King's Prince Yuia [Yuya], prince of Zahi." This discovery led to the conclusion that because Zahi (Tjahi in Egyptian) was on the Phoenician coast of the eastern Mediterranean, Yuia was a Syrian chief married to the Egyptian lady Tuyu.[16]

In a 1987 publication Ahmed Osman advanced a most interesting theory, that Yuya was the Joseph of Genesis: "It is impossible to examine the lives of Joseph and Yuya without also being struck by the remarkable number of similarities between them."[17] Oddly enough there are variant spellings of Yuya's name on the objects within his tomb, which Osman believes may be due to different scribes trying to render a foreign name, perhaps "YuSeph," into Egyptian hieroglyphics.[18] He adds a citation by Manetho mentioning two viziers, Yu and Seph, in Amenhotep III's time.[19]

Three views of the mummified head of Yuya. Found in a richly furnished tomb in the valley of Kings at Thebes, he was not a royal person but is thought to be of Semitic origin. Yuya was an advisor to and father-in-law of Amenhotep III and the grandfather of Akhenaten. There is presumptive evidence that he was the Joseph of Hebrew Scripture.

Photos Courtesy of The Egyptian Museum, Cairo.

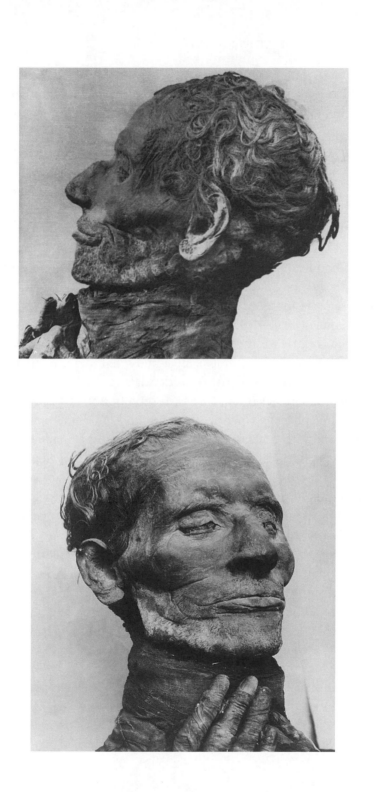

In Gen. 45:8 Joseph reveals himself to his brothers, stating "and He [God] has made me a father to Pharaoh, lord of all his household, and ruler over the whole land of Egypt." Part of the same phrase is found inscribed on Yuya's many possessions. Osman maintains that Joseph was the only person in the history of Egypt from the Hyksos through the New Kingdom who carried "a father to Pharaoh" title.[20] The parallels continue in Gen. 41:42, where pharaoh gave Joseph his own signet ring and put a gold chain around his neck. The signet ring could well have been the seal that is mentioned in Yuya's titulary, and a gold necklace, which had been missed by early vandals, was indeed found lying beneath the body in the coffin. Yuya's close association with chariotry may be matched with Joseph's reportedly frequent use of that vehicle (Gen. 41:43, 46:29, and 50:9). Joseph is said to have purchased cattle for the pharaoh in exchange for food during the period of famine (Gen. 47:17), an activity that might relate to the two cattle references in Yuya's credentials.

When Jacob dies (Gen. 49:33), Joseph honors his last wish by requesting pharaoh's permission to take his father's embalmed remains back to Canaan for burial. The request is made through an intermediary, which seems unusual in light of Joseph's easy entrée to the royal presence. In Gen. 50:4 Joseph "spoke to the household" of pharaoh, asking an unnamed person to speak "in the ears of pharaoh."[21] The phrase "household of pharaoh" in Egyptian usage was a euphemism for his wife,[22] and a queen would certainly be closer to pharaoh than any vizier. Also, "in the ears of pharaoh" suggests an intimate situation in which such a request might be more readily granted. But if Yuya's prestige in Egypt depended to some extent on his daughter as queen, how could he be Joseph, who had no known daughters? Osman suggests that either the writer of the Joseph tradition or a later editor may have deliberately omitted her existence because such a close familial relationship to the Egyptian royal house would have tainted the purity of an Israelite genealogy.[23] We shall see comparable distortions of memory in Moses' and Joseph's Egyptian backgrounds.

Tuya's presence in the tomb further supports the identification of Yuya with Joseph. In Gen. 41:45 pharaoh gave him the daughter of Poti-phera, priest of On, as a wife. The city On, in Lower Egypt at the head of the delta, had always been the center of worship for the sun god, Re. Its later name, Heliopolis, was the Greek translation for "city of sun." There is no indication who Tuya's father was, but Osman reasons that her position as "Mistress of the Harem" indicates that she came from a priestly background. Her brother, Anen, was also a priest by heredity through their father, confirmed by a statue of Anen in Turin identifying him as a priest of On.[24]

There are other commonalities in the revealed life of Yuya and the story of Joseph, but some of these tend to be arguments ex silentio and as such are much more speculative. In any event the honors bestowed on Joseph would make an interment like Yuya's quite plausible.

Osman does not believe that Joseph's bones were taken back to Canaan by Moses, which had been his plea to the sons of Israel in Gen. 50:25.[25] Valuables were customarily placed in the tomb along with the body, and therefore there was great secrecy about its location. How likely would it be that Moses knew where to find Joseph's body after at least four generations had passed, especially after the tenth plague had given such short notice before departure in Exodus? Although Osman implies that Joseph's remains were unavailable for transport, a Haggadic tradition acknowledges the problem but arranges for an occult solution at the same time. The legend typically mixes a hint of reality with an overlay of magical happenstance. Moses knew that Joseph had been interred in a mausoleum along with the Egyptian kings, but there were so many bodies that it was impossible to identify his. With the help of Jochebed, his mother (and also Joseph's niece), it was found very deep within the earth but could not be reached. Moses had to call to the body, reminding it of Joseph's living wish to be buried back in Canaan. With that, the coffin raised itself to the surface, where it could then be carried away.[26]

The redactors of the Bible may not have understood the process of embalming after so many years had elapsed, or they would have known that mummification does not yield bones as in the unembalmed state. It has also been suggested that a later editor knew of only two trips back to Canaan, one for Jacob's burial and the other for the Exodus. In that case Joseph's body had to be added to the Exodus trip if it were to be deposited in Canaan.[27] Perhaps it was unseemly to the early writers that so important an ancestor as Joseph should have been allowed to remain buried in a foreign land. Osman, however, resolves the problem succinctly: Joseph was never taken back to Canaan but rather continues to reside in the Cairo Museum.[28]

The thesis that Joseph's entry into Egypt occurred during the Hyksos reign, when a warm welcome might have been given to a fellow Semite, has been all but discarded recently. The attitude toward foreigners during the New Kingdom was rather benign, especially after the memory of the Hyksos experience faded somewhat. Perhaps the imperial expansion policy overcame the vaunted xenophobia of the earlier Egyptians. It is certain that there was considerable immigration of Semites, not restricted to only the eastern delta region. Joseph's phenomenal rise to power could have easily taken place during the midperiod of the XVIIIth Dynasty.[29] Osman suggests that Joseph was appointed vizier by Thutmose IV when there was considerable political turmoil between the royal and priestly factions.[30]

The story of Joseph, like that of the patriarchs, is not solid history. Many obvious embellishments have been added to rational details. The proto-Israelites of Asia found their eponymous ancestors in a Mesopotamian or Aramean milieu, whereas those of Egypt seem to have chosen to take root from Joseph. Whether the Egyptian Yuya is in reality the Hebrew Joseph or merely a model from which a great ancestor was patterned should be inconsequential to us an eon later. However, it is reassuring to note that as we pursue this quest for reality in early Israel, the crucial persons and commemorative events involved have more probability than mere mythic tales. The importance of a Joseph story is to establish a proud relationship for a group of people who will be leaving Egypt a hundred years later. When they needed an epic tradition to confirm their genealogical equality with the other peoples who were merging with them into Israel, Joseph became their illustrious ancestor, close to patriarchal status.

Amenhotep IV (Akhenaten)

The Amarna Age is most remarkable for the enigma surrounding the Pharaoh Akhenaten. He has been labeled more recently as "the heretic king" because of his radical departures from the traditional religions of Egypt. The central issue is whether his conception of one all-powerful deity was a revolutionary progression in the ongoing search for spirituality or merely the delusion of a disoriented fanatic. A degree of religious fanaticism cannot be denied, given his single-minded pursuit of a new vision and the forceful suppression of the rest of the Egyptian pantheon. But was his monomania justified in the creation of a single force in the heavens, replacing the bewildering multiplicity of animal-headed icons? A review of available data should indicate where he belongs on the philosophical scale.

Akhenaten was born to Amenhotep III and Queen Tiy rather late in their marriage. After several daughters had survived, they finally were rewarded with a male heir. It would be reasonable to assume that the long-awaited prince was treated with an exaggerated indulgence. A now mellow Amenhotep allowed the capable Tiy to provide the major influence over their son. The young prince's upbringing was thus dominated by the feminine, largely foreign influence in the harem.[31] The harem consisted not only of Amenhotep's partly Semitic queen but also at least one Mitannian wife who came with a female staff of hundreds. Queen Tiy still had importance even in her old age. This can be surmised from a letter to her reigning son by the Mitannian king, Tushratta, in which he seems to speak of her as still the de facto

power in Egypt. Akhenaten's taste for mysticism and his supposed lack of aggressiveness are thought to stem from this early
protective ambiance.[32] There is no evidence that his hunter-
father ever introduced the boy to the manly arts.

In our age of psychological imperatives his early upbringing
has been probed and diagnosed far beyond the historical capacity of the data. Through his mother's family he was strongly
influenced in his formative years by the priests of On, the most
ardent of the sun-worshipping cultists. Ma'at, the ancient goddess of truth, justice, and righteousness, was closely associated
with On, and it was during the Amarna Age that Ma'at assumed
an ethical quality not associated with her previous character.[33]

The ancient Egyptians recognized the immense power of the
sun god for the benefit of mankind, and On became the center
for its worship. This city's priesthood commanded an authority
that was never matched by other cults, even when there were
power shifts among the various cities and their patron gods. If
Akhenaten's loyalty to the teachings of the On school was fixed in
childhood, it is likely that he came to resent the power and wealth
of the Amen priesthood in Thebes. The supremacy of the god
Amen, often merged with Re as Amen-Re, reached its pinnacle of
importance in the early part of the XVIIIth Dynasty, when the
wealth of Asia flowed back to Thebes and its priesthood.

Sun worship was part of Egyptian religious practice as far
back as the middle of the Third Millennium. Even at that early
time kingship was closely identified with Re. Later the source of
all energy and power was the sun god, Re-Harakhte, who was
pictured as a man with a falcon's head. The god Osiris continued
to dominate the nether world of death while solar gods were
becoming important to eternal life. During the XVIIIth
Dynasty, private tombs were designed to propitiate these special
deities. Appropriate hymns and pictographs ensured that the
deceased would accompany the sun god from its birth in the
morning through its magisterial trajectory across the sky to its
rest at night and its rebirth the following day.[34] Relief drawings
on one side of the entry chamber pictured the owner striding

out of the tomb to join the god during daylight; on the opposite wall the owner was shown reentering the tomb when the sun god disappeared into night.

Interest was developing in Aten at the same time that the cults of many deities were flourishing. Amenhotep III is known to have built a temple to Aten in Thebes, although the god had been mentioned only sporadically before then. When the pharoah created a huge pleasure lake for Tiy, the royal barge was named Tehenaten, meaning the Radiance (or Splendor) of Aten. He even invoked Aten's name for his youngest daughter, Baktaten. Private inscriptions by his courtiers also cited Aten frequently.[35]

An active debate still rages about whether Akhenaten was appointed co-regent early in life or assumed the throne only at his father's death. Co-regency was a particularly Egyptian arrangement whereby the older pharaoh appointed his successor to rule with him, usually in response to a perceived threat to the government. The younger man might serve as a staff of old age, as happened with Amenhotep II and his father, Thutmose III.[36] In general, the junior pharaoh frequently functioned as the warrior-king while the aging senior continued with administrative affairs and foreign policy. In other examples of co-regency the motivation was to secure an uncontested succession, especially when civil strife was a threatening factor.[37] The distribution of authority between the two rulers had no traditional pattern and usually was determined by the circumstances that demanded the co-regency in the first place.[38]

The first two-thirds of Akhenaten's reign could have been spent as the junior partner in a co-regency with his father, whereas in the last few years a co-regency existed with Smenkhkare, supposedly his son or son-in-law.[39] This conclusion is not uniformly held, as the evidence for it is weak. Proponents of a long, earlier co-regency offer it to buttress the view of Akhenaten as weak and vacillating, in need of a strong, experienced paternal hand. Others feel that Amenhotep approved of his son's proposed schism and even lived in the new city that the latter built.

The persona of Akhenaten has been the subject of such scholarly disagreement that this book can add little new to it. Fortunately there are some major details of his life that all parties concede. Akhenaten probably lived no more than thirty-five years. He was married to Nefertiti, made famous by the beautiful painted stone bust found in the abandoned studio of an Amarna sculptor. She was possibly a Mitannian princess, although her name would suggest an Egyptian origin. Another theory holds that she was the daughter of Aye, a later XVIIIth Dynasty pharaoh. They produced six daughters but no known sons. Akhenaten was thought to be monogamous, but an inscription on a coffin found in another tomb indicates that he had a wife named Kia, about whom very little is known.[40] Also, he inherited one of his late father's wives, Taduhepa, when her father, Tushratta, passed her on to him.[41]

There is some indication that Akhenaten did have sons, even though no direct pictographic or textual evidence has been found. Letters to him from several Near Eastern kings inquired about "your sons." It is most unlikely that these kings would have mentioned them unless it were a known fact. A mummy whose identity had been conspicuously obliterated and now thought to be that of Smenkhkare has a remarkable physical resemblance to Tutankhamen's mummy. Also, test results, as well as the similar appearances, indicate that they were closely related. The fact that these two pharaohs were quite young and followed Akhenaten in respective order suggests that they may have been his sons by Kia.[42]

Akhenaten lived most of his early life in Thebes, the power center of the Amen cult. Egypt's deities seemed to have had a regional orientation: On/Heliopolis was the center of the sun cult, with Re as the chief god; Memphis was the seat of Ptah. In Thebes Amen held sway and gradually merged with Re to become dominant early in the XVIIIth Dynasty. The Theban priesthood had become very independent during the reign of Hatshepsut, because she had to purchase their support for her questionably legitimate rule. The extensive ownership of land

and wealth led to the increased power of these minions, who proved adept at using the role of syncretism to further their own goals.

The circumstance surrounding Thutmose III's election to kingship foreshadows the increased political clout of the Amen priesthood. He was the son of a royal concubine and therefore without special priority to the throne. However, he had already been an Amen priest and as such was targeted by them for the divine blessing, which ensured his investiture just as it commanded his loyalty. Thutmose IV, Akhenaten's grandfather, first shook up the vested interests by appointing his own high priest. Amenhotep III also had a large number of successive high priests, many of whom were connected to the god Ptah rather than to Amen. Perhaps this was the way to reassert the royal prerogatives.[43]

There can be little question that the two pharaohs prior to Akhenaten struggled to contain the power of the Amen priests. If his grandfather and father increasingly acknowledged the importance of Aten, he must have assumed the throne either as co-regent or as ruling pharaoh while this struggle was still in progress. His unswerving devotion to this god therefore does not appear to be an unheralded break with tradition but rather a calculated theological commitment in support of a political strategy.

In the fourth year of his reign Akhenaten decided to remove himself physically as well as emotionally from Thebes and the cult of Amen.[44] At least two more years passed before he could occupy the new city of Akhetaten. Why he decided to abandon the ancient capital, with its proximity to the buried glory of Egypt, for a small, isolated habitat that commanded legitimacy only through his presence there is uncertain. Was this an inward withdrawal in the face of an intransigent priesthood, or was it part of a planned, tactical retreat to achieve a strategic victory? The new city, unsullied by previous gods, was more likely symbolic as a holy site belonging to the new god.[45] It is also possible that he conceived it as a unifying national symbol for the religion of Aten.

Akhenaten also may have wanted to escape from the hostility of the priests of Amen because he lacked a solid grasp of the tenets of political power with which to press his rule. This could have happened by an earlier exclusion from decision making by his father or by his obsession with religious and philosophical issues. It has been suggested that Akhenaten was out of touch with the world around him, delegating the responsibility for governing to subordinates.[46] One author assumes a long co-regency and feels that his father, the senior pharaoh, may have encouraged him to leave Thebes either for his own safety or for the good of the state.[47] Akhenaten's penchant for self-isolation was truly extraordinary in that once he occupied his new city, he never left it again except in death.

The inscriptions about Akhenaten cannot disguise his belief that he was one with Aten and his intermediary on earth. To the modern mind a man who is convinced that he is a deity usually bears the stigma of mental aberration. If this is what is meant by being out of touch with the world, as his detractors maintain, a distinction has to be made between the world of his time and that of our own. For well over a millennium before him the divinity of a pharaoh was a given. The people were always conscious of the difference between the two levels of godship, although the exact relationship was left undefined.[48] In this context Akhenaten was in no way radical or disoriented.

When Amenhotep died, Akhenaten may have inherited the old royal counselors and therefore sought a form of personal liberation through a new god and new officers and in a new city.[49] Embracing a more existential way of life on virgin soil does not have to imply the cowardice or defeatism suggested by some writers. It is conceivable that the new city beckoned as a unifying national symbol for the religion of Aten. The fact that there is no record of any civil disorder during his entire reign is strong evidence that he was in control of the major forces in Egyptian life.

This alone reinforces the picture of a positive rather than a weak, cowering ruler.

Akhenaten's life in his new city apparently was all that he could desire. Surrounded by his family and presumably like-minded subjects, he was insulated at the same time from the despised priesthood of Amen. Perhaps he recognized, prophetically as it turned out, that his concept might not survive in the face of the persistent older cults. He began to demote the temples of other gods all over Egypt by ignoring their priests and replacing them with Atenists insofar as possible. Inscriptions referring to multiple gods were effaced wherever they were found. He succeeded in anathematizing all the older gods of Egypt in the remaining ten or eleven years of his reign. For this functional sterilization of the heavens, he has been called an atheist![50]

Akhenaten, Nefertiti, and their six daughters apparently enjoyed a healthy and normal family life. They are extensively pictured in activities ordinarily associated with any nonroyal family, playing, eating, worshipping, and so on. A tenderness hitherto unseen in royal pictography is displayed as he gambols with his children and again with his wife sitting on his lap. This pictured informality is unique to the Amarna Age. The impression of a gentle father and husband seems incongruent with the widely held image of an implacably dissident ideologue. He has been considered a madman for destroying temples to other gods and obliterating all references to them while trying to enforce an intensely personalized and austere worship of Aten.

An objective and less doctrinaire view, if indeed such is possible given his uninvited intrusion into the history of monotheism, might see a gentle human being with a vision of a better world and the power and motivation to act on it. His reign also marked the beginning of new expressionist art forms whereby an exaggerated realism replaced the flat, stylized depictions of traditional Egyptian art. He proceeded to enforce his nontraditional beliefs, at first tentatively and later more urgently, but he never resorted to violence. There is no evidence that he ever killed or even harassed his internal enemies. Perhaps it is understandable why authors with a romantic outlook would refer to him as a pacifist or an idealistic dreamer.[51] His indifference to the pleas of his vassals that he fight in Syro-Palestine is compatible with such a point of view. However, recent evidence indicates that on both the Canaan and Nubian fronts, Akhenaten's reign showed "a modicum of activity" in military matters.[52]

Akhenaten propounded an early radical change that rejected any anthropomorphic representation of god. Human or animal likenesses of Aten were forbidden. He alluded to the sun-disc as "the one who built himself by himself, with his [own] hands—no craftsman knows him."[53] Only the depiction of a sun-disc, with its multiple rays, was permitted. These rays terminated in tiny hands, which was a small concession to tradition. Wherever the sun-disc was shown, the hands that pointed toward the pharaoh and his family held the sign of life, *ankh*. Although Aten's ray/hands are often compared to the biblical "hand of God," such emphasis is easily overdrawn, as the hand is usually the effective instrument in any symbolic presentation.

Akhenaten's physique, seen mainly in relief drawings, is usually pictured in bizarre proportions. The bodily deformities have been described as "enlarged breasts," "protuberant belly," "swollen thighs," and "spindly shanks." His whole person was "effeminate" and "dwarf-like." He was even dismissed as an "iconoclastic freak."[54] Medical diagnoses of endocrine disorders, such as Froehlich's Syndrome, have been offered despite the certain knowledge that he sired at least six children. One writer surmised that he was in reality a woman masquerading as a man. A precedent for this theory existed in Hatshepsut, the former queen, who ruled as pharaoh while wearing a false beard and having herself portrayed in male attire.[55]

Some of Akhenaten's statuary has been thought to reveal degrees of craniofacial abnormality. One bust from Thebes, now in the Cairo Museum, shows a markedly elongated face. However, the deviation from normal is extremely tenuous and certainly does not match any commonly known congenital anomaly. It is impossible to ascertain whether these portrayals are accurate

within the limits of artistic integrity or thinly disguised carica-
tures. A sculptor's bust of him showing no abnormality whatso-
ever, would seem to be conclusive evidence to end the debate.
The face is clearly that of a man, not particularly handsome but
in no way deformed. His mummy, which would help to settle the
matter, unfortunately has never been identified.

During the Amarna Age, a less heroic or idealized portraiture
was taking place, perhaps at Akhanaten's own direction. The
changes might well be due to a new freedom given to the individual artist or to a trend away from the traditionally stylized
representation of the human form.

He and his family are not the only persons singled out for this
treatment; most figures of the time show similar characteristics.
Also, the tomb drawings of his nobles seem to suggest that the
elongated head and flabby torso had become fashionable. There
is surely a discernible change from the mature, grandiose style of
his father's reign to the vaguely disturbing license at the peak of
the Amarna Age.[56]

An interesting theory has been offered recently for Akhenaten's alleged hermaphroditism: The god Aten is conceived in
both genders. This symbolism has textual evidence in the tomb
writings of Amarna: "You are mother and father of all you create"
and "You are the mother who bears everyone, the one who nour-
ishes millions by your *ka* [spirit]." This combination of masculine
and feminine function within the god, who by extension of divinity is also Akhenaten, may underlie the portrayal of the king as
also having dual sexual characteristics.[57] Perhaps the feminine
lines of his body are a symbolization that the father-god's creative
force is inclusive and does not depend on specific gender. If the
pharaoh did not approve of the sculptors' representations of him
and his family, it is unlikely that they would have survived.
Therefore one can fairly conclude that Akhenaten supported the
stylized images that were made.

The pseudodeformities of face and torso have been used by
some authors to project a personal instability and even a mental
illness as the cause of his radical religious position. There have

Two views of a statue showing the head of Akhenaten in the style characteristic of the Amarna Age. Note the elongation of the face and the exaggerated features. This stylization was also used in the portrayal of the body, giving rise to theories about Akhenaten's physical deformities.

Photos Courtesy of
The Egyptian Museum, Cairo.

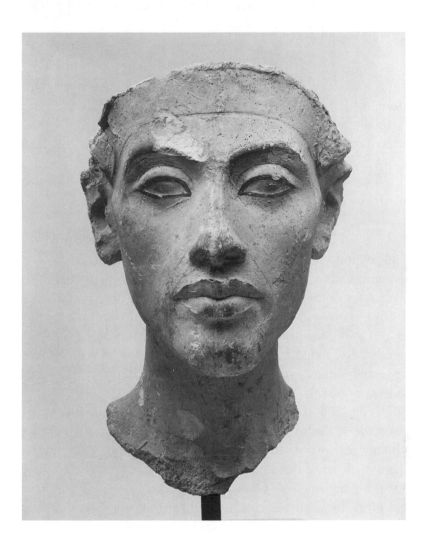

A life-size plaster cast of Akhenaten, excavated from a sculptor's studio at El Amarna. Modeled from real life, this cast is probably a good representative image of the pharaoh. Note that it shows no gross craniofacial deformity.

been suggestions that he was driven by paranoia. One writer states that "the fanaticism of Ikhnaton [Akhenaten] resulted more from a disordered brain than policy."[58] To permit his anti-establishment activities to impugn his mental or physical integrity is an offense against logic. With his pacifistic lifestyle, it is not difficult to see him as a dreamer or visionary given to excessive spirituality. Regardless of the underlying motivation, his actions reduced the worship of regional, highly personal gods to a belief in a single, all-powerful one.

That Akhenaten's life of reform still has the power to arouse dark passions in some scholars must indicate a reluctance—even an emotional intransigence—to accept his precedent role in the evolution of monotheism. Surely the artfully crafted religions of the modern world will not disintegrate simply because his concept of a single god with some ethical qualities can be shown to antedate our Judeo-Christian traditions. However, it is crucial to try to understand how Akhenaten's concepts impacted the development of Israel.

The lengthy paean to Aten, called "Great Hymn," that clearly foreshadows Psalm 104 is attributed to Akhenaten personally but without real proof. It was found in the tomb of Aye, the last pharaoh closely connected with him, who tried to salvage something of Atenism. The Great Hymn portrays Aten as the power that gives life to the earth and to all natural processes that exist. The universal ideal that all nations are creatures of the same god pervades the text. No other gods are mentioned. Its conception of Aten as the god of the cosmos is remarkably similar to the God in the Bible. This similarity could be merely a coincidental evolution of the same idea, but as it existed earlier in Egypt, a direct influence would seem to be more logical. Donald Redford feels that Akhenaten's concept of god involved universalism, dependence of life on the sun, transcendence, creativity, cosmic regularity, and absolute power.[59]

Unfortunately Atenism remained essentially a court religion without resonance among the common people. The ordinary Egyptian did not embrace these new ideas, perhaps from inertia

GREAT HYMN	PSALM 104
You [Aten] are beautiful, great and glorious, You are exalted over every land, Through your rays encompass the lands To the limit of all you have made. (lines 5–8)	O Lord, my God, You are very great; You are clothed in glory and majesty, wrapped in a robe of light; You spread the heavens like a tent cloth. (1b–2)
Your setting is on the western horizon, While the earth is in darkness in the fashion of death . . . Every lion has come forth from his den, As for all the serpents—they bite. (lines 13f, 19f)	You bring on darkness and it is night, when all the beasts of the forest stir. The lions roar for prey, seeking their food from God. (20f)
In the underworld you create the Nile, So that you may bring it, according to your desire, to sustain mankind. (lines 72f)	You make springs gush forth in torrents; they make their way between the hills, giving drink to all the wild beasts; the wild asses slake their thirst. (10f)

or the inability to comprehend an intangible god. The presence of *ushabtis* (small figurines representing personal deities) in Egyptian burial places during the Amarna period indicate that the common people could not accept the new religious austerity. Even some of Akhenaten's retainers may have paid only lip service to the changes.

When Akhenaten died, his reforms withered rapidly, and within twenty years he was himself anathematized. Perhaps it was economic chaos, resulting from his single-minded pursuit of religious reforms, that allowed his ideals to be reversed so precipitously after his death.[60] Yet could such a fundamental advance in spiritual awareness be lost completely? As one pertinent comment suggests, "There must have been among Akhenaten's courtiers sincere men who shared his convictions and were whole-hearted in following a charismatic leader."[61] It is therefore quite possible that some of these men might have gone underground during the active period of his damnation, resurfacing only at the time of the Exodus.

* * *

The suggestion that Akhenaten's monotheism was influenced by his maternal grandfather or the Asian practices brought with the Mitannian entourage of his father's harem has no factual basis. Certainly the concept of henotheism was present for a long time in Asia as it was in Egypt. However, monotheism in an Asian locus was unknown until the arrival of Israel about a century after the Amarna Age. There is little disagreement that Akhenaten's religion was monotheistic, but contentious debate still persists about the transcendent quality of that monotheism.

The relationship of his monotheism to that of early Israel is an issue that requires assumptions to be made about his personal worldview. If we could be certain that he had a philosophical vision embodying universality and ethical standards, it might be easier to place him at the vanguard of religious thinkers. On the other hand, if his interest was only in buttressing his own divinity by becoming one with an all-encompassing deity, he could stand only with those historical figures who inadvertently triggered later change. What is germane to our understanding of early Israel is not which goal he sought but rather that the obvious parallels be recognized in the concepts of both religions.

The Aten of Amarna was conceived as a living deity who stood alone. He was not framed in anthropomorphic terms. This defined a true monotheism, perhaps the most advanced conception that the Egyptian mind of the time could encompass.[62] The ethical value of pursuing truth and righteousness in life is expressed on the wall of a courtier's tomb: "I have come to thee, O living Aten; Maat has made her seat in me. I have not defrauded, I did not do falsehood." Although these tomb writings were prayers to Aten and his representative on earth to allow the supplicant's *ba* (the external form the person assumed after death) to roam during the day, it is obvious that they represent a new standard of ethical behavior, presaging demands by the later God of Israel.

The words of the Great Hymn and the prayers inscribed in the Amarna tombs were not written to impress posterity but to express the spiritualism of the time. These show similarities to the texts of Israel in the conception of both kingship and divinity. Some lines from the Great Hymn as translated by Vincent A. Tobin[63] and verses of Psalm 104 will illustrate this.

Aten, like the later God of Israel, had no associated mythology. Each deity was responsible for the purposeful creation of the world and all the things in it. Each did so by the medium of the spoken word. In Genesis 1 the repetitive phrase is *v'omer elohim* (and God said), whereas the Great Hymn states, "it is from your mouth that they [things that did not exist] have come forth." Thus the creative power of the spoken word is also attributed to Aten.[64]

The symbolism of light is another aspect of the remarkable likeness of both deities. "Let there be light," in Gen. 1:3a, is arguably the most widely known line in the entire Bible. Aten, as the sun-disc, already embodies the light of creative energy. The Great Hymn confirms this aspect of Aten: "Your rays nurse every field when you rise" (line 86). Also, "Your rising is their life ["millions of forms"]; your setting is their death" (line 110f).

A question often is raised whether a mechanistic symbol, such as a sun-disc, is appropriate to carry the visionary message of a universal god. It is quite clear, however, that the sun-disc is not the god itself but only a face, or representation. This point is supported by the fact that the real deity is inscribed as "the living Aten," or "the great living Aten," whereas the sun-disc is merely "the Aten."[65] The God of Israel, also unavailable to human senses, is represented by a screen of fire and smoke.(Exod. 3:2, 19:18). People still had to have a tangible expression of the abstract principle of universal divinity.

This identification of deities in familiar objects was the norm throughout the ancient world, whereas Yahveh, as the God of Israel came to be called, supposedly had a more transcendent function. As an authentic, implacable cosmic force, it had no need for the familiarity of an earthly form. However, there is compelling evidence to the contrary. Solar reference in the worship of Yahveh was widespread in northern and southern Israel, at least during the Monarchy period, and it is highly probable that the experience in Amarna was carried over directly in those Hebrews who left Egypt with Moses.

Solar metaphors for Yahveh abound in biblical literature: "for the Lord God is sun and shield" is one example (Ps. 84:12). The equation of Yahveh and the sun is clearly seen when Joshua "addressed the Lord; he said in the presence of the Israelites, 'Stand still, O sun, at Gibeon, O moon, in the Valley of Aijalon'"(Josh. 10:12,13). One wonders about the likelihood that Moses' chosen successor would openly pray to the sun (and moon) if a solar cult were not part of the group's practice. J. Glen Taylor's comment on the issue is, "On the basis of Josh. 10:12–14, it would appear that the link between Yahweh and the physical sun was relatively more direct at Gibeon (perhaps something not all that different from the cult of Aten?)."[66]

Not only were Yahveh and the sun closely identified in Gibeon, but also, for a period of time, the Tabernacle and the burnt-offering altar were located there (1 Chron. 16:39, 40; 21:29). These cultic objects, sacred to the religion of Israel and residing in a place where there was solar worship, are further implicated in the construction of the Temple in Jerusalem (mid-Tenth Century). Solomon "and all the assembly with him" went to the shrine at Gibeon to make "a thousand burnt offerings" on the bronze altar that "was also there before the Tabernacle of the Lord" (2 Chron. 1:3–6). When he later decided to build the Temple (2 Chron. 1:18), it is uncertain whether he moved the great bronze altar to Jerusalem or whether he used the commemorative altar that David, his father, had built in that city on the threshing floor of Araunah, the Jebusite (2 Sam. 24:25).

During the first half of the twentieth century, several authors postulated an east-west axis of orientation for Solomon's Temple.[67] These constructions suggested that on certain days, namely, the vernal and autumnal equinoxes, the first rays of sun rising over the Mount of Olives would shine unobstructed into the Holy of Holies, the sacred abode of Yahveh.[68] That the Temple hierarchy was associated with a solar cult is demonstrated in Ezek. 8:16: "Then He brought me into the inner court of the House of the Lord, and there, at the entrance to the Temple of the Lord, between the portico and the altar, were about twenty-five men, their backs to the Temple of the Lord and their faces to the east; they were bowing low to the sun in the east." The twenty-five men had to be priests of Israel, because no one else was allowed into those precincts.

Recent scholarship has indicated that a degree of sun worship was merged with Israel's God for several hundred years, at least until the Babylonian exile. As the religion evolved during this period, the priestly faction tried to repress the cultic manifestations but could not eradicate all traces that remained in the earliest literature. It was probably not until the Fifth Century that all pockets of solar worship finally disappeared.

The characteristics of the godhead in both the Amarna and Israelite religions are comparably transcendent. Aten is patently a universal god, as Yahveh later becomes. The introduction to the Great Hymn refers to Aten as "Lord of all that the Aten encompasses, Lord of heaven, Lord of earth. . . ." Gen. 24:3 contains almost identical wording: "the God of heaven and the God of the earth. . . ."

The foregoing presentation of the Amarna Age, along with a consideration of the uniqueness of Atenism, underscores the fundamental question: Was Akhenaten's a true monotheism? It appears that the Great Hymn is unambiguous on the issue: "How numerous are the things which you do, although they are hidden from sight, O sole god, who has no other face. After your own desire, you create the earth, although you are alone" (lines 57–60). As unequivocal as these lines are, many authorities who accept the evidence as presented still hesitate to confirm that

Aten was the single god, the universal god, and the only god of Amarna. One has to wonder whether this reticence does not depend more on a deeper emotional loyalty, a subconscious protectionism, than on available evidence.

Akhenaten's move away from the traditional Egyptian religious pattern, disavowed as it later was, nevertheless initiated farreaching change. By the beginning of the XIXth Dynasty, the rejuvenated Theban priesthood was acting again as a state within a state, becoming a rival political force to succeeding pharaohs.[69] For unspecified reasons the traditional proximity of royal power to its religious arm was permanently abrogated early in that dynasty. Thebes was downgraded to a mere religious center as the new pharaohs shifted their capital to Lower Egypt.[70] Undoubtedly the precedent for this was set by Akhenaten. The well-documented royal move into the delta region holds important implications for the time of the Exodus.

The "heresy" of Akhenaten represents a monotheistic concept far beyond anything that Egypt had previously known. Surely he was not alone in appreciating the logic of this advanced religious thinking. One person may enunciate the principle, but there are always others who recognize its validity. When Atenism was officially banished, its adherents were faced with the alternative of giving up the exciting new idea or trying to keep it alive quietly within themselves until a more receptive time appeared.

Moses was one who chose the latter course.

Notes

1. E. D. Oren, "The Ways of Horus in North Sinai," in *Egypt, Israel, Sinai*, ed. A. F. Rainey (Tel Aviv: Tel Aviv Univ., 1987), pp. 69–119.
2. D. B. Redford, *A Study of the Biblical Story of Joseph* (Leiden: E. J. Brill, 1970), p. 198.
3. J. Baikie, *The Amarna Age* (New York: Macmillan, 1926), p. 139.
4. D. B. Redford, "An Egyptological Perspective on the Exodus," in Rainey, op. cit., pp. 137–161.
5. M. Greenberg, *The Hab/piru* (New Haven: American Oriental Society, 1955), p. 81.

6. Ibid., p. 81.
7. N. K. Gottwald, *The Tribes of Yahweh* (New York: Orbis Books, 1979), p. 458.
8. D. B. Redford, *Akhenaten, the Heretic King* (Princeton: Princeton Univ. Press, 1984), p. 28.
9. Baikie, op. cit., p. 121f.
10. F. J. Giles, *Ikhnaton* (Rutherford, NJ: Farleigh Dickenson Press, 1970), p. 126.
11. Ibid., p. 93.
12. R. David, *Cult of the Sun* (London: J. M. Dent, 1980), p. 161.
13. A. E. Weigall, *The Life and Times of Akhenaton* (London: William Blackwood, 1910), p. 32.
14. Ibid., p. 32.
15. A. Osman, *Stranger in the Valley of Kings* (London: Souvenir Press, 1987), p. 124.
16. H. R. Hall, "Yuia the Syrian," *Proceedings of the Society of Biblical Archeology* 35(1913):63–65.
17. A. Osman, op. cit., p. 121.
18. Ibid., p. 122.
19. Ibid., p. 126.
20. Ibid., p. 16.
21. *Holy Bible*, Revised Standard Version (New York: Thomas Nelson, 1952).
22. A. Osman, op. cit., p. 130.
23. Ibid., p. 130f.
24. Ibid., p. 129.
25. Ibid., p. 15.
26. L. Ginzberg, *The Legends of the Jews*, vol. 3 (Philadelphia: Jewish Publication Society, 1911), p. 5.
27. D. B. Redford, *Joseph*, p. 163.
28. A. Osman, op. cit., p. 15.
29. H. H. Rowley, *From Joseph to Joshua* (Oxford: Oxford Univ. Press, 1950), p. 134.
30. A. Osman, op. cit., p. 14.
31. J. Baikie, op. cit., p. 236f.
32. R. Hari, *New Kingdom Amarna Period* (Leiden: E. J. Brill, 1985), p. 4.
33. R. G. Bonnel, "The Ethics of El-Amarna," in *Studies in Egyptology*, ed. S. Israelit-Groll (Jerusalem: Magnes Press, 1990), pp. 71–97.
34. C. Aldred, *Akhenaten* (London: Thames and Hudson, 1988), p. 238.
35. F. J. Giles, op. cit., p. 120.
36. W. J. Murnane, *Ancient Egyptian Coregencies* (Chicago: The Oriental Institute, 1977), p. 240.
37. Ibid., p. 255.
38. Ibid., p. 257.

39. Ibid., p. 232.
40. G. Perepelkin, *The Secret of the Gold Coffin* (Moscow: Nauka, 1978), p. 74.
41. W. H. Stiebing, "The Amarna Period," in *Palestine in Transition*, ed. D. N. Freedman and D.F. Graf (Sheffield: Almond Press, 1983), pp. 1–14.
42. Ibid., p. 5.
43. D. B. Redford, *Akhenaten*, p. 159f.
44. Ibid., p. 20.
45. R. G. Bonnel, op. cit., p. 84.
46. D. B. Redford, *Akhenaten*, p. 168.
47. F. J. Giles, op. cit., p. 133ff.
48. V. A. Tobin, "Amarna and Biblical Religion," in *Pharaonic Egypt* ed. S. Israelit-Groll (Jerusalem: Magnes Press, 1985), pp. 231–278.
49. D. B. Redford, *Akhenaten*, p. 165.
50. Ibid., p. 234.
51. J. Baikie, op. cit., p. 234.
52. T. Dothan, "The Impact of Egypt on Canaan during the 18th and 19th Dynasties in the Light of the Excavations at Deir el-Balah," in *Egypt, Israel, Sinai*, ed. A. F. Rainey, p. 123.
53. D. B. Redford, *Akhenaten*, p. 175.
54. Ibid., p. 158.
55. Aldred, *Akhenaten*, p. 231.
56. Ibid., p. 232f.
57. V. A. Tobin, op. cit., p. 253f.
58. F. J. Giles, op. cit., p. 113.
59. D. B. Redford, *Akhenaten*, p. 177.
60. C. Aldred, "Egypt: The Amarna Period and the End of the Eighteenth Dynasty," *Cambridge Ancient History Series* 2, part 2 (Cambridge: Cambridge Univ. Press, 1975), pp. 49–97.
61. C. Aldred, *Akhenaten*, p. 248.
62. L. V. Zabkar, "The Theocracy of Amarna and the Doctrine of the BA," *Journal of Near Eastern Studies* 13(1954):87–101
63. V. A. Tobin, op. cit., pp. 234–237.
64. Ibid., p. 251.
65. Ibid., p. 259.
66. J. G. Taylor, *Yahweh and the Sun* (Sheffield: Sheffield Academic Press, 1993), p. 142.
67. F. J. Hollis, "The Sun Cult and the Temple at Jerusalem," in *Myth and Ritual* ed. S. H. Hooke (London: Oxford Univ. Press, 1933), p. 99f.
68. J. Morgenstern, *The Fire Upon the Altar* (Chicago: Quadrangle Books, 1963), p. 7f.
69. R. Hari, op. cit., p. 6.
70. F. J. Giles, op. cit., p. 113.

Moses,
Sire of Israel

9

The defining moment in the history of Israel occurred when the figure of Moses took shape. Prior to this time there were only ancestor narratives to indicate the earliest currents of a new religion. The patriarchs were the lusty and exclusive fathers of the "chosen" people, but their spiritual beliefs were not presented as part of a comprehensive theology. Their religion seemed to be a variation of the regional polytheism practiced by neighboring peoples, but the patriarchs achieved special status by developing a contractual intimacy with a god who promised them perpetual ownership of the land, which stands as their major contribution to later Israel. These Semitic progenitors showed little pretense to ethical behavior and certainly nothing of the nobility ascribed to them later. It is likely that their traditions were enshrined when an earlier linkage was needed to root the people in the soil they coveted. The alignment of Israel with God by means of a thorough commitment to the Covenant was mediated only through Moses.

The patriarchs as ancestors were both real and generic, and Moses must be considered in the same light. His dominant role in the formation of Israel has been buttressed by a remarkable accretion of legends, which undermine his real credentials as they apotheosize his mission. In the Torah he survived a mythic birth to achieve a heroic maturity and then to experience an unfathomable demise. To recreate a semblance of realism in this fanciful biography, we must accept the premise that the epic qualities assigned to him are subjective embellishments, at once ordinary and inspired, in the later recollection of a life. The persona of Moses is encumbered today with a massive overlay of speculative material that we will try to analyze by asking figuratively, "Will the real Moses please stand up?"

The Nile valley and delta region had always been a magnet for the people of neighboring southwestern Asia because of a favorable climate and unlimited water. Unlike merchants or conquerors, unskilled immigrants often had to resign themselves to the lowest rung of the Egyptian occupational ladder, characteristically brute labor. The widespread use of Asiatics in the construction industry from the time of Thutmose III to the end of the New Kingdom is well attested.[1] Exod. 1:11–14, in which the Hebrews are laboring to build pharaoh's store-cities in Pithom and Ramesses, appears to describe the local scene quite realistically. Making the Hebrews into slaves is probably a later subjective interpretation, because a neutral reading of Exodus does not reveal them to be prisoners under tight military or police discipline. Indeed there is no evidence from any source other than the Bible that abject slavery was widespread in the late XVIIIth or early XIXth Dynasties.

Exodus reports a pharaonic scheme whereby hard labor was to be the vehicle for containing the sullen slave populace. However, this carefully crafted picture begins to fade when we learn in Exod. 5:15 that the Hebrew leaders have ready access to pharaoh, an unlikely perquisite offered to slaves. The presence of two Hebrew midwives (1:15) receiving discretionary orders from pharaoh himself suggests that they represented a small self-contained enclave of the body politic. Further, to assume that the midwives could ignore a royal request to allow all newborn Hebrew males to die without incurring considerable jeopardy to themselves is unrealistic, and there is no mention that the orders were carried out or that the midwives were punished. These interactions would be far more probable if the Semites were a free and legally accepted group within Egyptian society, and we have already seen how prevalent assimilation was by Semites.

The Moses traditions must be framed within a reasonable time period to validate their historical context. Unfortunately no identifiable pharaoh or other known person is named in Exodus, and applicable data needed to influence our thinking are vague, indirect, and often conflicting. To authenticate a Mosaic period, we must come to terms with essential uncertainties, although most scholars today place Moses and the Exodus within the latter half of the Thirteenth Century.

The propensity of Ramesses II (1290–1225) to build monuments and cities to his own glorification is well known, but he was not unique among the pharaohs in this pursuit. The recent location of a city, thought to be Pi-Ramesses, in the eastern delta region lends support to the biblical notation that the Hebrews labored there. Pithom is also believed to be in the same area but more to the east. The Mosaic traditions are thus appropriately linked to the eastern delta and within the Thirteenth Century.

Exod. 1:8 states that "a new king arose over Egypt who did not know Joseph." Given Joseph's preeminence in the land, it is safe to assume that if the new ruler did not know of him, more than a few generations had elapsed and a new dynasty was in power. The arrival of Hebrews who were unfamiliar with Egyptian customs can be set very logically in the Amarna Age.[2] Only four lineal generations are described between Joseph and Moses, a gap of about 100–150 years. If Joseph was the remarkable man who served Amenhotep III as vizier and father-in-law, as now seems possible, the theory that Moses dealt with Ramesses II or his son, Merneptah (1225–1215), musters strong arithmetical support.

The strongest evidence for this notion is the mention of Israel on the stele of Merneptah, which text describes his conquests in the Syro-Palestine area. When pharaohs recorded their personal achievements in stone, they were usually more concerned about posterity's image of them than about any accuracy of detail. This particular paean to Merneptah's military prowess has been dated to about 1220 B.C.E. without significant dissent. A people or a region in Canaan, already bearing the name Israel, had attracted his attention and was on the list of Canaanite political entities he had vanquished. The stele lends undeniable evidence that an Israel of some kind was present in the Near East by the end of the Thirteenth Century.

Moses was a man of mature years when he received God's call to return to Egypt, although the eighty years allotted to him in Exod. 7:7 appears to be biblically contrived. Harold H. Rowley noted that Moses' life has been conveniently divided into three forty-year periods in Egypt, in Midian, and in the wilderness.[3] Ramesses II reigned for sixty-five years, so it would be possible for Moses to have been born and raised to manhood in Egypt and still return to confront the same king, now in his old age. However, when God told Moses that those "who sought to kill you are dead" (4:19), it could have meant that he would be dealing with Merneptah. But whichever pharaoh was then in power, we are still safely within the Thirteenth Century. Also, the mention of Edomites and Moabites as obstacles to Israel's passage into central Canaan via the eastern shore of the Dead Sea supports this projected time frame. When Moses asks the king of Edom to allow them to march peacefully through his territory, the refusal (Num. 20:18, 20–21) implies strength to the Edomites and a relative weakness in the Exodus group. Significantly this kingdom had not been established before the Thirteenth Century.

In dating the Moses traditions, nineteenth and early twentieth-century scholars usually produced a much earlier Exodus, based on data that have since been critically reevaluated. Where the 430-year sojourn in Egypt (Exod. 12:40) is used as the primary factor, the identification of their arrival and departure becomes an exercise in manipulative projection. Several authorities have localized the patriarchs in Canaan throughout the first half of the Second Millennium.[4] For example, if they are placed near the beginning of that period, specifically at the time of Hammurabi, the Exodus would have taken place in the Amarna

Age. The Hab/piru activity in Canaan at that time then becomes "proof" of the conquest details in Joshua and Judges.

But this construction is very difficult to defend if the conquest is uncertain, as we shall see later. If Joseph and the descent into Egypt are made coincident with the Hyksos hegemony, a position still held in some quarters, a Thirteenth Century Exodus after four centuries is quite reasonable. However, a sojourn of that duration becomes more problematic if the beginning is assumed to coincide with Jacob, as the Bible states, while the end occurs with Moses leading the Exodus. Exod. 6:16–20 clearly defines only four generations in Egypt: Levi, Kohath, Amram, and Moses, and four generations in four centuries is untenable unless we revert to the exaggerated generational intervals of early Genesis. It is much more reasonable that the Exodus group represents four generations in Egypt, whereas the 430-year tradition uses a much earlier Semitic experience, probably the Hyksos period. The patriarchs can now be accorded a much more logical date, as Hab/piru in the Fourteenth Century.

The Birth Story: Myth and Reality

Can any person have missed the story of Moses' birth, with his concealment at home for three months and subsequent discovery floating on the Nile River in a basket? Although it may excite the imagination of children, it is patently flawed history. The tale reproduces the classic pattern of hero myths as the "exposed child" or the "foundling child." These tales have been known from the literature of ancient cultures since scholars decoded the long-forgotten languages in which they were written. The plot similarities betray their common mythic origins. From an anthropological perspective, the hero myth is the remnant of a ritual enactment whereby the designee had the magic power to achieve what it was that the group wanted. It has been suggested that, "we shall probably not err in assuming that many myths, which we now know only as myths, had once their counterpart in magic; in other words, that they used to be acted as a means of producing in fact the events which they describe in figurative language. Ceremonies often die out while the myths survive, and thus we are left to infer the dead ceremony from the living myth."[5]

Hero myths seem to have arisen among early peoples because of a basic urge to believe, to understand, and to act effectively in their own perceived destiny. These universal needs were readily converted into myths with the same symbols, regardless of the eccentricities of time and place. They routinely begin with an ominous birth into implied danger. The procreative act is often illicit or involved in shame. The newborn child, commonly fated to commit parricide, is hunted and has to be removed or hidden, commonly by a stranger, human or animal, who rescues and rears him as a foster child. He ultimately returns with a significant victory, frequently over the king/father, and rules in his stead. Marriage to a desirable woman, often related to his predecessor, is usually included. He reigns successfully and lawfully until he is overthrown. Death is mysterious, usually on a hilltop, and without burial. Children rarely succeed him.

Lord Raglan's classic monograph of 1936 describes twenty-two "incidents" that constitute the general pattern of a hero myth.[6] He analyzes the tales of many heroes from the world's literature but predominantly in Greek mythology. Not every hero experiences each of the incidents, but the fraction is large enough to leave no doubt that the hero qualifies for the myth. The one hero who most exemplifies every incident is Oedipus, although several others also rank very high on the scale. Contributions from Greek, Hebrew, Celtic, Roman, Teutonic, and even Javanese literature justify the conclusion that hero myths have a universal appeal. They also express commonly recognized human motifs even when divinities are involved.

To students of psychoanalysis, the near-perfect score made by Oedipus is more than fortuitous; it is inevitable. About twenty years before Lord Raglan's work, Otto Rank considered the problem in "The Myth of the Birth of the Hero."[7] He analyzed fifteen examples in which premonitory dreams, abandonment, chance nurture, and return to ultimate success play dominant roles. The male childhood fantasies that name the Oedipal theme course through all the tales. The success of a son's childhood wish for possession of the mother, accomplished through the father's death, becomes possible only in the anthem of a nonthreatening hero myth. It has been argued that the heroes of tradition are really heroes of myth linked to cultic rituals and therefore have no historicity.[8] On the other hand, if we accept that the Oedipal wish exists as part of the universally repressed masculine psyche, the hero myth represents the expression of what is otherwise unacceptable and becomes the heroic quality of the real character.

The issue of historical reality in hero myths is not to be relegated to recondite dialectic, because progress in Western civilization has come about by heroic activity of real persons on whom legends of mythic proportion have been grafted. Real heroism can be understood only when plain fact is separated from noble fiction. Many of the heroes of literature are easily characterized as mythic, regardless of the source. Whether for ceremonial rites, grandiloquent tribal festivals, or as displaced repression, the likes of Zeus, Oedipus, or Dionysios can easily remain in a fictitious realm without dissent. Others, such as Moses or Jesus, demand confirmation of their historic contributions. This presents less of a problem if we believe that humankind strives to transmit history without recourse to conscious falsification. Valid traditions, along with prescriptive modifications, have created a body of contradictory knowledge about them that now needs critical reevaluation, and the direction of that effort must be toward the separation of one aspect from the other. To deny an original reality is to demean the heroic in history. But to uncritically accept the literary accretions of unknown sources is to subvert intellectual discipline.

The figure of Jesus is not germane to this book except as it parallels the mission of Moses in mediating Godliness. The stories of both men bear more than a passing semblance to each other, and both are easily categorized as heroic with supernatural elements. Using the criteria of Raglan's outline, one scholar concludes that Jesus belongs squarely in the hero tradition.[9] However, because the historicity of Jesus is so critical to the Christian faith, it is noteworthy that Raglan, for whom heroic activity was unhistorical, omits him from his list. He does, however, use Moses as a prime example. If this implies a lack of concern about the historicity of Moses, the same is not true among most Jewish writers. They generally avoid critical evaluation of Mosaic traditions for the same reason that motivated Lord Raglan, a Christian, to overlook the hero myth manifestations in the figure of Jesus. Neither position respects objectivity.

The circumstances of Moses' birth and early life are almost identical with those of Sargon I, King of Akkad. Very little is certain about Sargon except that he was a Semite who conquered the Sumerians sometime in the Twenty-Fourth Century. His own description of his life includes being placed in a basket of reeds made waterproof by pitch and then abandoned in the Euphrates River, where he was rescued by Akki, a humble water carrier who raised him to manhood. He became king and reigned for forty-five years.[10] In the Semitic culture of Mesopotamia, his heroic life was undoubtedly transmitted as part of the regional folklore, making it available as a model for the later Hebrews who wished to commemorate a more recent leader with almost divine qualities. If they were concerned that Moses' origin was indistinct or inappropriate, the parallel to Sargon's early obscurity must have suggested itself.

The legend had to be modified slightly to align Moses' childhood with a contemporary setting. The details of his story in the first two chapters of Exodus would be confused, inconsistent, and illogical if measured without the prompting of creedal tradition. The Egyptian locus, with its long history of Semitic immigration, lent itself well for the creation of a hero of Israel, although the details invite skepticism even as they are plausibly presented. If Moses were to be saved from death, why did he have to be set on the bank of a presumably crocodile-infested river and in the vicinity of the palace from which his death had been decreed? And is it reasonable to believe that Moses' rescuer would not suspect his Hebrew parentage? Exod. 2:6 itself supplies the answer when pharaoh's daughter remarks, "This must be a Hebrew child." It would appear that she was either unaware or unconcerned about the death edict her father had issued. Both alternatives lack credibility, as do other charming and inventive touches that amplify the text. There is no reference from any source other than the first two chapters of Exodus that the Egyptians tried to destroy the Hebrews at this time.[11] Even the method of population control described in the Bible seems incredibly naive.

Abandonment of the hero in infancy usually fuels the hero myth. A recent study of thirty-two such tales found that twelve of them involved abandonment in water, mainly rivers.[12] Although Rank's suggestion that a basket on water is equivalent to the womb and amniotic fluid may be psychoanalytically cogent, it is totally irrelevant in a historical perspective. Exod. 2:3, in mimicking the Sargon legend, merely informs us that that a known literary device is being used to modify Moses' real background. The adoption practices widely followed in the ancient Near East for a foundling child are also reflected in the Moses story. After the discovery of an abandoned child, a wet nurse would be found to raise him for three years. Afterward he would be returned to the owner to be legally adopted and named.[13] This is the precise pattern in Exod. 2:9, 10.

The ambiguity of the tradition has been a source of concern to scholars, perhaps within a few generations after Moses' suspicious death. Recognizing the need for explication, they used colorful, folkloristic details to soften the harsh contrasts. Their preoccupation with diluting a pervasive Egyptian contribution in favor of an essentially Hebraic origin seems to indicate a coverup of unpalatable secrets.

Several strands are common to the extrabiblical legends about Moses. One deals with premonitions of greatness in his future. His mother, Jochebed, knew of it because she had no pain during the pregnancy or in the birth process. At Moses' first appearance, "the whole house was filled with radiance equal to the splendor of the sun and the moon." When he was but a day old, besides walking and talking, he refused to nurse at his mother's breast, a statement patently at variance with Exod. 2:9. The Egyptian princess who rescued him perceived the *shechinah* (God's Holy Spirit) lying beside him in the river basket.[14]

Another trend converts non-Hebrews who were affiliated with him into "God-fearers." The princess rejects the idol worship of her father's palace, and as a reward God adopts her with the name Bithiah (daughter of God).[15] Jethro, the Midianite priest who later becomes Moses' father-in-law, also rejects the idol worship of his own cult. His conversion to "God-fearer" is certified by additional Hebrew names: Jether (additional part in the Torah), Hobab (beloved son of God), Reuel (friend of God), and Putiel (he who renounced idolatry).[16]

In Midrashic literature the name of Moses undergoes similar multiplication. His father called him Heber, to indicate that he and Jochebed had become reunited after their failed attempt to practice birth control by separation. Jochebed's name for him was Jekuthiel because God returned him to her care. His sister, Miriam, named him Jered to indicate that she had descended to the riverbank to watch over him.[17] The number of Hebrew names pinned to his cloak raises further suspicion that later Israelites felt a vague discomfort with a name of obvious Egyptian etymology.

Moses is a common Egyptian name suffix meaning "son of" or "born to," as in Ah-mose, Thut-mose, or Ra-mose (Ramesses). Most Jewish authorities insist on reinterpreting Moses from a Hebrew root indicating that he had been "drawn out of [water]."[18] They point to Exod. 2:10, where the Egyptian princess named him Moses because "I drew him out of the water." Why she would offer a meaning derived from Hebrew in place of the standard Egyptian one is unfathomable except that the Hebrew meaning was probably added by later writers. Semites were given Egyptian names, especially as native-born children, but a name suffix standing alone would be inexplicable unless the original prefix was forgotten or consciously suppressed.

A third demonstrable trend resolves Moses' extensive Egyptian and Midianite relationships into a Hebrew matrix. The Egyptian princess, as his stepmother, enters the family of Israel in Num. 13 and 14 by marrying Caleb, of the tribe of Judah, and one of Moses' trustworthy scouts.[19] Another legend tells about a sacred rod that God first gave Adam, which had the Ineffable Name (Yahveh) inscribed on it, as well as the ten plagues that would ultimately descend on Egypt. Jethro, then a scribe in pharaoh's court, stole the rod, which promptly rooted itself in the ground, and when he demanded that his daughters' suitors pull the rod out, it devoured them all. Moses was able to uproot it, thereby getting a Midianite wife, and at the same time reclaiming the sacred rod.[20] Here is an unmistakable parallel to legends from Celtic and Teutonic sources, whereby the sacred sword can be drawn out only by the anointed person. It is a neat, circular symbolism that endows the rod Moses will use later in commanding the miracles of Exodus. It also cast a Midianite shadow by transforming itself into a serpent in pharaoh's presence.

Moses' wives further expand his foreign connections. In Exod. 2:21 he marries Zipporah, daughter of the Midianite priest Jethro. His father-in-law is also identified in Judg. 1:16 as a Kenite, Heber (Hobab). As this is one of the names associated with Jethro, and as Kenites and Midianites seem to be used interchangeably, it is not unlikely that these are the same people but reported from different perspectives. There is also an implication here that different peoples contributed to the genesis of Israel.

The Bible does not suggest that Moses had ever been to Ethiopia, yet in Num. 12:1 he is faulted for having a "Cushite" (Nubian/Ethiopian) wife. Extrabiblical legend explains this reference by describing his march at the head of an army, presumably Egyptian, to subdue rebellious forces in Ethiopia and remaining there for forty years as the ruler. When he finally leaves after a native-led coup d'état he is sixty-seven years old.

Still fearful of punishment because of his murder of the overseer in Exod. 2:12, he avoids Egypt, moving instead directly to Midian.[21] How ingeniously this tale threads its way between a potential germ of history and the biographical demands of a later national consciousness!

As an Egyptian of royal parentage, Moses might well have led one of the frequent military expeditions to control the people at the headwaters of the Nile. A native wife would come as no surprise under such circumstances. However, after offering a plausible aspect of Moses' adult life, the legend then complicates its message with a distinctly absurd suggestion—that in forty years of marriage to his Cushite wife, he did not cohabit with her, because he feared God.[22] We would be perfectly justified in wondering what had changed in his fear of God when we are introduced to his Midianite wife and their two sons in Exod. 2:21, 22 and 18:2, 3.

Moses is still a child when he is delivered to the princess who then "made him her son" (Exod. 2:10). By that tradition he is afforded an Egyptian youth spent in the royal palace. We have already learned of the diverse mixture of children growing up in the royal circle, where princes shared company with future priests, officers, officials, and sons of foreign vassals. Certainly the adopted son of a princess would be part of this privileged group. Yet according to Exodus, he never forgot his roots, so he could kill an abusive Egyptian "beating a Hebrew, one of his kinsmen" (2:11). Such an emotional attachment would be remarkable, considering that he had no contact with Hebrews from infancy to adulthood. The gratuitous phrase "one of his kinsmen" is another indication that his identity with the Hebrews is being flourished.

Moses obviously has been smothered in Hebrew symbolisms, yet his original name, truncated as it was, did not totally repress his Egyptian past. Again we witness scribal tenacity in adhering to the principle that traditions must be recorded as they exist. The pooled traditions of the merging groups who were to become Israel served to deliver this central figure into the wider communal mainstream. He soon became Hebrew, of the tribe of Levi, and Midianite by marriage. But if his Egyptian association could not be denied, it was at least presented as a forced adoption. That Moses was not assigned a wife from an Israelite tribe in addition to Zipporah, if only to ensure an appropriate lineage to his sons, is strong indication that his spawn would not occupy a place of honor in future Israel. That indeed happened.

Inexplicably the parents of Moses remain unnamed until he is well into his seniority and contending with pharaoh about the Exodus. Even then his Hebrew ancestry is revealed only within a clan list (Exod. 6:18, 20). This indifference is perplexing, given his undeniable status as the founding hero of Israel. The late mention of siblings and the absence of a detailed genealogy, when so many lesser figures are meticulously traced, strongly suggests that the mystery surrounding him was purposeful and necessary. It is not unlikely that his mythic birth story and placement in the tribe of Levi were secondary traditions because his parentage and place of birth were entirely unknown.[23] We shall see in chapter 12 how important the militant Levites were to the success of his mission. Even the redundancy in Exod. 4:14, ". . . your brother Aaron the Levite," intentionally belabors that tribal association.

The invocation of a mythic birth story is meant to certify Moses' Hebrew origins, perhaps as a balance to his association with Egypt, which is clearly central to the history of Israel. It is very strange that the oldest source, J, has no name for Moses' parents beyond "A certain man of the house of Levi went and married a Levite woman" (Exod. 2:1). Only after his membership in the tribe of Levi was established do we discover that his father and mother were respectively the great-grandson and granddaughter of Jacob himself. At that time, 100 or more years after Joseph and his triumphs, a closer relationship to the patriarchs could hardly be imagined. Two older siblings were then added to represent depth of family and to establish cultic leadership through Aaron.

* *
*

Before proceeding further into the reconstruction of a more historically cogent life and career for Moses, we should pause to
reflect on the story so far. There are two possible explanations
for the derivative features of the hero myth that attend his birth
and early life. First, the details at some point were no longer
known, although a dramatic beginning to any religious epic is
obligatory; second, his parentage was Egyptian and therefore
unacceptable in the context of later Israel's declared genetic
purity. Moses' contribution was so essential to the evolution of
Israel that only an ancestry relevant to the rest of its history could
be permitted. He simply had to become indisputably Hebrew.
But how was this to be done if his nativity would not cooperate?
Fanciful interpretation—"spin control" in contemporary
terms—was even then a time-honored method of redefining
unhelpful facts.

Sigmund Freud in 1939 suggested what had been unthinkable. Psychoanalytic research applied to the freely associating
text of the Bible led him to the conclusion that Moses was an
Egyptian, perhaps both a priest and the governor of the province
of Goshen, but certainly a prince.[24] Freud was vilified in both
religious and literary circles for his temerity in expressing a theory that Moses was not a Jew at all but rather an Egyptian. In a
vitriolic, almost hysterical attack, the following was said of him:
"Freud, the scientist, could not have committed this unforgivable
blunder, nor could he have been so unmindful of the very rudi-
ments of scholarly method and accuracy had he not been completely under the spell of the Jewish self-hatred complex which,
like every obsession, renders rational thinking impossible."[25]
Certainly it was not rational thinking that would misconstrue a
serious approach to a fundamental ambiguity in the Bible as an
attack on Judaism from ignorance and self-hatred! A recent work
strongly suggests that Freud had far deeper pride in his Jewish-
ness than has been commonly thought.[26] Freud's *Moses and
Monotheism* might well have drawn on material that time has
since rendered obsolete. However, his prescient observations

were based on sound research and psychological theory that still find support two generations after he wrote the book.

The suggestion that Moses was a member of the royal circle, and perhaps even a prince, gains substance in the legend in which the princess presents him to her father, saying that she "thought it proper to adopt him as my son and as the heir of thy kingdom." With that announcement pharaoh embraced the child.[27] This, of course, was the same pharaoh who ordered the death of all new-born Hebrew males!

Another Midrashic tale relates that Moses in his third year, while sitting beside pharaoh, playfully snatched the crown from the ruler's head and placed it on his own head. Consternation erupted among the court because of the symbolic transfer of power it represented. When pharaoh asked, "What is to be done to this Hebrew boy on account of this act?" it was decided to proceed with a "trial by fire." There are several versions of this episode, each substantially corroborating the others. Moses was to be presented with a choice of an onyx stone or a fiery coal. If he chose the precious stone, it would prove that he acted in a deliberate prophecy, and he would be put to death immediately to protect the pharaoh. If he reached for the coal, his transgression would be seen as an innocent childish act, and he would be spared. Moses started to reach for the onyx, but the angel Gabriel hastily guided his hand to the coal, which burned him. He quickly put the burned hand to his mouth, secondarily causing burns to his lips and tongue, so that for all his life he became "slow of speech" and "of a slow tongue."[28] In one of the many variants of this tale, it was Jethro, Moses' future father-in-law, who suggested the trial.

The mysterious speech deficiency is first encountered when Moses argues with God that he will be unable to persuade the Hebrews to follow him or to influence pharaoh to release them because "I am slow of speech and slow of tongue" (Exod. 4:10). Prior to this there is no mention of such a problem, although he was supposedly an adult of eighty years at the time of the burning bush (7:7). He reminds God of his impeded speech in 6:12,

30. It is generally accepted that the disability is but a metaphor indicating a real, if ill-defined, problem. The Targum Onkelos, an old Aramaic translation of the Torah, describes Moses' protest as "I am of heavy speech, and stammering tongue." Others read the pericope as a stereotypical literary device that ensures the sanctity of the mouth that speaks for God. George W. Coats finds hints of this position in Isaiah, Jeremiah, and Ezekial.[29] In the words of another long-standing tradition Moses says, "I am not well versed in the language of the Egyptians; I have forgotten it, for as a young man I fled from Egypt, and am now an octogenarian."[30] This position is an obvious attempt to prove that his primary language was Hebrew.

The most direct and logical explanation for the imputed speech defect is that Moses simply could not speak the language of the Hebrews, having been raised in the Egyptian palace. When God says, "Now go, and I will be with you as you speak and will instruct you what to say" (Exod. 4:12), it implies that the problem has nothing whatever to do with a physical incapacity to speak normally. Aaron assumes the role of interpreter when God says, "and he shall speak for you to the people" (4:16). Assimilated Semites undoubtedly spoke both languages. The suggestion that Moses needed a spokesman may have been a later priestly interpolation designed to augment the role of Aaron as progenitor of the high priesthood.[31]

Another indication of the lineal distance between Moses and the Hebrews can be deduced from his use of "your fathers" rather than "our fathers" when referring to the God who sent him to them (Exod. 3:15). If he were one of the Hebrews and urging them toward a mutual goal, it would have been most politic to use the first-person plural when referring to their common God. However, as an Egyptian, his use of the second person would be natural and appropriate.

Aaron's role as an interpreter between Moses and the Hebrews also finds support in Exod. 4:30. Both men assemble the elders of the people, but only Aaron speaks to them of God's plan. Moses remains silent. They also go together to meet pharaoh, but it appears that Aaron merely performs the signs that God commanded. There is no direct indication that he speaks, although God told Moses to tell him what to say (7:2). In the earliest confrontation the text stresses that both of them address and answer pharaoh together. However, by the second plague and until they leave Egypt, Moses alone speaks to pharaoh, an indication that he spoke fluent Egyptian, if not fluent Hebrew.

The Hebrews Are Freed

The liberation process for the Hebrews begins when Moses and Aaron confront the ruler of Egypt and ultimately unleash the first nine plagues. A point frequently overlooked is that before meeting pharaoh, Moses and Aaron first had to convince the Hebrews that God's plan was in their best interests. In Exod. 4:30 Aaron "repeated all the words that the Lord had spoken to Moses, and he performed the signs in the sight of the people, and the people were convinced." Would such a prescriptive harangue have been necessary if the Hebrews were slaves facing genocide? This prosaic episode becomes far more comprehensible if we realize that Moses needed Aaron to explain his risky plan of action to the wary Hebrews in their own language.

The episode in Exod. 2:11–14, in which Moses "went out to his kinfolk" and involved himself with them, is traditionally read as proof that he was rejoining his people in fulfillment of his destiny. But another explanation, more logical in the context of Moses' outsider status, is that he was trying to ingratiate himself with the Hebrews. Earlier, when he intervened to stop a fight between two Hebrews, one of them asks, "Who made you chief and ruler over us?" (2:14). The use of the Hebrew word *sar* (prince or minister) adds to the possibility that they regarded Moses' special status as alien to them. The question also implies a challenge by the very people he claimed as his own.[32] Moses was condemned for his lordly behavior in two of the many rebellions against him during the period of wandering (Num. 12:2,

16:13). His special status is also intimated in the statement "Moses himself was much esteemed in the land of Egypt, among pharaoh's courtiers and among the people" (Exod. 11:3). This popularity has been credited with making the Exodus possible,[33] but one has to wonder on what basis such esteem rested if he had just returned to Egypt after forty years and was now engaged in an adversarial relationship with pharaoh. The Bible offers little help with this question.

Pharaoh understandably refuses them permission for a three-day journey into the eastern desert to offer sacrifice to their God. Documentary evidence describes how a populace often went into the desert to pray for relief from a natural disaster. Grete Hort sees Moses and Aaron as pleading with pharaoh to let them go into the desert to pray for his relief. As long as his own magicians could induce or stop spells (Exod. 7:12, 22; 8:7), it was unthinkable that pharaoh would allow the Hebrew God to prove superior to his own.[34] But when they could no longer match the power of Moses' God (8:14), pharaoh began to take notice.

Pharaoh responded to the first request by punitively increasing the Hebrews' forced labor (Exod. 5:6–14). They angrily confronted Moses and Aaron, cursing them with "May the lord look upon you and punish you for making us loathsome to pharaoh and his courtiers—putting a sword in their hands to slay us" (5:20, 21). The people blamed Moses repeatedly throughout the subsequent wilderness journey whenever an obstacle was encountered. This apparent ingratitude is difficult to understand in people who were being offered a near-miraculous escape from slavery. It is more indicative of a sullen group, reacting adversely to a compact in which what had been promised was in danger of default.

The plagues are understood superficially to be miracles, evincing God's commitment to His people, but the descriptions of these are dramatic and somewhat overwrought. One scholar defines the essence of the plagues episode as "the grand and imposing struggle between the boundless power of the Omnipotent, and the refractory pride of a demented prince . . . between the Lord of the universe and the idols of a heathen country . . . the eternal struggle of Truth against Error, of Monotheism against Paganism."[35] An overwhelming mass of exegesis has accrued on this topic along two major themes. One involves simple explanations for what are assumed to be natural phenomena, whereas the other dismisses literal explanations as it seeks metaphorical answers.

The first nine plagues have been projected as combinations of natural phenomena arising from climatic events or hydraulic aberrations of the Nile River. An example of the latter theme assumes that at times of unusual flow, red algae in the Nile turn it into "blood," as in the first plague. Mud of the river bank is normally a breeding place for frogs, and deviations from any homeostatic factor might cause an excessive number of them, as in the second plague.

The next seven plagues—vermin, flying insects, cattle disease, boils, hail, locusts, and darkness—have been associated with natural or unnatural atmospheric conditions. Darkness, as in a prolonged solar eclipse, has tempted some astronomer-exegetes to try to calculate the year of the Exodus, with unconvincing results. Even the dense Saharan dust storms carried on westerly winds have had superficial appeal. Differences found in language and style between the first nine plagues and the last one suggest that these were added at varying times.[36]

The tenth plague is so obviously cultic in function that few have attempted to find correspondence in authentic events. Yet one author, after a detailed discussion, could write, "We have found that each of the plagues in its essential features describes correctly a natural phenomenon, which, though far from common, may yet happen in Egypt from time to time."[37] Even if we could bring ourselves to accept the natural origin of each plague, the possibility that they could all occur within the space of a few weeks or months is beyond statistical probability. Odds notwithstanding, the excitement that attends each new explanation about the meaning of the plagues is not easily brushed aside. Theoreticians do not simply withdraw when their ideas have been rejected. Instead they usually remain in a state of defiant hibernation while waiting for an unexpected technological innovation to grant them ultimate vindication, usually after they have modified the original conclusion significantly.

One recent theory that attained currency in some quarters suggests that the Exodus details can all be explained by the effects of the cataclysmic explosion on the Island of Thera (today's Santorini) in the Aegean Sea. The pumice layer on the island, reaching a depth of 150 feet (about ten times greater than that found at the base of Vesuvius), indicates that it had to be one of the most powerful volcanic eruptions in historical times.[38] Test borings from the floor of the eastern Mediterranean Sea reveal an ash layer of the same refractive index, suggesting that the volcanic clouds drifted southeastward, directly toward the Nile delta area.[39] For comparison, the wind-borne cloud of ash from the 1980 Mount Saint Helen eruption appeared several hundred miles to the east within a few hours.[40] The "pillar of cloud by day and the pillar of fire by night" described in Exod. 13:21, 22 as the Hebrews were preparing to cross the Red Sea is also tenuously connected to the same volcanic eruption. However, this neat bundling of a single cause with multiple effects unravels on serious analysis.

It has been estimated that the height of the volcano's plume extended well beyond the earth's curvature and therefore could have been visible in northern Egypt.[41] Even if the plume of smoke was seen, in itself most unlikely, a fiery glow certainly would not have been visible unless it extended at least 25–30 miles above the crater.[42] The massive cloud of ash that drifted over Egypt might have caused daytime darkness (plague nine), as well as severe skin disorders (plague six). The fearsome and destructive hail of the seventh plague as an equation with pellets of ash raining down from a volcanic cloud is tempting, except for the improbability that such dense aggregates could have stayed aloft against gravity for a distance of several hundred miles.

But the most serious problem in linking the volcano to the Exodus events is the divergent timing. The eruption at Thera is closely dated to the middle of the Fifteenth Century. The Exodus, in contrast, belongs to the Thirteenth Century. However, we shall see later that an indirect association with the volcano is not inconceivable.

The other explicatory theme of the plagues tradition is essentially allegorical. Their punitive power and general redundancy can be seen as a continuation of the "cursing" tradition of the Ancient Near East. This power to compel obedience is exemplified in the many Egyptian execration texts and the obligatory punishment clauses in the treaties of Mesopotamia. It was important to the later Israelites that the power of their "secret weapon" be acknowledged.

The plagues are not easily accepted as factual events except to religious fundamentalists. However, their use in the biblical narration lends a respectable cogency as witness to awesome events, especially when we know that no serious tradition starts de novo. A seed of reality, no matter how insignificant, can always be found in the most extravagant blossom, and to deny this is to diminish the native intelligence of those early ancestors who struggled to make sense of nature and the behavior of humankind. Subtle theological explanations have been given for the function of the plagues, mainly to prove the ascendancy of Israel's God over all others. Notwithstanding the importance of Egypt's gods, it had to be made evident that the Mosaic God was irresistible. The prolonged and repetitive dialogue obviously obscures the unusual debate between Moses and pharaoh that resulted in the Hebrews' departure from Egypt. The plagues became metaphoric in the struggle between them. With this perspective we can trace the outlines of the age-old technique of bargaining in the marketplace: Moses was the buyer of souls; pharaoh, the seller.

The conflict of wills satisfied the creedal requirements while emphasizing the importance of what would be achieved. Pharaoh, as the incarnation of the Egyptian pantheon, could not be shown without some respectable power, which was displayed by his prolonged resistance to Moses' importunate demands.

When pharaoh's sorcerers matched Aaron's trick of turning Moses' rod into a serpent, the world's first recorded example of one-upmanship occurred; his serpent swallowed theirs (Exod. 7:12). Pharaoh weakened at the second plague but retracted his permission when the plague disappeared. Moses' preliminary description of each plague represented an escalating offer, which pharaoh categorically rejected at first but then seemed to accept, only to reverse himself again on further reflection. Each succeeding plague increased the pressure on him to consider the threat more seriously. This "cat and mouse" game was essentially a stratagem for ratcheting up the price. After the fourth plague, pharaoh dangled a concession in front of Moses by allowing the people to go for worship but only within the land of Egypt. Moses held out, sensing that the other's resolve was beginning to ebb. Pharaoh then softened his position with the stipulation, "but do not go very far" (8:24). By the eighth plague pharaoh was beginning to deal seriously with Moses, probing for more advantages. Pharaoh offered to allow the "menfolk" to go into the desert to worship, but the families and flocks would remain behind as hostages (10:10, 11). Moses prevailed after the tenth plague, or more accurately, pharaoh finally capitulated. In a modern idiom it could be said that they made a deal and Moses got what he bargained for: title to the people whom he would introduce to a new and higher ethic.

The fact that pharaoh did not summarily execute the presumptuous Moses but continued to see him despite the escalating threats is compelling evidence that Moses was well known and not easily dismissed. How else can we explain the tense and prolonged dickering, except that Moses too had royal status? Obviously pharaoh was not averse to letting the Hebrews go if the price were right.

Exod. 12:30, 31 describes how pharaoh finally consented after the first-born Egyptian males, man and beast, had been slain in the middle of the night. He ordered Moses and Aaron to leave, saying, "Up, depart from among my people . . . begone!" He then voiced a plaintive request, "And may you bring a blessing upon me also" (12:32). In the context of Second Millennium beliefs this can be seen as an admission of the superior power of Moses' God, and therefore he wanted to ensure a little divine benediction for himself. However, if the plagues tradition is a figurative expression to deflect embarrassment that the people were being purchased like a commodity, the blessing at the end finds consonance with the concluding handshake of a contemporary business transaction. Legend relates that pharaoh himself accompanied the Hebrews to make sure that they left the land.[43]

This construct admittedly has only conjecture as its basis, but nevertheless it uses projections from established data. Semites were concentrated in the delta region, with the least assimilated people doing the most menial work, probably building Ramesses' monuments. Moses' overwhelming Egyptian background had to be shrouded in a mythic birth, a classic expedient to convert his royal origin into one appropriately Hebrew. If he were also a covert devotee of Akhenaten's monotheism, which had been officially discarded a few generations earlier, it is not illogical that he might have sought out a group of people on whom to transplant that religion in a new setting. Philo refers to Moses "as a hierophant [a term that designates the highest officer of the heathen mysteries] who initiated the Jews into the mysteries. . . ."[44] He approached them with a proposition they could not refuse: passage back to Canaan in return for fealty to a new religious concept. Aaron, who is now thought to have already been a priest of the Hebrews, supplied the needed support and cooperation to convince the indentured people that Moses' plan for their repatriation could succeed. Once all the elders agreed to it, Moses approached pharaoh with the obverse of the proposition. He offered him an exchange for a group of restive Semitic laborers. We have no inkling what tender he might have used, but certainly it would not have been plagues. More likely it was land, money, or other physical assets that would have greater appeal to pharaoh. They haggled over terms, perhaps acrimoniously, but finally reached an accommodation. Without it Num. 33:3 would be meaningless: "It was on the morrow of the passover offering that the Israelites started out defiantly, in plain view of all the Egyptians."

An Unsavory Departure

The Book of Exodus contains many narrative episodes wherein the Hebrews act less than heroically. That these episodes were retained proves once again that when a tradition became fixed in the consciousness of the people, it would be faithfully reproduced in the canon. Perhaps the ancient scribes understood that by including human frailty in their epic history, people would be induced to seek greater understanding, and the Bible would never become a static document.

As early as Exod. 3:21, 22 the issue of "stripping the Egyptians" arises. God tells Moses at the burning bush that the Hebrews will not leave "empty-handed," because the Egyptians will be "favorably disposed" toward them. Each woman "shall borrow from her neighbor . . . silver and gold, and clothing" to put on her sons and daughters. The theme recurs in 11:2, when God orders Moses to tell the people to do it, and again in 12:35, 36 when it had been accomplished.

The repetitive emphasis on getting precious goods from the Egyptians, who will give them up willingly, is so irrational that it commands careful attention. And indeed it has been the subject of many nimble explanations. The Hebrew phrase that becomes "spoiling," "despoiling," or "stripping" also can be translated as "saving." The request for gifts of valuables that the Egyptians yield up, being "favorably disposed," can be viewed as clearing their name and reputation as oppressors. Handing over gifts is supposed to create goodwill and also fulfills the custom of giving a departing slave valuable gifts after many years of good service.[45] From this perspective the Hebrews can therefore be said to have "saved" the Egyptians from their own baser instincts.

Further Midrashic justification for the accrual of precious objects is that they were to be contributed to the building and furnishing of God's sanctuary in the desert (Exod. 25:2–8). The word *k'li* (objects, vessels, jewels), as used here, refers to special items for use in the cultic festival that was the original request for the people's departure. However, most commentators feel that the word does not imply unique goods beyond the wealth they represent. In Ps. 105:37 the term is omitted, further indication that they were readily usable things of value, not venerable objects.

Another point of view holds that the verb root *sha'al* (ask for, request of, borrow) is in expectation of a loan or a gift. This occurs in Exod. 11:2 and 12:35, where the request is active. It is also used passively in 12:36, where the objects are given to the Hebrews. But in the same verse it states explicitly, "Thus they stripped the Egyptians." The use of the verb form *nitzal* (exploit, despoil, strip) negates the idea of simple goodwill. Whatever changed hands was not likely to be returned.

God intervened to protect His people as He had promised; the Hebrews receive recompense for their years of impressment, and the Egyptians are justly punished for their cruelty. This indulgent point of view is weakened considerably by a Talmudic report in which the Egyptians come before Alexander the Great in the Fourth Century to demand indemnification for the goods the Hebrews took with them at the time of the Exodus. Obviously the plaintiffs did not view this transfer of wealth as a form of justice. The Jewish spokesmen supposedly had little difficulty in convincing the Greek conqueror that it was themselves, rather than the Egyptians, who deserved compensation for the long years of slavery.[46] The theologically contrived doctrine that God dispenses justice even in punishment rinses the whole episode of its mendacity.

However, the deception issue cannot be so easily editorialized. Although the biblical words imply a seemingly unexceptional request of compliant Egyptians, there is little likelihood that it would have been granted. Why would ordinary people feel guilty enough to make restitution for pharaoh? And if it were in the nature of a neighborly loan, we already know that the Hebrews will not return to Egypt. Also, they pointedly took possession of the valuables just prior to the tenth plague (Exod. 11:1, 2). The people, preparing for a permanent departure from the political control of Egypt and knowing that they had the protection of an authority who could successfully bargain with pharaoh, might well have concluded that they were owed something more than just a release from bondage. The risk in stealing valuable goods from the Egyptians would be minimal if they left immediately for the interior of Sinai, where they would find safety. One author contends that a conscious deception or diversionary trick was needed to facilitate the planned, not-so-secret escape.[47]

The contrivance of having the Hebrews ask their neighbors for gold, silver, and clothing, together with the ready acquiescence of the neighbors to honor the request, is easily recognized as an exculpatory rationalization. The biblical writers glossed an embarrassing felony by creating an implausible social interaction. The logical conclusion to the whole episode is that later generations were unable to expunge the memory of a shameful action and experimented with a cosmetic facade. Readers will be hard-pressed not to see looting as the reality behind "despoiling."

A remarkable lack of rapport becomes evident in the subsequent relations between Moses and the people, with the frequent episodes of "murmuring" against him. An early example is contained in Exod. 14:11,12 when the Hebrews are about to cross the Red Sea. Suddenly aware of the advancing Egyptian chariots, they complain bitterly that Moses recklessly enticed them into the desert, where they will surely die. The implication is that they would have been better off had they remained in Egypt, where things really had not been so bad after all. A legend related by Louis Ginzberg expresses the peoples' fear of retribution: "What hast thou done to us? Now they will requite us for all that hath happened—that their first-born were smitten, and that we ran off with their money, which was thy fault, for thou didst bid us to borrow gold and silver."[48] Can any words be more indicative of the guilt and scapegoating that commonly accompany being caught red-handed?

The celebration of Passover, highlighting the escape from Egypt is a primary injunction of the Israelite religion. Yet there are indications that the Passover episode itself, described in Exod. 12, 23, 34; Lev. 23; Num. 28; and Deut. 16, has been woven together from several earlier traditions. The cultic sacrifice of an unblemished young animal was common to pastoralists, along with the apotropaic daubing of blood. The meat had to be consumed at the festal meal, and any remains had to be burned the next morning (Exod. 12:10). It was obviously a one-day festival. On the other hand, the seven-day Feast of Unleavened Bread had a different source. Unleavened wafers (*matzot*) were baked when the arrival of unexpected guests required food to be served quickly (Gen. 19:3). This urgency lent itself admirably to a tradition in which there was little time to make good an escape from Egypt. Also, unleavened bread was a part of other sacrificial rituals.[49]

These dramatic experiences were easily used in persuading the Hebrews of the redemptive power of God. Smeared blood on the doorposts became the code mark for sparing their first-born, although it bears a suspicious connection to the primitive sacrifice of first-born sons. Unleavened bread that can be prepared quickly provides the perfect symbol of the Divinely arranged window of opportunity. The people were to celebrate the first Passover meal with "your loins girded, your sandals on your feet, and your staff in your hand; and you shall eat it hurriedly" (Exod. 12:11). The varying traditions gradually merged into a single regenerative rite. Although Exod. 12:2–12 indicates that the Hebrews had at least fifteen days to prepare for departure, one might say that the urgency of a different tradition (12:30–34) gave rise to unleavened dough!

*   *
*

A trait of late twentieth-century society seems to be the pervasive fascination with conspiracy theories. Even biblical history is not exempt. In 1990 a book was published suggesting that the Exodus was a consummate Egyptian plot to rid the country of its Semites. Moses, as a loyal functionary, ingenuously fomented the rebelliousness in the wilderness so that he could massacre the largest number of people in the name of discipline. Whoever remained alive when the thinned-out ranks were finally deposited in Asia would then become a human barrier to any future invasion of Egypt from the east. Admittedly the margin between derivational logic and frank license can be narrow, but the retrograde suggestion of an early, planned "final solution" is unmistakable.[50] As a suggested explanation for population control, it certainly has more in common with Assyrian mentality than with Egyptian.

We may well ask ourselves about Moses' motive in assuming the leadership of this alien group of people. Why did he undertake to lead them out of Egypt? What was in it for him? If he were indeed an Egyptian of royal family, what would have persuaded him to renounce his special position in a cultured society in order to shepherd a group of unruly strangers across hundreds of miles of forbidding terrain just to deposit them in an uncertain venue along the eastern shore of the Mediterranean?

Of course, no one can presume to expound on another person's mind-set, especially when it happened so long ago and after so much veneration has ennobled the deed. But such considerations of motivation are necessary to fully appreciate the story. Like the contemporary murder mystery, there must be a clear motive in order to solve it. If Moses acted solely from political ambition, we should be able to discern what it was he wanted to achieve. Perhaps he was moved simply by a variant of the noblesse oblige principle, but given his alternating frustration and rage, he was more likely obsessed with the survival of the group. What appears most historical about him suggests that he harbored an implacable moral sense, as expressed in the Decalogue. If he did hear God speaking to him, as Exodus relates, he listened and he responded.

The "heresy" of Akhenaten represents one of the fundamental innovations that mark the episodic history of ideas. That it occurred in an Egypt of static conservatism was fatal to its survival. His vision of a single, universal god scarcely outlasted him. But it is certain that there were persons in the generations exposed to this early monotheism who recognized it as a giant step forward for humanity. During Horemhab's reign, Atenism was officially proscribed, and therefore any of its loyal adherents would have had to go "underground." Certainly Moses could have been a secret disciple of Akhenaten, convinced that there would be no resurgence of monotheism in Egypt and that he might soon be forced to flee.[51] His royal birth and experience in court circles protected him and ultimately offered him a unique opportunity to carry out that pharaoh's vision.

Is it beyond the realm of probability that Moses, as a son of privilege, could be passionately devoted to an idea that the life of humankind would be advanced by reverence for a single God who dispatched compassion and justice equally to all? And might Moses not have sought and found an underprivileged group who could be aroused to embrace the egalitarian religion he envisioned? Indeed the "chosenness" concept that heralded Israel at the beginning of its history and became such a unifying force, as well as an eventual burden, may have begun at the point when Moses targeted this people for himself. Only later was the choice ascribed to God.

But Moses' greatest achievement, as well as his tragic end, still lay ahead of him.

Notes

1. D. B. Redford, "An Egyptological Perspective on the Exodus," in *Egypt, Israel, Sinai*, ed. A. F. Rainey (Tel Aviv: Tel Aviv University, 1987), p. 145ff.
2. H. H. Rowley, *From Joseph to Joshua* (London: Oxford University Press, 1950), p. 134.
3. Ibid., p. 136, n. 5.

4. N. K. Gottwald, *The Hebrew Bible—A Socio-Literary Introduction* (Philadelphia: Fortress Press, 1985), p. 164ff.

5. F. R. Raglan, "The Hero: A Study in Tradition, Myth, and Drama," in *In Quest of the Hero* (Princeton: Princeton Univ. Press, 1990), p. 95.

6. F. R. Raglan, *The Hero: A Study in Tradition, Myth and Drama* (London: Methuen & Co. Ltd., 1936).

7. O. Rank, *The Myth of the Birth of the Hero* (New York: Journal of Nervous and Mental Disease Publishing Co., 1914).

8. F. R. Raglan, *The Hero: A Study in Tradition, Myth, and Drama* (New York: Vintage Books, 1956), p. 173.

9. A. Dundes, "The Hero Pattern and the Life of Jesus," in *In Quest of the Hero* (Princeton: Princeton Univ. Press, 1990), p. 191ff.

10. J. B. Pritchard, *Ancient Near Eastern Texts*, 3rd ed. (Princeton: Princeton Univ. Press, 1969), p. 119.

11. B. S. Childs, "The Birth of Moses," *Journal of Biblical Literature* 84(1965):109–122.

12. D. B. Redford, "The Literary Motif of the Exposed Child," *Numen* 14(1967):209–228.

13. J. S. Ackerman, "The Literary Context of the Moses Birth Story (Exodus 1–2)," in K. R. Gros Louis, J. S. Ackerman, and T. S. Warshaw, eds., *Literary Interpretations of Biblical Narratives* (Nashville, TN: Abingdon Press, 1974), pp. 74–119.

14. L. Ginzberg, *The Legends of the Jews*, vol. 2 (Philadelphia: Jewish Publication Society, 1911), pp. 264–267.

15. Ibid., p. 270.

16. Ibid., p. 290.

17. Ibid., p. 269f.

18. N. M. Sarna, *Exploring Exodus* (New York: Schocken, 1986), p. 32.

19. L. Ginzburg, op. cit., p. 270.

20. Ibid., p. 291f.

21. Ibid., p. 288f.

22. Ibid., p. 286.

23. L. Waterman, "Moses the Pseudo-Levite," *Journal of Biblical Literature* 59(1940):397–404.

24. S. Freud, *Moses and Monotheism* (New York: Alfred A. Knopf, 1939), p. 40 n. 1.

25. T. W. Rosmarin, *The Hebrew Moses: An Answer to Sigmund Freud* (New York: Jewish Book Club, 1939), p. 25.

26. Y. H. Yerushalmi, *Freud's Moses* (New Haven: Yale Univ. Press, 1991), passim.

27. L. Ginzberg, op. cit., p. 271f.

28. Ibid., p. 274.

29. G. W. Coats, *Moses, Heroic Man of God* (Sheffield: JSOT Press, 1988), p. 68.

30. M. Kalisch, *A Historical and Critical Commentary on the Old Testament—Exodus* (London: Longman,1855), p. 70.

31. D. J. Silver, *Images of Moses* (New York: Basic Books, 1982), p. 10f.

32. G. W. Coats, op. cit., p. 50.

33. Ibid., p. 65.

34. G. Hort, "The Plagues of Egypt," *Zeitschrift für Alttestamentliche Wissenschaft* 70(1958):48–59.

35. M. Kalisch, op. cit., p. 117.

36. D. J. McCarthy, "Plagues and Sea of Reeds: Exodus 5–14," *Journal of Biblical Literature* 85(1966):137–158.

37. Hort, op. cit., p. 58.

38. I. Wilson, *The Exodus: True Story* (San Francisco: Harper and Row, 1985), pp. 92, 100.

39. Ibid., p. 93f.

40. Ibid., p. 116.

41. Ibid., p. 113.

42. Ibid., p. 112f.

43. Ginzberg, op. cit., vol. 3, p. 6.

44. L. H. Feldman, *Jew and Gentile in the Ancient World* (Princeton: Princeton Univ. Press, 1993), p.67.

45. J. H. Hertz, *The Pentateuch and Haftorahs*, 2d ed. (London: Soncino Press, 1969), p. 216f.

46. Ibid., p. 217.

47. G. W. Coats, "Despoiling the Egyptians" *Vetus Testamentum* 18(1968):450–457.

48. L. Ginzberg, op. cit., vol. 3, p. 14.

49. N. M. Sarna, op. cit., p. 86.

50. F. X. Foulke-ffeinberg, *Moses and His Masters* (Edinberg: Cui Bono Books, 1990), passim.

51. Freud, op. cit., p. 44f.

Exodus:
The Long March

10

L ed by Moses, a motley group of Semites left Egypt to return to their ancestral homeland, Canaan. The trials they endured during the wilderness trek were balanced by several wondrous events, the most dramatic of which was the parting of the sea, allowing them to pass on dry land. That "miracle" occurred in Exod. 14:21–29 and is always cited to prove God's commitment to the people. However, natural and more prosaic forces can readily explain these lyrical passages, because elements of reality flicker within the Torah traditions even if original details have been transformed. The unique geography of the Suez isthmus provided a realistic ambiance to which the later storytellers added divine mystery. The growing belief that miracles happened because the people were chosen for greatness by a new and omnipotent God was the cord that bound them to one another. They recorded the dramatic events in story and song, and although they emphasized the miraculous, enough reality was maintained that a historical episode can be at least partially reconstructed.

A broad geological trench, running from the Gulf of Suez northward to the Mediterranean Sea, provided a natural cleavage between Egypt and Asia. Prior to the construction of the Suez Canal in the 1860s, a strand of contiguous lakes, swamps, and marshes dotted this massive north-south swale. The isthmus of

Suez had always presented a significant barrier to human traffic. Along its entire length only three relatively secure crossings were known during the historical period. By tradition the waters of the Red Sea parted somewhere along this depression, allowing the Hebrews to pass through on dry ground.

An analysis of the topography of the area reveals that the event could well have happened without the intervention of God.

Geographic Considerations

The Red Sea and its direct longitudinal extensions, the Gulf of Suez to the northwest and the Gulf of Aqaba to the northeast, define a unitary, elongated sea basin that measures 1200 miles long by no more than 200 miles wide. Superficially it appears to be merely a digital extension of the Indian Ocean. However, an extensive undersea shelf coincident with the Bab al Mandab Strait at its southern extremity indicates that its origin was distinct from that of the adjacent and much older ocean. The Red Sea rift valley probably formed in the Mesozoic era 180 million years ago, when the land masses of Africa and Arabia began to wrench apart. The earth's crust thinned out along the fault line and sagged, creating the deepest part of the tectonic trough that today runs through the horn of Africa northward to both the Jordan River valley and the Mediterranean Sea.[1] In the Miocene period of 30 million years ago, the triangular peninsula of Sinai developed, with the Mediterranean and Red Seas still connected.[2,3] The present Gulf of Suez would then have been technically the Strait of Suez. The upthrust of magma, which gradually repaired the integrity of the earth's broken crust on the western side of Sinai, partially fused the two continental masses.[4] Asia and Africa were thus reconnected by a shallow and incomplete land bridge. Five million years ago a further continental separation occurred that created the deep central trough of the Red Sea and the Gulf of Aqaba but left the Gulf of Suez intact.

Later changes in the topography of the area came about by climatic and oceanographic factors. Following the last Ice Age, the Red Sea reached its present level, but the southern end of the isthmus was still being augmented by the effect of surface waves. The configuration of waves as they strike a shoreline determines whether the land builds up or erodes. Low waves with long wavelengths on a shallow shore profile tend to build up land. As the waves crest and spill rather than break forcefully, they deposit a greater amount of the sandy sea floor material on the shore in their swash phase, because less of the sand is returned in the backwash, and the shoreline builds up.[5] This process, going on for millennia while the frequent windstorms over the surrounding desert deposited massive amounts of additional sand, has created vast tidal flats. It is the unusual configuration of the shallow Gulf of Suez, with its axial winds and surging tides, that may account for the miraculous escape of the Hebrews.

The Exodus began in the city of Pi-Ramesses (Exod. 12:37). The Egyptian prefix *pi* or *per* indicates "the house (city) of" the person named. There the Hebrews labored to build a garrison or store-city for the pharaoh, who most probably was Ramesses II (1290–1225). The biblical "Land of Goshen," where most of them resided, was an ill-defined area thought to lie in the Nile delta near the isthmus of Suez. The name Goshen is not an Egyptian designation but is found in the Masoretic Text of the Hebrew Bible (ninth century). In the Septuagint (the early Greek translation of the Hebrew Bible, dating from the Third Century), it is called "Land of Ramesses." Access to its eastern boundary was along a branch of the Nile River, the Wadi Tumilat. This was an east-west depression contiguous with an ancient trans-Sinai road, the Way of Shur. The road mentioned in Gen. 16:7 was a preferred route from the Negev region of southern Canaan to Egypt.[6] Within the Goshen area two more of the biblically named cities have been tentatively identified, Pithom and Succoth.

The site of Pi-Ramesses has been almost certainly located on the old Pelusiac branch of the Nile River, about 70 miles north of present-day Cairo, in what is now designated as the Qantir-Khatana area. This easternmost branch, now long silted up, ran northeastward from the Nile to the Mediterranean Sea. The particular site had been an important urban and sea-trading center from at least the XIIth Dynasty on. As the capital of the Hyksos empire, it was called Avaris. The city lost its regional preeminence after the Hyksos were defeated, and it was not resettled until the reign of Horemhab (1320–1305).[7] Seti I (1305–1290) began the rebuilding process as the concentration of Egyptians shifted northward into the expanding delta. The city regained its importance when Ramesses II made it his capital by instituting a massive building program there.[8]

The identification of the city was called into question recently when archeological investigations at Tanis, a city 15 miles downriver, showed unquestionable traces of Ramesside activity. Many monuments to him suggested this site as the biblical city of Ramesses. However, further excavation revealed that the earliest stratum of human habitation extended back only as far as the XXIst Dynasty (1070–950), seriously undermining the conclusion that Tanis was the site of Pi-Ramesses.[9] Apparently the Pelusiac had silted up enough within a few hundred years to render Avaris less useful as a port. Tanis was then built closer to the Mediterranean Sea, where it could continue to be a major hub for sea trade with the Aegean world and western Asia. Scholars were misled because much of the stone building material of the new city included commemorative material that we now know was scavenged from Avaris. It is quite certain that the real city of Ramesses in which the Hebrews labored was in the Qantir-Khatana region. Here was a large population center, with buildings spread out as much as 2 miles along the course of the river.[10] Large quantities of ornamental brick were found at this site where Exod. 5:7–20 describes the Hebrews laboring at the same kind of work.[11] The other designated locus of Hebrew slavery, Pithom, is not so clearly established and plays no further role in the Exodus story.

A proximal branch of the Pelusiac River, one of the several major streams formed at the delta by the diverging Nile, ran due east, emptying in the region of Lake Timsah along the trench where the Suez Canal is now sited. This fertile flood plain, the Wadi Tumilat, provided the shortest and preferred route from the copper and turquoise mines of the Arabah and the Sinai peninsula to the heart of Egypt via the delta region. The area today is marshy, whereas in former times its waters were navigable and used in the shipping trade between Egypt and the Mediterranean Sea.[12] Despite later topographical changes brought about by natural hydraulic pressures and silt deposition, the area continued to provide a major land thoroughfare between Asia and Egypt. Pharaoh Necho II, at the beginning of the Sixth Century, and Darius I 100 years later sought to deepen the channel and to reopen an east-west commercial route between the Nile and the Red Sea.[13]

In the Wadi Tumilat are several tells representing the debris of earlier settlements. One in particular, Tell er-Retabeh, is the site of a large fortress located midway along the wadi. This whole area has been variously documented in early Egyptian records as Tjeku, Tjkw, or Thuket and is associated with Ramesses II's son, Merneptah (1225–1215). Succoth, the first named encampment on the Hebrews' outward trek (Exod. 12:37) and a Hebraization of an Egyptian name, may have been here. This settlement declined several hundred years later as another one at the eastern extremity of the wadi expanded and was called "Pr-Itm." The latter site, today called Tell el-Maskhutah, was abandoned from the Middle Bronze Age until the Seventh Century.[14] Its identification as the Pithom of Exod. 1:11 therefore may be anachronistic.

An Egyptian text speaks of "the lakes of Pithom," which accords well with a known overflow lake in the western half of the Wadi Tumilat.[15] Etham, perhaps a distortion of Pithom, was the next stop along the Exodus route and appears to have been in the same general area.[16] However, there is enough uncertainty about the origin of the name, a Hebraization of the Egyptian word for fort, that it is safer merely to say that Etham was "on the edge of the wilderness."[17] It may be tempting to assume that because only two encampment sites are mentioned, the trek took a mere two days to that point. The text does not mention time, and therefore other interval sites may have existed and been forgotten or deemed too unimportant to record.

The last place-name of the Exodus itinerary in Egypt proper is Pi-hahiroth. From there the Hebrews crossed into Asia. If Pi-hahiroth could be located accurately, the site of the crossing episode would be more easily identified. The importance of this particular site can be surmised from the fact that two other localizing hints are given: "between Migdol" and "before Baal-zephon" (Exod. 14:2, Num. 33:7). A tablet from the Ptolemaic period (323–30), uncovered during the excavations in the region of Tell el-Maskhutah, speaks of another place nearby called Pi Kerehet. Identification with Pi-hahiroth on the basis of similar sounds can only be tentative. However, Pi Kerehet was the site of a temple of Osiris, who was later worshipped by the Greeks and Romans as Serapis. The temple would then be called a Serapeum.[18] A town by that name, lying between Lake Timsah and the northern edge of the Bitter Lakes, was still shown in a map published 125 years ago.[19]

Migdol merely means tower in Hebrew, and where the rift valley presented more than one access point, it is likely that watchtowers and custom house forts would be located at each of these. Without a modifier the place-name Migdol has no geographic context. However, a reference from the reign of the Assyrian king Esarhaddon (699–681) informs us that it was a city guarding Egypt's frontier just north of the Bitter Lakes.[20] Baal-zephon is thought to represent a long-forgotten shrine to a Semitic (Canaanite) god, probably one of many in the eastern delta. In a papyrus document that mentions four towers in association with the lakes, one is the "tower of Baal-Zephon."[21]

As we have seen many times before, solid proof is elusive when dealing with matters that occurred more than 3000 years ago. To verify the authenticity of place-names, we often have to use documentary evidence that is itself ambiguous. The Exodus

narrative, beginning at 12:37, describes sequentially the supposed route that the Hebrews used in leaving Egypt and is
repeated with minor variations in Num. 33:3–8. Given that the
J, E, and P sources are evident in the narratives of both books,
the similar route descriptions probably have some historical
basis. The problem in accepting the Torah's geographical details
is the inability to identify them in terms of more recent reference. Even the final redactors of the original traditions may
have had difficulty in identifying place-names that had been
dropped or changed in the intervening centuries. The biblical
descriptions using names that prevailed in the traditions were
already out of date by several hundred years. Whatever other
historical data the Exodus stories might contain, it is quite likely
that the geographic details were drawn from the contemporary
knowledge of the post-Exilic period (539–200).[22] The completion of the Torah in a fixed form occurred in the first century
after the exiles returned from Babylon. How well these details
correlated with the situation that existed in the Thirteenth Century remains moot.

Gordon I. Davies in a solid monograph highlights the uncer-
tainty of any location on the Exodus route.[23] His sources include
Jewish, Christian, and Arabic documents, along with ancient
Greek, Hebrew, and Aramaic literature, both canonical and non-
canonical. The sequential progress from Ramesses to Succoth,
Etham, and Pi-hahiroth has to be accepted as an uncertain route
through northeastern Egypt to Yam Suf (Red/Reed Sea), where
Moses and the Hebrews are said to have crossed over into Sinai.
It was from the events at this body of water that the tradition of
God's commitment to His people became an article of faith.

The meaning of the Hebrew word *suf* holds the key to that
part of the isthmus through which the people escaped from
Egyptian territory. Yam Suf in Exod. 13:18 seems to indicate a
large body of water with vegetation that extends above the surface. Because papyrus is a fresh-water plant indigenous to Egypt
and therefore is a defining factor, the locus was assumed to be an
inland lake.[24] A recent generation of scholars began to refer to a

"Reed Sea" as the point of crossing rather than at the traditional Red Sea. The topography of the ancient rift allowed the Wadi Tumilat to deliver fresh water to the area of Lake Timsah and the Bitter Lakes. Other branches of the Nile supplied water in large quantities to the rest of the northern isthmus. However, *suf* is also used in Jonah 2:6, where it means "entangling weeds" at the bottom of the sea. Obviously a fresh-water connotation is not explicit in the word.

Another location for Yam Suf can be derived etymologically. The Hebrew root *sf* with a different vowel becomes *sof*, which can mean end or ending. This translation in a geographic context would suggest a crossing at the Red Sea, because the word could then mean "at land's end."[25,26]

Yam Suf is also encountered in Exod. 23:31 and Deut. 1:40 and 2:1, where it unequivocally refers to the Gulf of Aqaba. This narrow extension of the Red Sea that bounds the east coast of the Sinai peninsula replicates the Gulf of Suez along the west coast of the same peninsula. The contiguity of both gulfs was surely known to the ancients and would allow both prolongations to be logically considered as a single body of water. The contemporary translation of Yam Suf as Reed Sea therefore seems to have no more to recommend it than Red Sea. Reeds do not grow in either gulf, and it will be shown that a northerly extension of the present Gulf of Suez is the most reasonable point of crossing.

The topography of the area at that time limited the routes by which the Hebrews could leave Egypt, regardless of their status as free people or as fugitive slaves. Their caravan consisted of persons young and old, strong and infirm, taking with them all their possessions, including domesticated animals. Even if the group numbered no more than a few hundred instead of the traditional 600,000, the route would have had to offer subsistence as well as reasonable surface conditions. These minimal criteria were not widely available in this arid and upthrust region. Precipitation in most of Sinai today averages less than 4 inches annually, far less than is needed for any widespread vegetation. Fortunately the water table is often closest to the surface in the low-lying valleys and especially in the wadis that traverse them. Whatever plant life exists in Sinai tends to be in these areas.[27] It is thought that in the time of Moses, there was much more subsurface water than today, which would have yielded a vegetative cover capable of supporting many game animals.[28]

Beyond the rift barrier, Sinai offered Moses but three paths to Canaan. In the extreme north was the "Way of the Land of the Philistines" (Exod. 13:17), also known to the Egyptians of antiquity as the "Way of Horus" and to later Rome as the "Way of the Sea" (Via Maris). This main military and commercial highway from the eastern delta to Asia bristled with a network of man-made defense points. The best known of these was the fortress city of Sile (Zaru, modern Qantara), which straddled the western terminus of the road.[29] This northern route was the shortest and most level, as it followed the Mediterranean coastal plain.

In reality there were two northern routes, one of which began at the ancient city of Pelusium and traversed the narrow ridge of land out over the water, threading its way between Lake Sirbonis (Bardawil) and the Mediterranean Sea. However, this road was too uncertain for military or commercial purposes because of frequent washouts by wind and tide. The other route followed the shoreline that was contiguous with the Sinai land mass. The pharaohs of the XVIIIth and XIXth Dynasties, who were often involved in Asian adventures, used this latter road beginning at Sile.[30]

The scholars who equate Yam Suf with Sea of Reeds believe that the crossing had to have a fresh-water source and therefore would be within the interior of the isthmus rather than at the sea, north or south. The flood levels of the Nile were very high in predynastic times but decreased significantly throughout the First Intermediate Period (around the turn of the Twentieth Century). The floods were high again during the Middle Kingdom (2000–1700), only to fall in the later Ramesside period (1220–1000).[31] These cyclical inundations created many temporary lakes and fresh-water swamps at the periphery of the northeastern delta flood plain where papyrus could grow. The area around northern Lake Ballah has been referred to as "Papyrus Swamp."[32] Also, Lake Menzaleh is a vast lagoon jutting out into the Mediterranean Sea, into which a significant portion of the Nile effluent discharges. Even Lake Sirbonis is thought to have received fresh water from the Pelusiac branch at one time.[33] The northern route thus recommends itself to many authors for whom the reeds are the essential landmark. If the Hebrews wanted to avoid passing through the Egyptian fortifications at Sile on the northern route, they could have turned south and passed through the nearby lake area of Ballah. Some think that this is the most likely Yam Suf.[34]

There are also compelling arguments for a midisthmus crossing around Lake Timsah and the Bitter Lakes. In Exod. 15:22, after Miriam's triumphant song that praised God's power in saving them while the pursuing Egyptians drowned, Moses turns and leads the people on into the "wilderness of Shur." As *shur* in Hebrew means wall, and a range of hills is just east of the midisthmus lakes, it is not unreasonable that the crossing could have taken place in this vicinity. A fortification known as the "Wall of the Prince" was begun at the eastern edge of the Wadi Tumilat in the Xth Dynasty (2150–2050) to interdict caravans from Asia.[35] Another point in favor of a crossing here is that the ancient road called the "Way to (of) Shur" (Gen. 16:7) had a terminus just east of the northern edge of Lake Timsah. This road led to the Negev region of southern Canaan, where Moses and the Exodus group were later reported to be. This road paralleled the "Way of the Sea" about 30 miles to the south. Given the flow of fresh water through the Wadi Tumilat into Lake Timsah and perhaps also into the Great Bitter Lake, papyrus and other grasses that thrive in brackish water might well have grown in sufficient profusion for the area also to be considered the Sea of Reeds.

Late in the nineteenth century it was widely held that the Hebrews crossed over into Sinai at the southern port of Suez. At that time there were two well-established fording places, one just north of the city and another to the south. The distance at the northern ford measured two-thirds of a mile to the opposite shore and included two small islands. The other ford, about 2 miles wide, apparently never really had shallow water, although it could be crossed at low tide.[36] When Napoleon I visited Suez in 1798 to evaluate the possibility of reconnecting the Red Sea to the Mediterranean via the Nile River and the ancient canals of Darius, he found a silted-up harbor. However, the dream to conquer the East and to open India to French commerce was irresistible. He crossed over the narrow ford to Sinai on horseback with his engineers and surveyors to inspect the nearby Wells of Moses. When they began the return trip several hours later, the rising tide almost overwhelmed horses and men. The potential disaster prompted Napoleon to exclaim, "Did we come here to perish like Pharaoh?"[37]

Today the biblical story of the escape from Egypt bears an overwhelming burden of inspired exegeses by theologians, by scientists, and by scholars. If the number of authorities who support a particular version adds merit to its cause, a central or midisthmus sea crossing would become the most likely candidate. But however many may subscribe to a common position, numbers alone cannot certify an exclusively rational conclusion. And where so many potential crossing sites exist, none carries the unchallenged imprimatur of truth. The following explanation corroborates the basic tradition of a hasty water crossing as a logical and realistic happening.

The Exodus Trail and Crossing the Red Sea

The Exodus narrative begins as the people leave Pi-Ramesses and go to Succoth (Exod. 12:37, Num. 33:5). These sites were within the Wadi Tumilat floodplain, the former near its western edge and the other closer to its eastern extremity. The distance between them could have been as much as 25 miles. We can only speculate whether the children and elderly persons of the group could have covered this distance in what seems to have been a single day. We are told in the same verse (12:37) that the group numbered "about six hundred thousand men on foot, aside from children." Adding a similar number of adult females plus an assumed three children for each, the group then totals an astonishing three million persons. If the ancient road allowed them to march eight abreast, itself quite unlikely, the distance such a line would cover between the first rank and those in the rear would be about 225 miles. The last rank would not be able to leave Pi-Ramesses until several days after the first one had moved. Surely there would have been no need for pharaoh to chase them all the way to Yam Suf to recapture them!

Scholarly calculations about the number of people involved in the Exodus have centered on the meaning of the Hebrew word *elef*, which is most often assumed to mean "thousand." The text in Exod. 12:37, *b'shaish ma'ot elef*, has been translated as "six hundred thousand." Because the word can also refer to a clan or family group, Nahum M. Sarna uses this alternative definition to calculate the exiting group at 5550 persons in 598 units.[38] Although such mathematical precision may seem unsupportable, nevertheless his numbers are certainly more reasonable than the Bible's. The only rational position to hold on this issue is that the true number was far less than 600,000 and probably no more than a few to several hundred.

A "mixed multitude" joined the marchers in leaving Egypt (Exod. 12:38), indicating that Moses' group was not the exclusive and interrelated family of twelve tribes that the Torah implies. In Num. 11:1 the comment "The people took to complaining bitterly" is followed in 11:4 by "the riffraff in their midst ["mixed multitude" in some translations] felt a gluttonous craving." The importance of the reference is its suggestion that early Israel was made up of many diverse and unrelated peoples. Certainly the Exodus group likely had social divisions as well as ethnic diversity. One cannot but wonder whether the later elite of Israel found it convenient to blame an intrusive foreign or socially undesirable element for the ingratitude and religious recidivism of the people on the wilderness trek. Tcherikover quoted Philo, who stated that "with the Jews there left Egypt a mixed mob of various people born of marriages between Hebrews and Egyptian women." He may have been extrapolating from the experience of his own time,[39] but the possibility that the mixed multitude may have been converts was suggested again more recently.[40]

Moses followed a circuitous route in arriving at a spot in the rift valley where the people could cross the water barrier into Sinai. This raises an intriguing question: Why didn't he proceed directly, or was there an unexpected problem? From Succoth they marched to Etham, which logically should have been closer to the expected point of crossing. But a sudden change of plans occurs between Etham and the actual crossing, which takes place very late the next night. God tells Moses in Exod. 14:2 to "turn back and encamp before Pi-hahiroth," explaining that the reversal is to highlight the coming miracle He will perform. The change of direction is also mentioned in 13:18, where "God led the people roundabout" by way of the wilderness at Yam Suf, explaining that the Hebrews would be frightened when they faced the formidable Philistines and would scramble back to Egypt (13:17). The miracle motif is priestly in origin, whereas the other explanation is from the E source, whose writer was obviously unaware that the Philistines were not settled in the land until a hundred years later. However, there can be no doubt that an abrupt change in the planned route occurred.

When pharaoh, frustrated and chastened after the tenth plague, ordered the Hebrews to leave his land immediately, it implies that they were free to go and did not have to take flight. Legally released, they would surely have sought the shortest and safest road to Canaan, the "Way of the Sea." In a planned emigration, as the Exodus was, a time-consuming maneuver to change course without a cogent reason, once the route was chosen, would be incomprehensible.

What momentous circumstance was responsible for the sudden change in the line of march? Pharaoh possibly had second thoughts about the deal he made with Moses, which is suggested in Exod. 14:5: "When the king of Egypt was told that the people had fled, Pharaoh and his courtiers had a change of heart about the people and said, 'What is this we have done, releasing Israel from our service?'" When news of the widespread despoilment of the Egyptians reached pharaoh, it surely would have been an affront to his office, demanding immediate retribution. Pharaoh's decision to rescind the Exodus by mobilizing his chariot force and giving chase is contained in 14:5–7. His change of mind should come as no great surprise, since he reneged several times previously on promises made to Moses.

Moses, on the other hand, faced a much more difficult decision when he discovered that his people had robbed the Egyptians. He knew that the agreement with pharaoh, so painstakingly wrought, would be renounced even if he could get the Hebrews to return their stolen treasures to the aggrieved parties. We can well imagine the concern Moses felt for the success of his mission at the moment he learned of the affair. His decision was to save the project at any cost. Once they were safely in the Sinai wilderness, the ethical question could be finessed by forcing the people to contribute their stolen treasure to enhance the religious appurtenances that would be needed for their worship of God. These "voluntary" gifts and the sacred objects to be made from them are described in detail in Exod. 25:1–39.

Moses knew that the pursuers would be coming soon and that he would have to outwit them to escape being recaptured. The speed of the chariots would soon overtake his group if he continued along the same route, despite their two-plus-day advantage. His best chance lay in a sudden change of direction toward the interior of Sinai, where the topography would nullify the Egyptian military preponderance and speed. Pi-hahiroth, most likely located in a central part of the isthmus as it then existed, became the new objective. In one view it stood on the west shore of the Bitter Lakes, where the ruins of an old tower can still be seen, perhaps the Migdol of Exod. 14:2.[41] A careful reading of Exod. 14:16–29 provides all the details necessary for a reconstruction of the Red Sea crossing.

The Hebrews were encamped at Pi-hariroth toward nightfall when they spotted the pursuing Egyptians. The Hebrews were spared an immediate attack because of impending darkness, described in 14:19f as due to "the pillar of cloud . . . so that the one could not come near the other all through the night." Then Moses raised his rod over the sea, causing a strong east wind to blow all night. The wind "turned the sea into dry ground" and "the waters were split" (14:21). This beautiful imagery has endowed a prosaic, diurnal event with a spectral charm that will stimulate the imagination of humankind forever. Certainly the manifest power of God in the service of the people makes the story much more compelling than the mere coincidence of an ebb tide that left patches of bare shore between pools of water.

The tidal flow has been a consideration in many exegetical studies, but the effect of wind has been highlighted even more often. Generally the tidal effect has been rejected simply because it is not mentioned in the text, whereas the wind carries biblical support.[42] One text states, "Shallow water of this kind may easily be driven back by a strong wind, leaving the sand bare. With the dropping of the wind the water returns."[43]

The Hebrews fled across the dry sea bed during the night, and in the morning the Egyptians followed them. The next verse describes how the chariots became mired in the sand. Moses then administered the *coup de grace* in the name of the Lord: He "held out his arm over the sea, and at daybreak the sea returned to its normal state" (14:27). Although the Egyptian soldiers fled at the sea's approach, they were drowned (14:28), and their bodies washed ashore to be viewed by all Israel (14:30).

There is a belief in some quarters that the Hebrews were not as passive as the biblical description implies. Citing the use of phrases with military connotations (in the RSV Bible), such as "equipped for battle" (Exod. 13:18), "encamp" (14:2), "fight" (14:14), "host" (14:20), and "rout" (14:27), one author constructs a scenario whereby the Hebrews cross over and lie in wait for the Egyptians.[44] He sees Hebrew archers taking deadly aim at the exposed and immobilized Egyptian charioteers, killing them all.

This guerrilla style of battle is an interesting conjecture, finding support in the generally accepted military tactics of besieged defenders against more disciplined attackers. Given the generations of slavery that the Hebrews were supposed to have experienced, their panic at the sight of a pursuing army is not unreasonable. What seems most incredible is that they would stop to engage Egypt's highly trained professionals even if they had significant weaponry. With no mention of a battle other than in the subsequent paean to God (Exod. 15:1–18), the resistance theory must remain a novel assumption.

* * *

The implications of a great miracle incited countless storytellers to further explicate the extraordinary events that happened at the Red Sea. Until the recent contributions of science became available, most explanations struggled to identify common events that would fit the biblical descriptions. The "pillar of cloud by day . . . the pillar of fire by night" used in 13:21 and other passages indicated God's presence at the head of His people. This image with added theological overtones had a clear historical association. It was a custom of the Persian armies when on the march to affix a brazier of combustible material at the top of a tall pole and to carry it at the head of the column. The pole would then be visible at the rear of the line as smoke during the day and as a fiery glow during the night. Xenophon described a Spartan functionary, called the "fire-bearer," who preceded the king on military expeditions, carrying the flame taken from the altars of sacrifice.[45] And of course there is always the image of volcanic activity.

A storm sequence, whereby the clouds darken the daylight while lightning creates the surreal at night, also suggests the presence of God. In the ancient religions of this area sudden storms often presaged such theophanies.[46] There are many examples in the Bible of God's power to unleash the skies and rattle the earth (Pss. 18:8, 9; 29:2–5).

The suggestion that a massive seismic wave (tsunami, or tidal wave) created by a tectonic disturbance of the ocean floor could explain the crossing opportunity of Exod. 14:21–28 is very ingenious. Speeding in the open ocean at around 400 miles per hour, the wave slows down as it approaches land. It gathers height as well as volume by siphoning away the water from the shore as it approaches land. Because so much water is drawn into the towering wave, occasionally reaching a crest of 100 feet in shallow waters, it exposes increasingly vast areas of the sea bed ahead of it.

Pliny the Younger described the effects of the Vesuvius eruption in 79 C.E., when the sea withdrew, exposing sea creatures beached on the widened shore.[47] Ian Wilson quotes a Syrian historian on the sea changes that preceded a tidal wave in 365 C.E.: ". . . the sea with its rolling waves was driven back and withdrew from the land, so that in the abyss of the deep thus revealed men saw many kinds of sea creatures stuck fast in the slime; and vast mountains and deep valleys which Nature, the creator, had hidden in the unplumbed depths, then, as one might well believe, first saw the beams of the sun. Hence many ships were stranded as if on dry land, and . . . many men roamed about without fear in the little that remained of the waters, to gather fish and similar things with their hands."[48]

If a tidal wave were the basis of the phenomenon at the Red Sea, it would have required a miraculous coincidence for the Hebrews to be poised to cross at the first moment the water began to recede. After crossing, they would also have had to be far enough away and on high enough ground not be swept away by the wave's landfall. The characteristics of even the largest wave would allow them very little time to cross the dry sea bed to safety. This critical time factor is highlighted in a description of the effect of a seismic wave that occurred in Lisbon in 1755. Curious people were drawn to the suddenly exposed bay floor only to be drowned when the wall of water "arrived only minutes later."[49]

Before subscribing to a tidal-wave theory, we should recall that the eruption at Thera in the Aegean Sea occurred at least 200 years before the Exodus. Also, those who would accept this explanation for the crossing of the Red Sea necessarily must postulate that the Hebrews took the northern route of escape. The wave effect could have happened only at the Mediterranean shore, the route we have seen was the least likely under the circumstances. In some quarters the idea of a volcanic tidal wave was so enthusiastically embraced that the date of the Exodus was recalculated, using the eruption as the primary reference point. One author attempted to prove that the Exodus took place in the first half of the Fifteenth Century,[50] to which a reviewer commented, "This book . . . may best be characterized as an exercise in wishful thinking."[51]

Yet it is possible that the consequences of the Thera eruption do underlie some aspects of the Exodus stories. Semites who lived in the delta region when the volcano occurred and witnessed the awesome happenings would likely have assigned them a supernatural significance that persisted in the communal memory. It would then require only a small step to add these marvelous tales to the creedal aspect of God's deliverance of Israel.

Of all the tales showing God's unlimited powers and His desire to protect the people from their enemies, the most dramatic rescue occurred as the people stood on the western bank of the Red Sea, with the impenetrable water in front of them and the Egyptian army closing in from behind. The parting of the sea for the Hebrews to cross on dry land evokes a veritable water-walled canyon: ". . . the waters forming a wall for them on their right and on their left" (Exod. 14:22). It must be obvious to everyone who is not bound by the literal Word that such a representation can be only rhetorical. A temporary passage on dry land between two bodies of water, however, is infinitely possible.

With the known geological and oceanographic changes that modified the contours of the isthmus of Sinai, a crossing of the Yam Suf was possible anywhere from Lake Timsah south to Clysma, the present-day port of Suez. The Gulf of Suez pene-

trated 30 miles farther northward into the isthmus at the time of
the Exodus than it does at present.[52] It connected with the Bitter
Lakes and perhaps even with Lake Timsah. Shells have been
found on the floor of these lakes that are similar to ones found in
the Gulf of Suez, although such findings are considered by some
authorities to be too imprecise for use in proving the connection.[53] However, two stones of the Ptolemaic period, inscribed in
Latin, were found during excavation of Tell el-Maskhutah at the
eastern end of Wadi Tumilat. These stones indicate that the
marked site was at the head of the "Arabian Gulf" (Gulf of Suez).
Edouard Naville, citing "geological arguments," also supports
the idea that the Red Sea then reached as far as the northern
shore of the Bitter Lakes.[54] On the eastern side of the Sinai
peninsula the Gulf of Aqaba is also thought to have retreated
from its ancient shoreline but not as much as in the shallower,
western rift.[55] The southern half of the isthmus was an elongated
tidal swamp. At ebb tide much of the area would be exposed as
sandbars, only to be covered again at high tide. A sketch made in
1844, prior to the construction of the Suez Canal, showed the
southern part of the Bitter Lakes to be as shallow as 4 feet.[56]

A well-known feature of tidal ranges is that the amplitude is
greater at the head of a bay than at its mouth. The Bay of Fundy
is a clear example; the tide can rise 45 feet at the head of the bay
while measuring only 15 feet at its mouth.[57] The funneling effect
of tidal volume as it enters a long and narrow bay becomes
greater as it approaches the distant shore. The Gulf of Suez is a
relatively shallow, fingerlike body of water 200 miles long by 20
miles wide and only about 150 feet deep throughout its length.
Tides in the gulf have been estimated between 2 1/2 and 9 1/2
feet.[58] The average tidal range at the mouth of the gulf measures
less than 2 feet, but it increases to 4 1/2 feet at the port of Suez
during the spring.[59] By extrapolation the level of high tide 30
miles beyond Suez, at the northern edge of the Bitter Lakes,
would certainly be greater than at Suez.

Returning to the biblical story with this information, it
becomes evident that a crossing from Egypt to Sinai was quite

possible at any place where the mean water level was no more than 4 to 5 feet deep. The move would have to be appropriately timed to use the ebb tide and its briefly exposed seabed. Semites had been used for hundreds of years to guard the caravans bearing copper and turquoise from the Sinai mines to Egypt and would have been familiar with the various fording points and tidal patterns. Perhaps Moses could change course and head for Pi-hahiroth because some men in his entourage had this detailed knowledge.

The Hebrews were "encamped by the sea" (Exod. 14:9), waiting for low tide, when they spotted the pursuing chariots. Responding to the emergency, Moses elected to cross the sea as soon as possible that night in a forced march. The exposed sandbars at low tide and a knowledge of the terrain would allow them to cross on foot without difficulty. The Egyptians, following somewhat later, were not so fortunate.

Egyptian chariots, originally patterned after the Canaanite models, were modified late in the XVIIIth Dynasty. They became heavier, and the wheels were moved forward so that the driver's weight was directly over the axle.[60] This design, which is widely depicted on Egyptian monuments of the period, resulted in greater maneuverability while carrying more weight on the wheels. A chariot found in the tomb of Tutankhamen allowed two persons to stand side by side, and it would appear from the photographs that the wheel rims were little more than 2 inches wide.[61] There can be little doubt that the combined weight of chariot and passengers over thin wheel rims would have caused them to sink into the soft seabed.

The action of Exod. 14:21–25 took place during the night and the early daylight hours. The Hebrews logically moved under the cover of darkness; the Egyptians followed "at the morning watch" (14:24). Before the Babylonian exile, Israelite time divided the night into three watches, the last of which, the morning watch, would have ended with sunrise at about six o'clock.[62] Armies classically attack at dawn, and the Egyptians plunged into the ford, which could have been several hundred yards wide.

This was obviously a fatal mistake. According to the next verse, God "locked the wheels of their chariots so that they moved forward with difficulty" (14:25). An alternative translation reads, "He took off their chariot wheels, and made them drive heavily."[63] The image of chariots bogged down is unmistakable. The pair of powerful horses might have been able to continue on the downward incline even as the heavy vehicles began to sink deeper into the sand. But after they reached the middle of the tidal basin, it would have been impossible to pull uphill. There they were stuck, their wheels "locked." In the meantime the water of a spring tide was rising at the rate of almost 1 foot per hour. The Egyptian leader faced an awesome dilemma. His vehicles, as well as his quarry, would be lost if he did not get them moving ahead of the incoming tide. Undoubtedly he ordered all the charioteers to dismount and to begin to push, slipping and sliding as they sought firm footing under water. Progress was very slow, and the rising tide defeated the efforts of man and beast. When the water level reached waist height, the leader would have realized that the situation had deteriorated to an impending disaster. He ordered the men to leave the chariots and to hasten back to shore. However, wearing battle armor and struggling against a rapidly rising tide, perhaps already at chest height, it is not unlikely that most of them were overwhelmed and drowned before they could reach dry land.

The Hebrews standing on the far shore later in the day experienced a profound emotion. Exod. 14:30, 31 hints at the sense of awe felt by those who were recently hunted as they contemplated the bodies of Egyptian soldiers strewn about in the wet mud. Perhaps the Hebrews returned to the scene with trepidation, but there can be no doubt that they resumed their journey filled with a gratitude that their new God had indeed proved his favor. Their successful escape to Sinai, in contrast to the drowned Egyptians, convinced the group that their destiny lay in the adoption of Moses' God. It was the only moment of consensus that these Hebrews were to have for some time.

* * *

Of course, this reconstruction of the Exodus escape is highly conjectural but no more so than any other one that preceded it in history. It even has the probative advantage of using the plain words of text and natural explanations in place of fanciful sophistry. Also, it allows the poetic imagery of the canonical text to stand on its own historically. We do not even have to relinquish the elegant images to adopt a more mature understanding. Umberto Cassuto, unwilling to forego the miracle of the biblical account, nevertheless believes that its natural basis should be sought. He states that "it is clear that the Torah does not imply that laws of nature were changed but that a wonderful use was made of those laws."[64] Unfortunately when events are shown to

This two-horse Egyptian chariot (modern model of the XVIII Dynasty chariot of Yuya and Thuyu. Original from Thebes, Valley of Kings) was in use early in the Fourteenth Century. It belonged to Yuya, Akhenaten's grandfather. Note that the rider(s) stood over the axle, transmitting their full weight to the narrow wheel rims.

Photo Courtesy of The Metropolitan Museum of Arts,
Rogers Fund, 1921 (#21.2.61)

have a natural cause, the miraculous aspect is often exposed as a superfluous and factitious additive. By accepting a text that uses poetic license in elaborating on the laws of nature, the burden of creedal history becomes less imposing and can be borne with greater confidence.

With the Egyptian experience receding to the west, Moses and the Hebrews pressed onward into the interior of Sinai on their way to Canaan, the "promised" land. He planned to use the period of wandering to promote a sense of purpose and a more demanding spirituality than they would have likely known in the past. It is at this point that the Scriptures begin to deal with political and religious concerns of the struggling group. The wilderness would forge a nucleus of community that would progress over the next few hundred years to a wider nationality of Israel.

Notes

1. A. J. Edwards and S. M. Head, *Red Sea: Key Environments* (New York: Pergamon Press, 1987), p. 6.
2. M. Har-el, *The Sinai Journeys* (San Diego: Ridgefield, 1983), p. 12ff.
3. P. B. Kinross, *Between Two Seas: The Creation of the Suez Canal* (London: John Murray, 1968), p. 4f.
4. A. J. Edwards and S. M. Head, op. cit., p. 7.
5. M. A. Bradshaw, A. J. Abbott, and A. P. Gelsthorpe, *The Earth's Changing Surface* (London: Hodder and Stoughton, 1978), p. 233.
6. M. Har-el, op. cit., p. 305.
7. W. H. Stiebing, *Out of the Desert?* (Buffalo: Prometheus Books, 1989), p. 60.
8. H. H. Rowley, *From Joseph to Joshua* (London: Oxford Univ. Press, 1950), p. 132.
9. J. Van Seters, *The Hyksos* (New Haven: Yale Univ. Press, 1966), p. 131.
10. Ibid., p. 132.
11. G. V. Pixley, *On Exodus* (Maryknoll, NY: Orbis Books, 1987), p. 10.
12. M. Har-el, op. cit., p. 305.
13. J. Baines and J. Malek, *Atlas of Ancient Egypt* (Oxford: Equinox, 1980), p. 48.

14. D. B. Redford, "An Egyptological Perspective on the Exodus," in *Egypt, Israel, Sinai* ed. A. F. Rainey (Tel Aviv: Tel Aviv University, 1987), pp. 137–161.

15. M. Bietak, "Comments on the 'Exodus'," in ibid., pp. 163–171.

16. D. B. Redford, op. cit., p. 142.

17. G. I. Davies, *The Way of the Wilderness* (Cambridge: Cambridge Univ. Press, 1979), p. 80.

18. E. Naville, *The Route of the Exodus* (The Victoria Institute, 1891), p. 10.

19. *Wyld's Official Map of the Suez Maritime Canal* (London: James Wyld, 1869).

20. D. B. Redford, op. cit., p. 143.

21. U. Cassuto, *A Commentary on the Book of Exodus* (Jerusalem: Magnes Press, 1967), p. 160.

22. D. B. Redford, op. cit., p. 150.

23. G. I. Davies, op. cit., passim.

24. I. Wilson, *Exodus: The True Story* (San Francisco: Harper and Row, 1985), p. 131.

25. M. Copisarow, "The Ancient Egyptian, Greek and Hebrew Concept of the Red Sea," *Vetus Testamentum* 12(1962):1–13.

26. N. H. Snaith, "The Sea of Reeds: The Red Sea," *Vetus Testamentum* 15(1965):395–398.

27. Z. Garfuncle, "Geography," in *Sinai*, ed. B. Rothenberg (New York: J. J. Binns, 1979), pp. 41–60.

28. W. F. Albright, "Moses in Historical and Theological Perspective," in *Magnalia Dei, The mighty acts of God*, ed. F. M. Cross, W. E. Lemke, and P. D. Miller (Garden City, NY: Doubleday, 1976), pp. 120–131.

29. E. D. Oren, "The Ways of Horus in North Sinai," in Rainey, op. cit., pp. 69–119.

30. A. H. Gardiner, "The Ancient Military Road Between Egypt and Palestine," *Journal of Egyptian Archeology* 6(1920):99–116.

31. K. W. Butzer, *Early Hydraulic Civilization in Egypt* (Chicago: Univ. of Chicago Press, 1976), p. 106f.

32. I. Wilson, op. cit., p. 131.

33. M. Har-el, op. cit., p. 89.

34. M. Bietak, op. cit., p. 167.

35. J. Van Seters, op. cit., p. 18.

36. M. Har-el, op. cit., p. 144f.

37. P. B. Kinross, op. cit., p. 2f.

38. N. M. Sarna, *Exploring Exodus* (New York: Schocken, 1986), p. 99.

39. V. Tcherikover, *Hellenistic Civilization and the Jews* (Philadelphia: Jewish Publication Society, 1959), p. 353.

40. L. H. Feldman, *Jew and Gentile in the Ancient World: Attitudes and Interactions from Alexander to Justinian* (Princeton: Princeton Univ. Press, 1993), p. 289.
41. U. Cassuto, op. cit., p. 159f.
42. M. Kalisch, *A Historical and Critical Commentary on the Old Testament—Exodus* (London: Longman, 1855), p. 253.
43. T. H. Robinson, *A History of Israel*, vol.1 (Oxford: Clarendon Press, 1932), p.87.
44. L. S. Hay, "What Really Happened at the Sea of Reeds?" *Journal of Biblical Literature* 83(1964):397–403.
45. M. Kalisch, op. cit., p. 234.
46. N. M. Sarna, op. cit., p. 111.
47. I. Wilson, op. cit., p. 133.
48. Ibid., p. 133.
49. *Encyclopedia Britannica, Micropedia*, vol. 9, 15th ed. 1975, p. 35.
50. J. J. Bimson, *Redating the Exodus and Conquest* (Sheffield: Almond Press, 1981), p. 102.
51. A. F. Rainey, "Review of 'Redating the Exodus and Conquest' by J. J. Bimson," *Israel Exploration Journal* 30(1980):249–251.
52. P. B. Kinross, op. cit., p. 5.
53. M. Har-el, op. cit., p. 148.
54. E. Naville, op. cit., p. 9.
55. N. Glueck, *The Other Side of the Jordan* (Cambridge: American Schools of Oriental Research, 1970), p. 107.
56. M. Har-el, op. cit., p. 351.
57. S. Pond and G. L. Pickard, *Introductory Dynamic Oceanography* (New York: Pergamon Press, 1978), p. 208f.
58. M. Har-el, op. cit., p. 353.
59. Edwards and Head, op. cit., p. 65f.
60. Y. Yadin, *The Art of Warfare in Biblical Lands* (New York: McGraw-Hill, 1963), p. 87f.
61. M. A. Littauer and J. H. Crouwell, *Chariots and Related Equipment from the Tomb of Tutankhamun* (Oxford: Griffith Institute, 1985), p. 99.
62. m. Kalisch, op. cit., p. 253f.
63. J. M. Hertz, *The Pentateuch and Haftorahs*, 2nd ed. (London: Soncino Press, 1969) p. 269.
64. Cassuto, op. cit., p. 168.

In the Wilderness: 11
The Sinai Experience

P rior to the departure of a mixed group of Semites from Egypt in the Thirteenth Century, Israel did not exist even as a potential entity. But as Moses, Levites, and the emigrant Hebrews meandered through Sinai, the traditions of a coalescing people began to outline a popular history. These traditions, now codified in the Torah, do not represent conventional history by modern criteria. They do, however, convey a sense of purpose among people preparing themselves for a lifestyle governed by ethical principles. It is uncertain whether those people visualized their world as a self-contained unit or merely as a subset of a larger one. By carrying a singular religious concept, they hastened the birth of Israel.

We traced the geographical and racial origins of many peoples of Arabia and Mesopotamia migrating toward the western horizons during much of the Second Millennium. These peoples absorbed other groups along the way, developing vectored cultural patterns in the process. Occasionally smaller units broke away or reformed for more independence. This process was repeated endlessly, spreading topical aspects of a common culture. Only certain strands of this fabric were destined to arrive at a place and time where Israel would form. They came together from the melting pots of Egypt and Canaan to a locus in Sinai, most probably within the latter half of the Thirteenth Century.

The Torah proclaims that the people who had lived and suffered in Egypt for more than 400 years were already Israelite descendants of the patriarchs. The Exodus was hailed as the triumphant climax of God's promise to their ancestors. How likely that this is a valid historical picture rather than an apotheosized packaging of disparate traditions must be left to the judgment of each reader. The simplicity of preternatural events along with genealogical relationships that underlie the biblical narratives obviously met the emotional needs of people for thousands of years. But today, buttressed with multiple strata of knowledge, we have the option, and even the obligation, to dig deeper into buried reality.

The people who marched out of Egypt were split by the fault lines of economic and occupational differences, cultural levels, political experience, ancestry, and, not least, motivation. This is clearly intimated in the "mixed multitude" phrase (Exod. 12:38). The majority of the group were undoubtedly Semites, with a probable smattering of Hurrians and Hittites who found themselves in Egypt and yearned to return to native soils. The complex process of disengaging a number of people from an established society, moving them out of the country, and planning for their subsistence in the forbidding ambiance of the Sinai peninsula could not have been achieved without the organization and facilitation by knowledgeable, well-connected Egyptians. The Semites of the "mixed multitude" might have been the descendants of Amorites, along with Hab/piru and Shasu who came as migrants or as war captives generations before. Many had become mired in Egypt by declining economic circumstances, working mainly as laborers on royal or temple estates where they lived in isolated settlements.[1]

It is more logical to consider the term "mixed multitude" as encompassing the entire group rather than a separate addition to it. The use of "riffraff" and "Israelites" in the same figurative breath (Num. 11:4) would also indicate a diversity within the group. Moses, an ethnic Egyptian, was the leader, although his position was challenged repeatedly. Aaron was the other power figure in the group, probably as shaman for the unassimilated Semites. We shall see in the next chapter that many onetime soldiers were included because military experience was understandably valued in the hostile territory they would traverse. These men were the Levites who also served as Moses' praetorian guard.

The Exodus group unquestionably possessed a military capability, and there is ample historical precedent that some of the Semites in the exiting group could have been soldiers. Scenes from tombs that date back to the beginning of the XIIth Dynasty show oriental warriors fighting side by side with Egyptians,[2] and records from the Akhenaten period reveal Asiatics as "spearmen, shield-bearers, swordsmen, charioteers, etc."[3]

Moses and the Hebrews left Egypt "troop by troop" (12:51), and again in 13:18 they "went up armed." In the latter verse the term *hamushim* denotes war equipment or a readiness for war. A. S. Yahuda, in his classic text on the language of the Pentateuch, finds its origin in an Egyptian loan word meaning "a weapon, a sort of lance or harpoon;" in many Egyptian wall sculptures the leading soldiers are shown carrying long thrusting weapons.[4] Another scholar translates the phrase to mean "in orderly array," implying a proper military formation.[5] It has even been suggested that the linguistic features of a wandering tradition in the form of an itinerary is indicative of a military expedition.[6]

The first clue to the Levites as soldiers is found in references to the sword. This weapon was used in Asia as early as the Middle Bronze Age (2200–1500), but it first appeared in Egypt only during the New Kingdom, becoming a symbol of pharaonic authority.[7] The sickle sword, its sharp edge now on the convex surface rather than on the inside like the older agricultural tool, became the simple weapon that increased the fighting efficiency of the foot soldier in close combat. Although such weapons were not readily available in a slave household, former soldiers certainly would have had access to them. The golden-calf episode clearly demonstrates this point. In Exod. 32:26–28 every Levite has a sword, and together they slaughter "brother, neighbor, and kin," with no mention of any casualties of their own. The distinct onesidedness of the action would be inexplicable if all the people had similar weapons. Between the Amarna period and the Exodus Semites had time to become soldiers, assimilated and disciplined to the extent that they would predictably serve the interests of an Egyptian leader.

Moses' reluctance to assume the leadership role suggests that he knew the difficulties he would face leading the fractious group. Several hints in the early chapters of Exodus suggest that Moses did not think that he could successfully communicate with the Hebrews or that they would trust him. The success of the movement required their unity and loyalty, which were clearly equivocal. Indeed the frequent insurrections provide evidence that there were intercurrent antagonisms between Moses and his charges. The idea that Aaron and the swords of the Levites were there to provide "health and accident" insurance for Moses is not far-fetched.

Moses and the Hebrews were now in Sinai, free of any Egyptian influence except what they carried subconsciously. Disengaged from an established government, they faced new challenges for which they had little preparation. Social and political rules had to be established to replace the ones they left behind. Although some remnants of previous experience would find expression in their behavior, the leadership had to create a power structure appropriate for the new circumstances. New group dynamics had to be acknowledged and channeled constructively. Yet there was insufficient time to completely repudiate the older dependencies.

With Egyptians, assimilated Egyptian Semites, recent Semitic immigrants, and perhaps some non-Semites making up the group, a pattern of collectivity had to be established quickly. A layered, hierarchic society was illogical and even antithetical, as the essence of the new belief held all people to be intrinsically equal. Any residue of Semitic tribalism also would have commended a more egalitarian structure. The need for survival suppressed ancient antagonisms at the same time it absorbed diverse traditions. However, at this early stage the various peoples could not yet feel a whole-hearted unity. Egyptian leadership over a Hebrew corpus still constituted a reminder of impressment or at least social dependency. It is unlikely that Moses could have been a popular leader for long. Nevertheless the Book of Exodus documents progress within this diverse group as its members struggled with physical disabilities and their atavistic urges while slowly acknowledging an interlocked destiny.

The prior religious practices of the group are unknown but probably entailed worship of multiple, regional, and categorical gods of the Semitic Near East. It is not unlikely that other persons besides Moses, who had been exposed to the recent history of Egypt, carried the seed of Akhenaten's monotheism. As the people picked their way across Sinai, encountering indigenous nomadic and seminomadic groups, the uniqueness of their newly acquired universal God must have appeared as a singular estate. They were now different from others, their mutual obligations being fixed in a tight-fitting morality. But something remarkable was happening to this mixed group; they stayed together despite their differences. The universality of the new God allowed for a broader sense of community, which in turn exerted a gravitational effect on the individual. The concept that they were now the favored children of one just God must have generated a desire to remain part of the greater whole.

Their first several weeks on the trail can be understood as a "shake-down cruise," in modern naval parlance. Moses' leadership was challenged frequently by both internal and external forces. The people's anger and ingratitude were monumental. By the third day after the escape into Sinai, Moses faced his first mutiny, and two chapters later he had already dealt with five episodes of rebellion and insubordination. A profound lack of rapport is evident by the hostility directed toward him from the time he tried to stop the two Hebrews from fighting in Egypt until he finally reached the vicinity of the Promised Land. One author characterizes the relationship by noting, "What appears to Moses as ingratitude based on insatiable appetite seems to the Hebrews a result of insatiable demands made on them by Moses."8

As the Hebrews left Egypt, Moses seemed to be firmly in charge of the operation. He had Aaron as interlocutor, and the loyal Levites provided crowd control. No sooner had the Exodus begun than the pent-up servility that characterized the Hebrews' response to the Egyptians exploded into anarchy. They had been deferential in Egypt out of fear, but in a new venue they grumbled, defied, and even rebelled. The people harassed Moses by invidiously comparing the harshness of Sinai with their now roseate memories of Egypt. However, it should be noted that although they threatened to return to Egypt, they never carried it out.

Despite the heroic aura surrounding the biblical Moses, he appears as an insecure leader, perhaps daunted by the overwhelming challenge he had undertaken. His diffidence in the face of personal insults parallels his earlier trepidant response to God's call. Num. 12:3 explains, "Now Moses was a very humble man, more so than any other man on earth." When Aaron and Miriam tried to undermine his leadership, he did not respond directly, and when his authority was again challenged by a dissident group under Korah, Num. 16:4 reports, "When Moses heard this, he fell on his face." It was God's wrath that then settled the issue. Moses preferred to consider popular sentiment, prompting one author to comment that "compromise rather than implacability, is the common Mosaic mode of resolving conflict."9 Only his response to the golden-calf episode can be seen as both immediate and decisive.

The most personal of the internal challenges came from Aaron and Miriam, his erstwhile siblings. First they tried to undermine his moral standing by pointing out accusingly that he had married a "Cushite" woman. There is a possibility that Cush does not refer here to Ethiopia but rather to the tribe of Cushan, which the prophet Habakkuk (Hab. 3:7) relates to Midian.10 If this was a reference to Zipporah, his Midianite wife, the purpose of their accusation is unclear. They also questioned the exclusiveness of his relationship with God, implying that they had it as well (Num. 12:1–2). Their attempt to grab power during the second year of living in the wilderness is foiled when God again intervenes on the side of Moses. Miriam alone is punished, with a temporary leprous condition, while Aaron remains unscathed. That he manages to avoid punishment after betraying Moses should alert the reader that the relationship between them is far more complex than Exodus allows.

The most famous episode of religious perversity, the worship of the golden calf, is traditionally used to illustrate Moses' unrelenting ethical stance. In chapter 12 it will become very clear that Aaron precipitated the episode entirely for his own interests, which raises the suspicion that he was less a loyal brother than a powerbroker in his own right, carrying an agenda that was at variance with Moses'. Again he escapes punishment, and although his challenges to Moses were unsuccessful, they did not derail his eligibility for future cultic leadership. This surprising immunity can only mean that Aaron had power of his own, the source of which is left unexplained in the Torah.

Moses faced a serious challenge from Korah, a great-grandson of Levi and therefore an erstwhile cousin. Korah was supported by three Reubenites—Dathan, Abiram and On—who may have felt that leadership of the Exodus group belonged to them by right of primogeniture. After all, were they not descendants of Reuben, Jacob's oldest son? David Daiches feels that the rebellion of Korah probably represented an internal power struggle among the Levites themselves.[11] Although it would be natural for the interests of group members to undergo realignment as they interacted with one another over the course of time, we would not expect to find the disciplined Levites deserting Moses in favor of other alliances. This realignment is also uncharacteristic of intratribal behavior, although it has already been suggested that a high degree of kinship did not exist within the group. Moses carried the day once more with God's help when Korah and his cohorts were swallowed up by the earth in the unmistakable image of an earthquake. The geological faults in this region have given rise to many earthquakes in recorded times,[12] but association with the punishment of Korah undoubtedly represents the creedal insertion of a dimly remembered event.

Moses knew that he would have to make significant compromises to get the people to accept the radical idea of a single, occult God, and certainly he knew of their susceptibility to magic in worship. Nevertheless he was determined to create a religion that would be at once evolutionary and transcendent. The people had to be maintained as an integral unit while he educated them in the demands and benefits of his ideals. Deviant or separatist behavior had to be restrained, and contact with other wandering polytheistic groups had to be closely monitored, especially where they recognized ancient blood ties. Moses understood the human need for psychic gratification and developed the role of charismatic leader by mediating Divine messages to them.[13] He adapted his intense spirituality to this role because the political leadership was beginning to stabilize around the elders and the more progressive younger elements in the group.

The primary motivation of the people who joined the Exodus is not at all clear. One would assume that those who had been the most disadvantaged would rejoice at the prospect of being freed of their despair. But remarkably few expressions of happiness or joyful anticipation are reported. The grumbling and insubordination against Moses clearly express the people's unfulfilled expectations. The lamentations of Exod. 14:11,12 and 16:3 are so accusatory that we have to wonder whether they also did not feel betrayed. Apparently Moses promised the Hebrews something special when he introduced the departure plan before going on to talk to pharaoh. If they had been promised temporal rewards and future greatness in exchange for following him, they may well have decided that the trade was worthwhile, even if their living conditions had not been as humble as that of slaves. But the inhospitable wastes of Sinai prompted a reevaluation, and they indulged in the most human of reactions—blaming someone else for their disappointment. We have to wonder about the real goals of these people: Was their concern only in getting out of Egypt and back to Canaan, or did they have any interest in embracing a new moral code? Sadly it would appear that Moses erred at first in assuming that the common people would recognize truth in the abstract. Yet as time went on, they drew closer to his concept of a just, if implacable, God.

The Torah implies that Moses had a clear plan and a definite destination as they walked into the Sinai wilderness after successfully eluding capture. Kadesh-Barnea, an oasis at the western edge of the Negev, was the cultic site that Moses had in mind when he asked pharaoh to let the people go to celebrate a festival in the desert.[14] This place of perpetual springs is referred to in Gen. 14:7 as "spring of judgment" and would certainly be a blessed site in a sere climate, as well as the most direct route other than by the Way of the Sea. The problem with this explanation is that he originally asked to go "a distance of three days into the wilderness" (Exod. 5:3), whereas Kadesh, lying about 125 miles from the eastern delta region, obviously would have required much more time. We do not know whether Moses had a closer site in mind or whether his request was merely an understated opening bid in the negotiation process.

Several circumstantial clues suggest that the people were prepared to go there. The text in Jud. 11:16 is very specific: "When they left Egypt, Israel traveled through the wilderness to the Red Sea and went on to Kadesh." A reasonable time to traverse the route from the Egyptian border to the oasis might have been several days. Therefore the unleavened bread they took with them might have been sufficient for the trip. It is interesting to note that the Feast of Unleavened Bread, later joined to the Passover celebration in commemorating the deliverance from Egypt, was a week-long festival (Exod. 12:15). But they did not go straight to the oasis. According to Num. 33:37, 38, they arrived there for the first time in the fortieth year. A forty-year sojourn in Sinai becomes difficult to defend without further supporting particulars. The biblical narratives detail only two years of wandering before both Aaron and Moses die, just prior to their entrance into Canaan.

Menashe Har-el has shown that the Way of Shur would have been the most direct route to Kadesh-Barnea and that it had the best water supply in northern Sinai.[15] The issue of water is germaine because the Exodus group found no water in three days, requiring the miracle at Marah (Exod. 15:25). This tradition, however, may come from a different group that fled Egypt at another time.[16]

Moses seemed to have no intention of leading them directly to Canaan. If the people were to adopt and practice a new and rigorously self-disciplining religion, much time would be needed for its inculcation. The longer he could delay their arrival at the Promised Land, the more confident he could be that the religion would survive him. Such was his supreme confidence in the appeal of ethical monotheism.

The route they took through Sinai has had an infinite number of imaginative reconstructions because of the specific place-names given in Num. 33:5–49. Many of the names remain undocumented and very likely represent the conflation of traditions from several proto-Israelite sources.[17] In fact the time spent wandering and the exact route taken are less relevant to the understanding of the whole event than are the internal dynamics of the group.

Moses' first order of business was to organize the disparate cliques into a politically functioning unit. At the same time, he had to convince them that his leadership goals were not incompatible with theirs and that he was essential to them, that without him they could not survive. He never openly expressed this position, but it had to be evident to all that the rescuing God spoke only to him. But the prospects of success were not promising. As an Egyptian he had been steeped in an imperial system of administration, emanating from a supreme royal source and mediated through an aristocratic and priestly hierarchy. Whatever political organization the Hebrews had was probably uncomplicated and participatory, as in most Semitic tribal cultures. The obstacles in constructing an orderly administration under extremely uncertain conditions are evident throughout Exodus and Numbers. Perhaps Moses was unwilling to flaunt his authority because civil control was already effectively in his hands through the Levites.

The aimless wandering of the Hebrews in the hostile environment of Sinai offered them ample opportunity to reevaluate their predicament. In Exod. 17:8 they were attacked en route by the Amalekites associated in the Bible with an unremitting hostility toward Israel. Before the battle we are introduced for the first time to the man who will succeed Moses. Joshua is from the tribe of Ephraim, of the house of Joseph, and he is bidden to pick men to fight the Amalekites while Moses goes to the top of a hill overlooking the field of battle. Moses is accompanied by Aaron and Hur, the latter from the tribe of Judah. According to the historian Josephus, Hur was also Moses' brother-in-law, having married Miriam.[18] In another example of proximate association Hur's grandson, Bezalel, was the master craftsman entrusted to make all the sacred objects that would become central to Israel's worship (Exod. 31:2). Talmudic opinion further complicates these projected tribal relationships by suggesting that Hur was not Miriam's husband but rather her son by Caleb, one of Moses' Judahite scouts.[19] Perhaps you will recall that Caleb also was said to be the husband of the Egyptian princess who adopted Moses. At this point it becomes anybody's guess who married whom in this idealized family.

Exod. 17:13 does not reveal who Joshua chose as fighters to defeat Amalek, but it is reasonable to assume that they were mostly Levites given to him to command in that emergency. There may have been other men among the Hebrews who had fighting experience, and they certainly would have been welcomed. Biblical references mention no tribe other than Levi using swords (except in Gen. 34:26, where they were joined by Simeon at Shechem). Bows, spears, or javelins might have been available to all Hebrews, because these weapons also had utility in gathering food.

* * *

The classical configuration of Israel by tribes is in reality a much later development. Rowley believes that only Levites and members of the so-called Joseph tribes came out of Egypt.[20] Judah, who did not come out of Egypt, or at least not at the same time, ultimately became the most powerful tribe in southern Canaan. When the United Monarchy divided at the end of the Tenth Century, the southern kingdom took that tribal name. Ephraim was the comparable force in the northern kingdom, which adopted the name Israel. Gen. 48:3–20 foretells this when Jacob mysteriously crosses his hands in blessing the two sons of Joseph, his right hand giving Ephraim priority over first-born Manasseh.

The Levites assumed control of all cultic appurtenances to protect them and to preserve their holiness. This special function is consistent with the fact that warriors in Egypt typically occupied a higher hereditary caste.[21] Thus leadership roles for the three most powerful tribes in later Israel—Judah, Ephraim, and Levi—were being emphasized during the Exodus. As the Levites were being groomed for sacerdotal status, some of the other Hebrews began to assume civil duties.

Moses left Egypt with Levites and Hebrews, but they met other groups along the way, motley nomads and opportunists, who joined them for diverse reasons. His ability to integrate them and to control the centrifugal forces that were aroused in his band was being severely tested. He cried out petulantly to the people and plaintively to God on the many occasions when they threatened mutiny. Only the Levites and their weapons stood between him and sudden liquidation. But as time went on, internal alliances began to shift, and we shall see in chapter 12 how Moses adroitly compensated for the changes that occurred in the power balance.

The Midianites and the Adoption of Yahveh

Among Semites who traditionally occupied the vast area of southern Canaan, extending westward across the Negev and into Sinai, were the Midianites, or Kenites. It is thought that they came originally from northwest Arabia, although there is no certainty of this.[22] The land of Midian/Madyan stretched eastward from the Gulf of Aqaba, and throughout the Second Millennium its inhabitants flourished because of their location along the incense road from southern Arabia to Mesopotamia.[23] In Gen. 25:6 they roamed the Syro-Arabian desert after Abraham sent them away, in order to safeguard Isaac's patrimony.[24] Ancient campsites have been uncovered across the width of Sinai, from the eastern edge of the Suez Canal to Kadesh-Barnea.[25] The similarity of pottery discovered at Timna and at Tayma (Tema) in northwestern Arabia, and the unique earth from which it was made, point to the latter region as the source of the characteristically Midianite artifacts.[26]

The name Kenite supposedly comes from their eponymous ancestor, Tubal-Cain, "who forged all implements of copper and iron." (Gen. 4:22). The noun *keni* means "smith" in several Semitic languages.[27] It is widely held that these people were mainly copper metalsmiths, involved in the mining operations at Timna in the Arabah region north of the Gulf of Aqaba, perhaps even as partners with the Egyptians,[28] and were also associated with mining at Serabit el-Khadim in southern Sinai.[29] The recent finding of a gilded copper snake in the Midianite temple at Timna is most suggestive of the episode in Num. 21:8–9, in which Moses fashions a copper serpent and mounts it on a pole as an amulet against death from snakebite. That Jethro might have taught his son-in-law this trick is an intriguing connection.[30] However, their traditional occupation as journeymen metalsmiths and metallurgists rather than as shepherds has not gone unchallenged.[31]

The Bible uses the terms Midianite and Kenite almost interchangeably, although their true relationship is unclear. Enough similarities exist in descriptions of their leadership, geographic distribution, occupations, and contact with the Israelites that we can assume that they were at least collusive tribal elements within a Yahveh-worshipping confederation. An example of this is the name given to Moses' father-in-law: Jethro or Reuel as a Midianite, but Hobab as a Kenite. To lessen the confusion of dual terms as we explore their relationship to the Hebrews, only the Midian root will be used, regardless of the particular biblical reference. Midian is best viewed as an amorphous league of related peoples who ultimately disappeared from the pages of history, probably by submersion within Israel.[32]

The Midianites became closely related to the Hebrews and to the later Israelites at many levels. Contact, both peaceful and hostile, was intermittent for several hundred years from before Moses' time through the period of the Monarchies. Genealogical considerations begin in Gen. 25:2, with Midian as one of the six sons born to Abraham by Keturah, his second wife. Another early association is contained in a theory that the name of Moses' mother is Midianite in origin. Jochebed, a combinant with Yahveh, would indicate the preexistence of that version of God's name before Moses introduced it to the Hebrews.[33] There is a tradition that Moses fled from Egypt to his mother's people when he felt threatened and then conveniently married into her family. We have seen this pattern before, when Abraham's servant returned to Sarah's land to find a wife for Isaac, even including a meeting at the community well (Gen. 24:45, 46; Exod. 2:15–21).

The "mountain of God," located somewhere in the Midianite territory of Sinai, became the focal point of God's existence. That was the site where God first approached Moses to lead the people forth from Egypt (Exod. 3:1). Also, Moses was given the Law there to transmit to the people. Although God and Moses had consulted many times in places other than the imposing mountain, that particular site remained holy to Israel. The Hebrews were encamped there when the Midianites reappear in the Exodus story. At the defining moment of Israel's history, when God gave them the Law, it was deemed obligatory for them to gather at the mountain, where fire and brimstone would etch the experience in their memories. If only we knew which of the hundreds of peaks in and around Sinai or the Middle East was the supposed site of God's permanent home!

Sinai and Horeb are two names that the Torah uses for the mountain. Although the J writer preferred Sinai and the E writer used Horeb, they theoretically refer to the same place. Most of the Western world today casually accepts Jebel Musa (Moses' mountain, in Arabic) in south-central Sinai as today's "mountain of God," notwithstanding strong arguments against it.[34] Equally cogent reasons can be advanced for siting it in northern Sinai, the Negev, or in the Madyan (Midian) region of northwest Arabia. Because the text of Exod. 19:16–19 is usually accepted as reference to a volcanic eruption, some scholars prefer the latter site, where inactive volcanoes have been found.[35] None are known to exist in Sinai itself.

Romantic scholars and devout pilgrims of all faiths were usually certain that they had discovered the true site(s) of Exodus events in Sinai or southern Palestine. At least thirteen locations for the mountain, nine for the Red Sea crossing, and eighteen for the locus of Kadesh-Barnea have been identified.[36] This phenomenon of obsessively seeking biblical landmarks is relatively late in history, although some early descriptions date from the Tannaitic period (early in the Common Era).[37]

When the Israelites were encamped near the mountain, Jethro, the high priest of Midian, appears with his daughter and two grandchildren, who we already know to be Moses' wife and sons (Exod. 18:2–5). The text ignores the greeting Moses might have given his family, but by contrast his approach to Jethro is so deferential that we suspect the latter's patron god of having axiomatic importance for Israel. The many different legends of Jethro's affiliation to Israel offer corroboration of a deep-rooted relationship. The Midianites obviously had a significant claim on Moses and perhaps on Israel as well.

The visit of Jethro is condensed into two days and appears to be tangential to the main thrust of Israelite history. Yet the visit contains clues to a much deeper involvement than a mere in-law connection with Moses. The sequence in Exod. 18 implies that Jethro's visit preceded the great theophany, but Deut. 1:9–18 suggests that it came after the Israelites left the mountain. In either case the timing is symbolic for Israel's moment of revelation. The indisputable Midianite presence at Israel's convocation indicates that an expansion and modification in the group and its religion is about to occur. At this point we would be justified in thinking that the people are becoming Israelites, imbued with an ethic not shared by anyone else. The Mosaic Covenant is the primary factor that converted them from their past as Hebrews, Egyptians, Midianites, or other.

Exod. 18 contains many references to both Yahveh and Elohim as God, but Jethro apparently acknowledges the supreme power of the God of Israel. He then offers a sacrifice and partakes of a eucharistic meal with Aaron and the elders of Israel (18:11,12). Many rabbis assume that Jethro undertook to become a proselyte by this act.[38] Other scholars suspect that it was the high priest of the Midianites who bore the original Yahveh tradition, not Moses. It would be most unusual for a priest to officiate or to make a sacrifice to a god not his own.[39] In Exod. 18:12 Jethro sacrifices to Elohim, not to Yahveh, and Martin Buber uses this fact to suggest that Jethro could not have been a priest of Yahveh.[40] This position is neatly rebutted by Rowley when he writes that "it can hardly be supposed that the demonstration of the power of Yahweh in the deliverance of the Israelites would lead them forthwith to sacrifice to some other God. Nor is it clear why Jethro should officiate as priest and preside at the sacred feast unless his own God was being approached."[41]

The sacrifice and meal could also represent the making of a covenant between equals, as in Gen. 31:54, where Jacob and Laban agree.[42] This position finds support where God is used as a witness to the covenant, along with the widespread ancient practice of a sacrifice and mutual participation in the sacrificial meal.[43] So again, the canon enfolds a seemingly extraneous event in the historical tradition of Israel and in the process manages to elucidate a profound nuance within that tradition.

The major link to be established is the source of Yahveh, the new name of the God of Israel. The first evidence outside the Torah comes from commemorative lists found in an Egyptian temple. One is ascribed to the time of Amenhotep III, whereas another, similar list dates to the reign of Ramesses II. Both include reference to the "land of the Shasu Yahveh," as well as to the "land of the Shasu Seir." In this context it appears that the references are to geographic places within southern Canaan and Sinai. If the name Yahveh was used to denote a particular place, it would be a reasonable assumption that the region was defined by the particular god that was worshipped there.[44] Given the general area covered by the Shasu, which appellation could also include the Midianites, circumstantial evidence mounts that Yahvism was a long-established practice in the Near East and was introduced to the Hebrews when they passed through Sinai. This "Kenite (Midianite) Hypothesis" is compelling, but its certainty is by no means assured. Also, there is no evidence that Yahveh was the one and only god of the Midianites. The monotheistic principle, now using Yahveh as the sole God, seems to have been favored by Moses' Egyptian experience.

Textually the presumption is very strong that the pre-Mosaic Hebrews did not know God's name to be Yahveh. During the first interview at the burning bush, God introduces himself as "the God of your father, the God of Abraham, the God of Isaac, and the God of Jacob" (Exod. 3:6). Here the term *elohai* is used with each patriarch, but we should recall that each of these Gods had different names at an earlier time. Moses asks which name to use when the Hebrews will surely ask who it was that sent him (3:13). God offers an enigmatic response, *"ehyeh, asher, ehyeh"* (3:14), commonly rendered "I am what I am" or "I will be what I will be." In the very next verse the name Yahveh is added to the three patriarchal God-names.

This ambivalent answer obviously demanded an explanation, and in the 3000-plus years since God is supposed to have uttered that first commentary, many others have been offered with infinitely less authority. Later in Exod. 6:2–3 God states that He is Yahveh but admits that He did not identify Himself to the patriarchs by that name, using El Shaddai (God Almighty) instead. This admission should be taken as further indication that the name of Yahveh became universal to Israel only after they were in the company of the Midianites. According to Daiches, there exists "a tradition of Yahweh worship among Habiru and Kenites long before Moses."[45] When God tells the patriarchs that He is Yahveh in Gen. 15:7 and 28:13 but in Exod. 6:3 denies that He was known to them by that name, an apparent contradiction is exposed. By now the reader should understand that consistency is not the norm in theological matters.

Rowley, along with other scholars, feels that the Hebrews settled in Canaan in at least two groups.[46] Moses was introduced to the worship of Yahveh in Sinai after the escape from Egypt, but other immigrant groups may have already worshipped this God, even if only as part of a pantheon. Clearly the Hebrews under Moses encountered Midianites and mingled with them. If the latter were Yahveh worshippers from earliest memory, it is not unreasonable to expect that the Hebrews might have adopted this name and assigned it retrospectively to their own beginnings. Perhaps the name Yahveh, already in wide use among the peoples of southern Canaan, provided the nexus that allowed Israel to form a broader and more imposing entity.

The suspected origin of the Midianites in northwestern Arabia has other ramifications for the religion of Israel. The theophany of Yahveh at the mountain of God came amid fire and thunder (Exod. 19:16,18). Fanfare of a deity's approach, including darkness, lightning, and thunder of a severe storm, is common to all ancient tales. The possibility that a god's anger would be recognized in a volcanic eruption is also widely accepted. This hypothesis is facilitated by the geological activity known in this particular area of the Red Sea rift, with its northerly extension through the Gulf of Aqaba, the Arabah, and the Jordan River valley. Sodom and Gomorrah, cities thought to be along the rift south of the Dead Sea, were destroyed by "sulfurous fire," leaving "all the land of the Plain . . . smoking . . . like the smoke of a kiln" (Gen. 19:24–28). Also, the only mountains that show any evidence of recent volcanic activity are not within Sinai but rather just east of the shore of the Gulf of Aqaba along the same fault. The Midianites, inhabiting this seismically active region, might well have carried the primitive tradition of a fiery god whose manifestation was in a volcano. Given their other influences on Israel, the contribution of such a tradition is most reasonable.

The impetus to create a more responsive governing structure within the Exodus group also came from the Midianites. Jethro saw that Moses was overwhelmed by the lonely responsibility he assumed and urged him to create a pyramidal structure whereby he alone would "bring the disputes before God" (Exod. 18:19). Moses would continue to instruct the people in the Law, but he would choose capable men to be "chiefs of thousands, hundreds, fifties, and tens" (18:20–22) who would adjudicate the lesser disputes. Moses appropriated this Midianite organization (18:24–26), which was politically more efficient and resembled military order.[47]

After the theophany, Jethro returns to his own land (Exod. 18:27), which is strange behavior, considering that the Midianites and Israelites had just affirmed the unity of their God and presumably now shared a common social structure. Legend offers several fascinating comments on the relationship of the two peoples. Jethro is supposed to have stayed with Moses more than one year and had chastised him for sitting "like a king on a throne," perhaps another allusion to Moses' royal origin. Moses urged Jethro to come with them to the Promised Land but warned him that he would have no claim on the land, because it would be divided only among the twelve tribes of Israel.[48] The final comment mentions that Jethro's descendants nevertheless "inherited his devotion to the Torah."

This episode illustrates a persistent ambivalence in dealing with the Midianites. An invitation to permanent subordination is hardly a friendly gesture, whereas the final comment is essentially a subsequent laundering of the whole affair. Moses' concerns are understandable in light of his need for expertise in desert survival on the one hand and his anxiety about the effect of Midianite worship on the still tentative monotheism of his charges.

Num. 10:29 has Moses asking Hobab, who is familiar with the terrain, to guide them to their destination and promises that they will be generous to him. Hobab is described as the "son of Reuel the Midianite, Moses' father-in-law," implying that he was Moses' brother-in-law. The apparent discrepancy in identification, according to Rabbinic sources, is that Hobab/Jethro was indeed his father-in-law but that his own father was Reuel. Father was often used in place of grandfather.[49] At first Hobab refuses to go, but when Moses promises him "the same bounty that the Lord grants us" (10:32), he apparently accedes to the request and joins them. Obviously this is in flat contradiction to the previous version, but it carries a more logical outcome, where the two peoples found common cause and merged.

It is extremely important to note that Exod. 18:27, where Jethro and the Midianites presumably take leave, comes from the Elohist document, which represents more of the viewpoint of the Joseph-descended people who left Egypt. This northern perspective would be likely to support Moses' primacy. The version in which the Midianites are welcomed warmly and join the Hebrews (Num. 10:29–32) is assigned to the southern-oriented J source, perhaps revealing a desire to cement a sense of unity with the more "chosen" group from Egypt. Rowley's contention is that the southern tribes of the later Israelite confederation entered Canaan during the Amarna Age, well before the Exodus.[50] It is therefore most reasonable that some Midianites merged with earlier Hebrews while others maintained a rival identity. This would explain why both the J source, and to a lesser extent the E source, portray the Midianites in friendly terms and without rancor (Exod. 2,18; Num. 10).[51] The P writers at a later time defend the concept of genealogical purity and implicate the Midianites as enemies to be dealt with harshly (Num. 25, 31).[52]

The issue of Midianites in forming part of Israel continues to simmer. Near the end of Moses' life relations between the two peoples deteriorated to a blood enmity (Num. 31:1–12). Num. 25 graphically describes punishment for an episode of intimacy between them. Later, after the death of Joshua, the descendants of the Midianites travel with Judah to Arad in the Negev (Judg. 1:16) and are found with the Israelites as they defeat the Philistines, a victory celebrated in Deborah's Song (Judg. 5:24–27). But Gideon, possibly a Midianite himself (Judg. 6:11, 25), defeats a hostile coalition including Midianites.[53] By the time of King Saul there is again friendship and consideration between the peoples. David, whose political interest was always contrary to Saul's, is found raiding their camps at about the same time (1 Sam. 15:6, 27:10, 30:29). Finally, the Midianites are installed as an integral part of the Judah tribe in the genealogical listing of 1 Chron. 2:55.

These conflicting versions have been scrupulously preserved by the ancient scribes, who certainly were aware of the intrinsic contradictions. Each version came from traditional sources and contributes a valid picture of the complex origins of Israel. However, the suspicion lingers that the Torah maintains a significant ambivalence about the relationship. The Midianites obviously represent a facet of Israel that formed early in the wandering period. Both text and legend suggest that they had a previous linkage with some of the people who made up the Exodus group, and it was renewed under Moses. His marriage to Zipporah (Exod. 2:21) can be cited in support of this thesis. Yet the subsequent interactions of reciprocal friendship and enmity must not be considered incoherent. One rational approach is to view the two peoples, whose territories intersect over a wide area, as reacting naturally to the cooperative necessities and inevitable frictions that occur between kindred peoples living in close proximity. Certainly international relations have always been subject to alternating periods of peace and belligerency.

Many scholars today accept the dictum that the Hebrews who left Egypt with Moses were polytheistic, like all their former neighbors, recent or remote.[54] As they wandered through Sinai, setting their sights on the land of Canaan, these proto-Israelites embraced the iconoclastic demands of monotheism, albeit fitfully. It was Moses who injected the seed of morality into an ambivalent or even reluctant communal psyche. But where did he get the ideas? Were they his ab initio, or did he modify someone else's thoughts? We can never know for sure, but we will not be alone in assuming that Moses had been exposed to the ideas of Akhenaten.[55] Experience suggests that momentous concepts rarely appear abruptly without some preliminary development. The chronology that relates Moses to Akhenaten's legacy is compatible with the conjunction at Sinai of monotheism, moral values, and Yahvism. Egypt's apparent priority for the beginning of monotheistic worship must be acknowledged, although Israel's religion evolved to a higher ethical level and exerted a much greater impact on civilization. It has also been pointed out that many of the laws of Israel were also Mesopotamian in origin whereas the sacrificial rituals might have been from Midianite sources.[56]

Given this variety of inputs, is it not therefore likely that the charismatic Moses, bearing a unique perspective on an earlier monotheistic experience, was the catalyst of a new religious outlook in a selected people?

Notes

1. D. B. Redford, "An Egyptological Perspective on the Exodus," in *Egypt, Israel, Sinai*, ed. A. F. Rainey (Tel Aviv: Tel Aviv University, 1987), p. 145.
2. G. Posener, "Syria and Palestine," in *The Cambridge Ancient History*, vol.1, part 2, 3rd ed. (Cambridge: University Press, 1971), pp. 532–559.
3. D. B. Redford, op. cit., p. 146.
4. A. S. Yahuda, *The Language of the Pentateuch in its Relation to Egyptian* (London: Oxford Univ. Press, 1933), p. 96f.
5. U. Cassuto, *A Commentary on the Book of Exodus* (Jerusalem: Magnes Press, 1967), p. 156f.

6. G. I. Davies, "The Wilderness Itineraries," *Tyndale Bulletin* 25(1974):46–82.

7. Y. Yadin, *The Art of Warfare in Biblical Lands* (New York: McGraw-Hill, 1963), p. 79.

8. A. Wildavsky, *Moses as a Political Leader* (University of Alabama Press, 1984), p. 174.

9. Ibid., p. 175.

10. R. de Vaux, *The Early History of Israel* (Philadelphia: Westminster Press, 1978), p. 331.

11. D. Daiches, *Moses, Man in the Wilderness* (London: Weidenfeld and Nicolson, 1975), p. 136.

12. K. M. Kenyon, *Digging Up Jericho* (London: Ernest Benn, 1957), p. 176.

13. A. Wildavsky, op. cit., p. 204.

14. G. Widengren, "What Do We Know About Moses?" in *Proclamation and Presence*, ed. J. I. Durham and S. R. Porter (Richmond: John Knox Press, 1970), pp. 21–47.

15. M. Har-el, *The Sinai Journeys* (San Diego: Ridgefield, 1983), p. 66.

16. J. Bright, *A History of Israel*, 2d ed. (Philadelphia: Westminster Press, 1972), p. 122.

17. M. A. Klopfenstein, "Exodus, Desert, Mountain of God," in *Sinai*, ed. B. Rothenberg (New York: J. J. Binns, 1979), pp. 17–40.

18. F. Josephus, *Jewish Antiquities*, transl. H.St.J. Thackeray (Cambridge: Harvard Univ. Press, 1978), III, p. 345.

19. M. Kalisch, *A Historical and Critical Commentary on the Old Testament—Exodus* (London: Longman, 1855), p. 310.

20. H. H. Rowley, *From Joseph to Joshua* (London:Oxford Univ. Press, 1950), p. 123.

21. M. Kalisch, op. cit., p. 244.

22. R. de Vaux, op. cit., p. 332.

23. E. A. Knauf, "Midianites and Ishmaelites," in *Midian, Moab, and Edom*, ed. J. F. Sawyer and D. J. Clines (Sheffield: JSOT, 1983), pp. 147–162.

24. W. J. Dumbrell, "Midian—A Land or a League?" *Vetus Testamentum* 25(1975):323–337.

25. B. Rothenberg, *Timna* (London: Thames and Hudson, 1972), p. 13.

26. G. Bowden, "Painted Pottery of Tayma and Problems of Cultural Chronology in Northwest Arabia," in Sawyer and Clines, op. cit., pp. 37–52.

27. G. V. Pixley, *On Exodus* (Maryknoll, NY: Orbis Books, 1987, p. 13.

28. B. Rothenberg, op. cit., p. 183.

29. I. Beit-Arieh, "Canaanites and Egyptians at Serabit," in Rainey, op. cit., pp. 57–67.

30. B. Rothenberg, op. cit., p. 183.
31. I. Kalimi, "Three Assumptions About the Kenites," *Zeitschrift für die Alttestamentliche Wissenschaft* 100(1988):386–393.
32. W. J. Dumbrell, op. cit., p. 327.
33. H. H. Rowley, op. cit., p. 159.
34. D. Baly, *The Geography of the Bible* (New York: Harper and Row, 1974), p. 105.
35. J. Bright, op. cit., p. 122.
36. M. Har-el, op. cit., p. 2.
37. G. I. Davies, *The Way of the Wilderness* (Cambridge: Cambridge Univ. Press, 1979), p. 14.
38. J. H. Hertz, *The Pentateuch and Haftorahs*, 2d. ed. (London: Soncino Press, 1969), p. 289.
39. H. H. Rowley, *From Moses to Qumran* (New York: Association Press, 1963), p. 52.
40. M. Buber, *Moses* (London: East and West Library, 1946), p. 95.
41. H. H. Rowley, *Joseph–Joshua*, p. 151.
42. E. Cody, "Jethro Accepts a Covenant with the Israelites," *Biblica* 49(1968):153–166.
43. F. C. Fensham, "Did a Treaty Between the Israelites and the Kenites Exist?" *Bulletin of the American Schools of Oriental Reasearch* 175(1964):51–54.
44. R. de Vaux, op. cit., p. 334.
45. D. Daiches, "The Quest for the Historical Moses," Robert Waley Cohen Memorial Lecture, 1974, p.11.
46. H. H. Rowley, *Joseph–Joshua*, p. 149.
47. G. W. Coats, *Moses, Heroic Man of God* (Sheffield: JSOT Press, 1988), p. 54.
48. L. Ginzberg, *The Legends of the Jews*, vol. 3 (Philadelphia: Jewish Publication Society, 1911), pp. 73.
49. J. H. Hertz, op. cit., p. 612.
50. H. H. Rowley, *Joseph-Joshua*, p .111f.
51. N. K. Gottwald, *The Hebrew Bible—A Socio-Literary Introduction* (Philadelphia: Fortress Press, 1985), p. 182f.
52. Ibid., p. 187.
53. E. J. Payne, "The Midianite Arc in Joshua and Judges," in J. F. Sawyer and D. J. Clines, op. cit., pp. 163–172.
54. H. H. Rowley, *Moses–Qumran*, p. 45f.
55. J. N. Schofield, *The Religious Background of the Bible* (London: Thomas Nelson, 1944).
56. W. F. Albright, "Moses in Historical and Theological Perspective," in *Magnalia Dei, The Mighty Acts of God*, ed. F. M. Cross, W. E. Lemke, and P. D. Miller (Garden City, NY: Doubleday, 1976), p. 128.

Levites: Egyptian Soldiers to Israelite Priests

The metamorphosis of Levi in Genesis into the Levites of Exodus is indeed dramatic. At first Levi is merely one of twelve brothers, all sons of Jacob, who together become the eponymous ancestors of Israel. Between the time the Levites leave Egypt as Moses' champions and resettle in Canaan, they assume the exclusive role of handling and protecting the cultic symbols of God's presence among the people. It is noteworthy that the Levites are the only tribe whose activities are extensively described in Exodus, and the reason given for their elevation to a sacerdotal caste is explicit; they believed in and obeyed Moses (Exod. 32:29).

Levi was the third son of Jacob by Leah, his unloved wife. We first encountered Levi with his full brother, Simeon, in the sordid episode at Shechem in central Canaan (Gen. 34:25). They are pictured as aggressive, acquisitive, and treacherous, which is also an unmistakable description of Hab/piru behavior in Canaan during the Amarna period. Moving on to Bethel, the brothers' reputation apparently preceded them: "As they set out, a terror from God fell on the cities round about, so that they did not pursue the sons of Jacob" (35:5). Simeon later disappears as a tribe, presumably absorbed by Judah. He is not mentioned in the Blessing of Moses (Deut. 33) or in the ancient Song of Deborah (Jud. 5).

It is commonly assumed that in the pre-Mosaic period, Levi also failed to secure any territorial stake in Canaan.[1] The reality of their low estate is mirrored in Jacob's deathbed curse: "Simeon and Levi are a pair; Their weapons are tools of lawlessness . . . I will divide them in Jacob, scatter them in Israel" (Gen. 49:5, 7). This testamentary tradition from the J source is probably a codification of the subsequent Levitical presence in all parts of Canaan but with no aggregate landholding in any region. It has also been used to imply that both tribes had to withdraw from Shechem to the south, much diminished in numbers and power.[2]

The lack of documentation of any tribal land rights for Levi may be due to the fact that some of them pushed on to Egypt when their numbers were further diminished. They had disintegrated into smaller groups after Shechem, and some of them returned to their original area in the south, whereas others migrated to Egypt.[3] Presumptive evidence for this is contained in Num. 26:58, where two of their clans, the Libnites and the Hebronites, are named by association with the cities in southern Canaan. Both places were included in a subsequent list of Levitical cities (Josh. 21:13). But two other clans, the Mahlites and the Mushites, both descended from Merari, a son of Levi, have names of Egyptian origin, indicating that they were part of the Exodus group.[4] Thus a continuity between the Levites of Genesis and those in Exodus is clearly established. The well-attested presence of Hab/piru in Egypt both before and after the sojourn[5] furthers the association of early Levites with Hab/piru.

The theory that Levi/Levites were one and the same people is also based on the assumption that the strong tribal consciousness of Semites would preclude the later formation of a pseudotribe ex nihilo.[6] More likely, a small group, aware of a regnant tribalism, would seek acceptance under the banner of an earlier brother tribe. The pattern of choosing an unrelated hero's name, as early Greek tribes did, has never been demonstrated in a Hebrew context. But the early storytellers were presented with a neat opportunity to refurbish the reputation of the descendants of the original Levi by casting them as the preferred of Moses.

One author who believed that the Levites represented an elite group among their brethren wrote, "Those who were in Egypt won recognition from the authorities and were exempted from slave labor" and "In Egypt, the Levites became the aristocrats of the Hebrews. They assimilated and mingled with the Egyptians, even adopting Egyptian names, and in general . . . [the Egyptians] treated them as a privileged class."[7] Unfortunately this description of their exalted status has no supporting reference.

The choice of the Levites for priestly honor is problematic in that there was nothing holy or exalted about their eponymous ancestor. The name Levi has been scrutinized etymologically for clues indicating an original cultic function, but none was found. The Semitic root of the name, like that of the other tribal ancestors, is found widely in the Near East.[8] The reasons that favored their later preeminence must rather be sought in a political context. Their loyal protection of Moses during the period of wandering demanded a special reward, and in the coin of that time a hereditary priesthood was an inestimable benefice.

In Genesis they were feral aggressors, whereas later tradition finds them as minions of God and part of His designated leadership. How this transmogrification was achieved in no more than a few generations is a mystery about which the Bible offers no clue. One authority holds that "it seems to be neither impossible nor improbable that there was in fact one tribe of Levi, which, at an early period, came to specialize in cultic functions."[9] This position simply assumes a coincidental specialization. It has also been suggested that the Levite response to the episode of the golden calf (Exod. 32:25–29) was a voluntary decision by individual men who were willing to undertake the obligations of a priesthood rather than as a tribal function.[10] Moses' description of Levi in his farewell blessing, "who said of his father and mother, 'I consider them not'. His brothers he disregarded, ignored his own children" (Deut. 33:9), supports such an understanding. It also suggests that the Levites originally functioned as soldiers of fortune without an overt tribal connection.

The pharaohs of the New Kingdom used mercenaries whenever possible, and the martial experience of the Levites as Hab/piru must have been an eminently marketable skill. Military men of Egypt could be expected to pledge their primary loyalty to the royal house, and it must be more than literary accident that the Levites, so disparaged by Jacob at an earlier time, now become essential to the Exodus project. Earlier immigrants could have become more native than Hebrew after several generations in Egypt. The Egyptian derivation of such Levitic names as Moses, Aaron, Hophni, Pinehas, and even Levi itself, is indicative of at least a considerable cultural assimilation.[11] The skilled and disciplined Hebrew/Egyptian Levites were readily converted into Moses' civil power, and grouped with Aaron as translator and mediator to the Hebrews, they created an adroit and compelling authority.

Early in Exodus (6:14–25) an oddly truncated genealogical listing interrupts the narrative flow. Only the heads of the clans of Reuben, Simeon, and Levi are represented. Reuben and Simeon are merely named, whereas a detailed list is given of the descendants of Levi, including the life spans of Levi himself, as well as Kohath, his son, and Amram, his grandson, the direct line to Moses and Aaron. Even the wives of Amram, Aaron, and Eleazar are specifically named, along with their fathers. Strangely Moses appears only once and then only as Aaron's brother. There is nothing about his wife or progeny, despite his preeminence within the designated family.

This surprising selection of names, drawn from the priestly (P) source, serves to highlight the special status of Aaron, the first in the priesthood of Israel, but also raises questions about its significance. Earlier in Exod. 1:1–7 all twelve tribes are accounted for within Egypt, and in Num. 1:1 twelve tribes are again enumerated. A rabbinic source believes that it was only these three tribes that preserved their genealogical purity while in Egypt,[12] an explanation difficult to accept at face value. The omission of Moses' family cannot be coincidental, as it underscores the ascendancy of the Aaronites.[13] But why were Reuben and

Simeon, tribes that had no special importance in later Israel, featured in tandem with Levi? One suggestion is that at some point in time they may have been linked by occupying land together in southern Canaan.

We saw in the previous chapter how the Levites functioned to channel the people's anger and to protect Moses from it. The critical event that led to the transformation of the Levite role was the episode of the golden-calf. It happened when Moses had gone up the mountain to receive the Law from God. Exod. 32 tells of the people's restlessness when he was "so long in coming down from the mountain" and their demand of Aaron that he "make us a god who shall go before us" (32:1). Tradition describes how he acquiesced by taking their "gold rings," which he "cast in a mold, and made it into a molten calf." When the people exclaimed, "This is your god, O Israel, who brought you out of the land of Egypt!" Aaron then "built an altar before it" and announced, "Tomorrow shall be a festival of the Lord!" (32:2–5).

God informed Moses of the terrible transgression that was going on back at the camp and said, "Now, let Me be, that My anger may blaze forth against them and that I may destroy them, and make of you a great nation" (32:10). The juxtaposition of "them" and "you" is another indicator that Moses was unrelated to the Exodus people. He pleads with God not to take such action, reminding Him of the promise He made to the patriarchs (32:11–14). One typically rabbinic explanation is, "Moses' love of Israel is such that he nobly and selflessly rejects God's offer to make his own descendants the sole heirs to the promises made to the patriarchs."[14] A more rational understanding of Moses' modest disclaimer is that as an Egyptian, he simply was not in line to receive the promise that Jacob's descendants expected.

Moses' reactions to confrontation with the Exodus people were usually timid or conciliatory. But in the golden-calf episode we see a more imperious personality—raging, vengeful, and even arrogant. At the sight of the pagan orgy he explodes, and in anger demolishes the tablets of God that were to make them into a moral force. He burns the idol, grinds it into powder, mixes it with water, and then makes the Hebrews drink the loathsome brew (32:19–20). This implacable Moses will brook neither a diversion from his goal nor a challenge to his leadership.

He calls for volunteers to slay the revelers, and all the Levites respond to his appeal to "put sword on thigh, go back and forth from gate to gate throughout the camp, and slay brother, neighbor, and kin" (Exod. 32:27). They killed 3000 persons (32:28), but it restored his authority in a convincing manner. The purge, however, was short-lived; the next day Moses addressed the people, saying, "I will now go up to the Lord; perhaps I may win forgiveness for your sin" (32:30). Perhaps Moses felt that his own leadership had been restored convincingly enough by the slaughter of the ringleaders that he could afford to placate the rest of the people. The number slain is small compared with the official census of the exiting group (Exod. 12:37, 38; Num. 1:17–46), but regardless of that there is no indication of Levite losses or of armed resistance to them. We can fairly conclude that only the Levites possessed the skills and the offensive weapons of war, a clear reminder of their occupational past.

It would be reasonable to expect that when Moses returned to camp, he would have taken Aaron to task for his role in the orgy. By actively participating in the return to idol worship, he undermined everything that Moses was trying to accomplish. Yet Moses' first words to him were, "What did this people do to you that you have brought such great sin upon them?" (32:21), obviously deflecting the implied rebuke toward the people. Aaron then entered an exculpatory plea that was as feckless as it was ludicrous. He told Moses that when he got their gold, "I hurled it into the fire, and out came this calf" (32:24). It appears that Aaron remained more renegade Semite than Mosaic monotheist. But the question remains: Why he was so readily exonerated when his guilt was so obvious?

Aaron's later investiture into the hereditary priesthood of Israel (Exod. 28:1), despite his culpability in the pagan rites, is even more puzzling. It has been suggested that the "house of Aaron" already occupied this position well before the Exodus, so Moses' action was no more than a confirmation of the existing priesthood.[15] This theory would explain Moses' need to have Aaron at his side when he first approached the Hebrews with the plan for an Exodus (4:29–31). The idea that the Aaronites were Semitic priests during the sojourn and then were converted to the Mosaic doctrine has a certain cogency. "Presumably, they were swayed by the message of Moses, supported him, and influenced the people to follow him" is how Yehezkel Kaufmann sees the dynamic.[16] Moses certainly would have had a more difficult time controlling the people without support from their indigenous leader.

Also meaningful is the pointed reference to Aaron rather than to Moses as the one who joins Jethro at the sacrifice to Yahveh (18:12). Aaron is unquestionably a central figure within the Hebrew element and able to command the allegiance of the people. This reference suggests how he could rebel against Moses by the egregious idolatry of the golden-calf and still avoid the punishment meted out to others. That he and his seed should therefore be awarded the high priesthood of Israel is not as surprising as it is redolent of a political compromise: Moses desperately needed Aaron's authority.

The sovereign skills that Moses possessed can best be seen in his manipulative use of the Levites. The situation must have been very tense after he had brutally suppressed Aaron's show of cultic independence, leaving the Hebrew survivors humiliated and vengeful. At that point Moses chose to ignore Aaron's complicity and instead ceremoniously elevated him and his sons to the official priesthood of the Israelites. By doing so he acquiesced to the indigenous structure already important to the people and at the same time allied himself with their cherished institution. At the beginning of the Exodus he tolerated the native priests solely for their political support, but now that his response to the golden-calf episode created turmoil, he had to embrace them. Perhaps in elevating the Aaronite family, Moses was merely acknowledging the limitation of his own position. Yet the move served to salvage and even to increase his authority.

Moses used another gambit to avoid subsuming his own leadership role as he placated the people by confirming their trusted priests. Previous menacing behavior by the people had been defused with promises and miracles. But the blatant rejection of his leadership, as implied in the golden calf, demanded an immediate response, provided by the Levites, who obviously were unconstrained by any emotional consideration of kinship. For that faithful service he awarded them participation in a valuable monopoly, the priesthood of Israel. But wait a minute, you say! What is going on here? Israel already had its priests in the family of Aaron and reconfirmed by Moses.

Moses evidently recognized that the people's future behavior as landed citizens would be influenced by the ministrations of a priestly class. Combining the Levites and the Aaronites in a unified cultic structure effectively neutralized the power threat of each force in a time-honored ploy. If the Aaronites were to freely use the apotropaic powers associated with primitive seers, a clash with Moses' own program for the divinity of God would be inevitable sooner or later. The appointment of the Levites provided the most diplomatic way for him to block the Aaronite influence until they could be convinced to promote his concepts wholeheartedly. The loyal Levites thus became integrated among the Hebrews as a spiritual force beyond their military function. Tension between the two priestly groups lasted well into the Second Temple period (515 B.C.E.–70 C.E.), making it doubtful that the Aaronites ever really accepted the Levites as authentic priests like themselves.[17] The elemental clash over the golden calf is best understood as a power struggle between Moses and the recidivist, native shamanism of Aaron.

The Levites can be said to have reached the stage of positive historical significance at the point where they were less enforcers of law and order than purveyors of God's service. However, the two functions were not yet mutually exclusive. Their military past can still be seen in the order of march as the people traversed the wilderness toward Canaan. Each of the tribes occupied precise positions both in camp and on the march: "The Israelites shall encamp troop by troop, each man with his division and each under his standard" (Num. 1:52). All the tribes were to encamp "at a distance" from the Tent of Meeting (2:2), also called the Tabernacle. Grouped in four "companies," each occupied one side of a square surrounding it. The maintenance and security of the Tabernacle itself, including its cultic vessels, were assigned to the Levites, who camped around its perimeter to "stand guard" (1:53). They alone were allowed to set up, take down, and carry the holy objects, acting as "essentially sanctuary attendants - not soothsayers, not diviners, not sacrificers."[18] The scene mirrors the bivouac pattern of the Egyptian army camp at the battle of Kedesh (circa 1274 B.C.E.),[19] a further suggestion that the Levites were soldiers who may have seen service there.

The primary duty of all Levites, whether in camp or on the march, was guarding the Sanctuary from encroachment. The Levitical perimeter outside the structure was a bulwark against physical contamination by the people.[20] This led one scholar to suggest that the Levites had been "trained guards."[21] A reading of Num. 18:1–7 leaves no doubt that they were subordinated to the Aaronite priests, the latter being responsible for the inviolability of the inside of the Tabernacle. The sons of Aaron were not involved in the portage of the sacred objects, but when the group broke camp, they carefully packed and covered them for the Kohathites (the clan of Moses and Aaron) to carry. Other Levites carried the less awesome parts of the Tent. Only the priests could officiate at sacral ceremonies held within the Tabernacle, and in camp their position at its entrance kept the inside holy. One duty of ancient priests was as doorkeepers at a sanctuary to protect the resident divinity from harm.[22]

Sanctuary, as used in the Bible, indicates a holy place where God is to be found. Although it also may refer to spatial areas within the compound reserved for the Divine presence, it is generally not specific for any location within it. The Tabernacle, a tentlike structure with a detachable wooden frame measuring 45 feet long, 15 feet wide, and 15 feet high, was wholly lined with fine linen cloth except at the front end. Surrounding the linen was a layer of goathair cloth and outside of that another layer of tanned ram skin. Finally, an outer covering of dolphin skin protected the contents from the elements. A curtain of fine linen with a design of cherubim on it hung 15 feet from the rear of the Tabernacle. This screen enclosed a 15-foot cubic space that contained the Ark and was known as the "Holy of Holies." No person except the high priest could enter this space without suffering immediate death.

The Ark was a portable chest, or cabinet, made of acacia wood and housing the symbol of the Covenant, the Decalogue tablets. The remaining space in front of the Holy of Holies was 30 by 15 feet and contained the incense altar, the lampstand (menorah), and a table with gold receptacles for ceremonial libations. Only priests could enter this part of the Tabernacle. Another curtain separated this anteroom from the outside courtyard.

The linen-girded courtyard, twice as long as it was wide, extended 150 feet from the front of the Tabernacle, and all Hebrews who were not ritually unclean could gather there. Although the courtyard had no roof, it was still considered to be part of the Sanctuary and included with the Tabernacle. For all intents and purposes such terms as Tent of the Pact, Tent of Meeting, and Tent of the Covenant are synonymous with Tabernacle.

A class with cultic responsibility was certainly known in the religions of the ancient world, but it usually consisted of soothsayers, oracles, or magicians. They were intercessors between people and their gods when the former needed specific help from the latter. People were awed by those who bore the mark of divine communication. If we think that such misplaced deference belongs only to an age of primitive awakening, one has but to look around today to find charismatics who promise certain grace in exchange for monetary offerings.

The religious activities of the Levites began when they were given the duty of recording and keeping the accounts of the building of the Tabernacle (Exod. 38:21). After the Korahite rebellion the entire tribe was remanded into Aaron's service to preserve the sanctity of the Tent (Num. 18:2–4). However, the same verses also have been used to cast doubt on an earlier relationship between the priesthood of Aaron and the tribe of Levi.[23] It is a critical question whether the Levites in reality were subordinated to the "house of Aaron" or whether it was a nominal assignment during the time they still maintained primary loyalty to Moses, as in Exod. 32:26. Because the apparent subservience to Aaron emerges from the later P source, a bias in favor of the Aaronites would not be unexpected. However, according to the JE source, which may be more historical, the Levite investiture following the golden-calf episode implies equality, not subordination. If they were delivered to Aaron's ultimate control, it could be indicative of shifting political realities within the Exodus group.

Distribution of the ritual benefits is another indication that Moses and Aaron had authority in different functional units. In Num. 18 the sacred gift offerings and tithes are precisely and specifically apportioned between Aaronites and Levites. This chapter is of P origin, and a separation between the two cultic groups is assiduously maintained, with the Aaronites holding the superior position. In Num. 18:8–20 God outlines what shall be the portion due Aaron and his family. But when God describes the gifts accruing to the Levites (18:21–32), He addresses Moses directly. The unmistakable conclusion to be drawn from this duality is that each of them represented a different constituency.

There is considerable ambiguity in the Torah about the specific priestly duties of Levites and Aaronites. The genealogical material, mainly from P, serves to maintain the distinction of Aaron and his descendants. When the Tabernacle was completed, they received special recognition: "This their anointing shall serve them for everlasting priesthood throughout the ages" (Exod. 40:15). Obviously the rest of the tribe was not included at that time. However, when Levites had the opportunity to assume priestly duties, they tended also to assume the appellation "sons of Aaron."

The special anointment of Aaron and his sons while the group was still in the wilderness of Sinai has a compelling logic. A single portable shrine, which was their cultic center, hardly needed a whole tribe of priests. But after they settled in the land, each tribe would want its own altar for convenience in offering sacrifices. Therefore a need for many and varied cultic services arose, which led to an increase and differentiation in Levitical roles. The range of duties seemed to extend from a priesthood restricted to "sons of Aaron," as defined in the P source, to the essential equivalence of the terms "priest" and "Levite" contained in Deut. 18:1; 21:5; 31:9.

In the course of the settlement many sanctuaries were established throughout the territory. The Ark of the Covenant, which was constructed in the wilderness of Sinai and attended by the Levites, arrived with them in Canaan. It was set up in Shiloh in the territory of Ephraim, becoming the earliest cultic center of the tribes. The original sanctuary in the wilderness became the archetype for each local shrine.[24] One theory that supports differences in cultic roles refers to priests who were in charge of services in the central sanctuary as "altar-clergy" and alternatively to "client-Levites" who worked elsewhere as teachers, preachers, or liturgical musicians.[25] The compilers of Deuteronomy, however, did not recognize any clerical distinctions, conceding the same priestly potential to all Levites.[26] Yet most scholars recognize functional differences between priest and Levite, which raises the question of when they occurred. Was a multilayered, priestly class the product of later Israel, or did it exist in some form from the beginning?

People always demanded cultic intercession, suggesting that a separate Hebrew priesthood functioned during the Egyptian sojourn and that it was led by the family of Aaron.[27] Their ceremonial adornment (Exod. 28), with emphasis on an oracular function exemplified by the *urim* and *thummim* (deterministic devices, sacred dice) carried next to the priest's heart (28:30), tends to imply such a past. That divination was part of primitive rites antedating the Mosaic religion can be surmised from the language: The Hebrew term for priest, *kohen*, parallels the Arabic *kahin*, which means diviner.[28] Kaufmann also believes that originally the priests and Levites were separate, the priesthood being indigenous to Aaron and his family. In the wilderness they were compelled to accept a partnership with the Levites, although they retained the sole right of access to the Sanctuary.[29]

The essential equality of priests and Levites was accepted by the Israelites in the early centuries of their history. Only the priests who traced their lineage directly to Aaron disagreed. The policy of cultic centralization in Jerusalem, with its concomitant suppression of local sanctuaries, began with King Hezekiah (715–686 B.C.E.). It created many "client-Levites" because there were then no other altars to approach, but Deuteronomy still recognized their priestly potential. The definitive split, where the Levites became Temple acolytes and minor service functionaries, occurred after the return from Babylonian exile hundreds of years later.

Originally a Levitical caste was created by the merger of the "priestly" Aaronites with the loyal militants of Moses. However, the priests from the house of Aaron persisted in defining themselves as the ceremonial elite. Later, when they were well represented in southern Canaan in the territories of Judah and Benjamin, envy for the more authentic origin of the northern priests arose, and they tried to secure the mantle of Aaron for themselves.[30] The opportunity occurred when David, the scion of Judah, became king and created the nation's capital city in Jerusalem. Much of the subsequent literary effort in recording the Torah traditions was the work of the southern priestly class, and not unexpectedly they favored their own view of Israel and Levitical status.

The heyday of the high priesthood, which began with the reign of King David, defined a particularly close association between Judah and Levi (via Aaron). Exod. 6:23 seems to presage this relationship by featuring Aaron's marriage to Elisheba, a daughter of the Judahite Amminadab. The Aaronite high priests could then boast of a blood relationship with David, who was of

the sixth generation after Amminadab. Also, a functional associ-
ation of Aaron and Hur portends a future priestly–Judahite axis.
Together they held up Moses' arms during the battle with the
Amalekites (17:10–12), and they jointly took charge of the
Hebrews when Moses went up the mountain to receive the
Decalogue tablets (24:14).

The narrative history of the Exodus indicates that Aaron's
family and the Levites remained with the main group as they
made their way north, toward the central highlands of Canaan.
Therefore they all should have been part of the northern
Israelites. But if they followed Moses to the central hill country,
how did some of the Aaronites find their way into Judah? There
is no biblical reference to a separate movement, but it is certainly possible that some of them, along with others of the Exodus group, elected to accompany the Midianites and to remain
in the south.

The Levites were excluded when the first census was taken.
God said, "Do not on any account enroll the tribe of Levi or take
a census of them with the Israelites" (Num. 1:49). In another
census "They [the Levites] were not part of the regular enroll-
ment of the Israelites, since no share [of land] was assigned to
them among the Israelites" (26:62). Thus the political organization of embryonic Israel was altered to create a uniquely
endowed class. This change in the critical service of the Levites,
along with their exclusion from the census, suggests that they
had always been a recognizably separate unit within the group.

The segregation was furthered when they were not awarded a
contiguous segment of the Promised Land. Instead the people
were to "assign, out of the holdings apportioned to them, towns
for the Levites to dwell in" (Num. 35:2). In addition, pasture
land around their towns was to be donated "for the cattle they
own and all their other beasts" (35:3). The contribution of cities
and land to the Levites had to be proportionate to each tribe's
total land holdings (35:8). If we can fathom the reason for this
fundamentally unequal distribution of assets, the true relationship of the Levites to Israel should become clear.

The Levites as soldier/priests, without any agricultural orientation, had no pressing need for extensive open spaces. The idea that the tribes would contribute to the needs of their resident Levites in proportion to their own wealth implies that the Levites were domiciled according to host tribal strength. It also suggests a continuing policelike function, wherein a prudent ratio had to be maintained between the enforcers and the general population. Otherwise it would be incomprehensible why the Levites, who contributed so much to the success of Moses' mission, would be rewarded only by cities with narrow rims of meadow land, in reality scattered nodules within the greater body of Israel.

The people who were to settle in Canaan had only a subsistence economy. Land was the most valuable asset they could have. However, the geographic assignment of land would always be a source of tribal ethnocentrism whether it was held individually or communally. The Levites, whose cultic function was practiced independently within all the tribal territories, were given a source of livelihood that isolated them from the competitive pressures of land ownership.

Six Levitical cities—three in Canaan and three in the territory across the Jordan River—were designated as "cities of refuge" (Num. 35:13, 14). These cities have been described as "extra-territorial zones, probably sites of national sanctuaries, wherein a manslayer may find refuge from the avenger of blood."[31] Vengeance has always been a potent force in personal injuries, requited only by shedding the offender's blood. The great ethical advance of the Mosaic order was in its recognition that injury or death could occur without malice (35:11). To prevent the avenger from killing the manslayer, the Levites were charged with maintaining the refuge cities, where the facts of the case could be investigated "in a trial before the assembly" (35:12). The Levites were particularly suited for this task of protecting the hunted, because they were not only facile with arms and familiar with defense strategies but also they were becoming the repository of laws that were applicable both to cultic observances and social behavior. Distributing the cities around the tribal territories ensured that shelter would always be accessible within the drastically foreshortened Near Eastern time frame between deed and dead!

There were other motives for dispersing the Levites among the secular tribes besides providing safety for the hunted during the cooling-off interval. Internal strife could be expected where contentious peoples may have had little in common except the new religion of Moses. The Levites could stand above the petty rivalries because they had an identifiably public role in the lives of all the people, and they were not bound by any mandated loyalty to the tribe in whose territory they resided. Also, as each competing group needed a manifestation of God's blessing before undertaking any hostile adventure, the "international" Levites represented a stabilizing, quasi-judicial force. The Levitical enclaves, although scattered within Israel, nevertheless formed an intertwined group bound together in a functional kinship. By sharing common sacral duties, they also eased the political isolation of the tribes. Their military prowess, still formidable if no longer absolute, was now augmented by access to cultic sanctions. The concentration of civil and moral power served to moderate bellicose intertribal behavior.

Forty-two Levitical enclaves in addition to the six cities of refuge made a total of forty-eight centers. These are listed in both Josh. 21 and 1 Chron. 6, but several are named differently, and the totals vary slightly. But their existence cannot be doubted, given the diverse sources of the tradition. Because they were widely distributed in the peripheral areas of the country but not at the center, they might also have functioned as defensive military outposts. Benjamin Mazar believes that the paucity of Levitical cities in the central part of Israel stemmed from the antagonism of the house of David for the house of Joseph, where a strong tradition of tribalism persisted.[32]

A full understanding of these cities' function suffers from a general uncertainty about accuracy in the lists. Many of the designated places, such as Shechem and Gezer, were not finally conquered by Israel until the time of the monarchy and therefore could not have been Levitical during the early occupation of Canaan. Many authorities believe that former cult centers became Levitical cities for the religious continuity it ensured, but this thesis is under challenge. Several shrine cities that figured prominently in the Israelite cult, such as Bethel, Gilgal, and Beersheba, did not appear in the lists, although the place where priests lived was not necessarily the place where they practiced.[33]

Dating each of the Levitical cities mentioned creates a significant problem in validating its true function. The omission of Jerusalem has been used as proof against both an early date and a late (postexilic) one. It would be inconceivable after David had made Jerusalem his capital and brought the Ark there that it would not have become the first city of priestly and Levitical function. This is a very strong argument against a late date for the city lists but would be consonant with the early settlement period, when Jerusalem had not yet been occupied by the Israelites. Another compelling theory is that the Levitical cities represent a historic pattern within the Solomonic period, when many organizational changes were taking place.[34] Priests and Levites willingly assumed the role of royal servants when the Temple was being built,[35] and their cities may have been expanded for provincial administration and to supervise royal lands.[36] In this context a similarity in function to the priesthood of Egypt is evident. Mazar is quite confidant that "a link will be established between Egyptian practice in Canaan as late as the Twelfth Century, and the national plan to build cities of Priests and Levites, carried out by Solomon in the tenth century."[37]

The failure of Moses, the most exalted Levite of all, to perpetuate a leadership role for his sons, Gershom and Eliezer, is difficult to fathom. It is unlikely that a Midianite mother would be the eliminating factor, as marriage outside the twelve-tribe consortium did not constitute an impropriety except at certain periods of ritual fanaticism or heightened xenophobia. There is also no prejudicial personal information that would render them unfit to assume at least a portion of their father's honor. Yet his sons inherit neither political power nor leadership within the priesthood. This unusual testamentary pattern indicates that Moses did not have sufficient power to bequeath privilege, as his close relationship with God might imply.

The general failure of his descendants to assume leadership roles is latent in a single reference in Judg. 17,18. A young Levite from Bethlehem in the territory of Judah finds employment as a priest in the household of an Ephraimite (17:10–12). He abandons his employer to join the tribe of Dan as they carve out a new territory in the north. We do not learn until 18:30 that the Levite is Jonathan, son of Gershom, and therefore grandson of Moses, whose name is written in the text as Menashe. Most scholars today believe that the superscribed *nun* (n) is a later attempt to gloss the name Moshe into Menashe. But why would Moses' name be consciously distorted? Was this another attempt to suppress his importance because of his Egyptian background? Was it embarrassment over the low estate into which the house of Moses had been allowed to fall? Or was there another, more ominous reason.

The historicity of this episode is provocative because it seems to serve no ulterior purpose except as a sign of the times. Without expansion we are allowed to glimpse a grandson of Moses as a house priest in tenuous circumstance. He fairly leaps at the opportunity to better himself by employment even within an unsettled tribe. After this chance episode the Bible never again mentions Moses' descendants. But some mystery still surrounds Jonathan's presence in Bethlehem, when we know that his grandfather led the Exodus group to central, not southern, Canaan. Perhaps after Moses' death his dispossessed sons or grandsons had to emigrate for political or economic reasons. Fundamental transformations were happening to society at that time within the land.

The last chapter of this book, covering the settlement period in Canaan, delves into the massive demographic changes that occurred when neighboring peoples were exposed to the immigrants' new spiritualism. This happened quickly as factions of the

Exodus group split away to enter Canaan from the south while the main body continued on to the north. Indigenous peoples all over the countryside, seeking security and a future to believe in, approached these zealous newcomers. Everybody wanted to be a part of the new religious awakening, with its egalitarian base and relatively classless society.

Here, at last, was a moral authority that embraced all peoples.

Notes

1. H. H. Rowley, *From Joseph to Joshua* (London: Oxford Univ. Press, 1950), p. 112.
2. E. Nielsen, "The Levites in Ancient Israel," *Annals of the Swedish Theological Institute* 3(1964):16–27.
3. H. H. Rowley, "Early Levite History and the Question of the Exodus," *Journal of Near Eastern Studies* 3(1944):73–78.
4. Ibid., p. 76.
5. L. Waterman, "Moses the Pseudo-Levite," *Journal of Biblical Literature*, 59(1940):401.
6. Y. Kaufmann, *A History of the Israelite Religion*, M. Greenberg, transl., and abridged (Chicago: Univ. of Chicago Press, 1960), p. 196, n. 12.
7. M. Berger, *Moses and his Neighbors* (New York: Philosophical Library, 1965), p. 36.
8. A. Cody, *A History of the Old Testament Priesthood* (Rome: Pontifical Biblical Institute, 1969), p. 33.
9. G. W. Anderson, *The History and Religion of Israel* (London: Oxford Univ. Press, 1966), p. 78f.
10. Nielsen, op. cit., p. 16.
11. A. S. Yahuda, *The Language of the Pentateuch in Its Relation to Egyptian* (London: Oxford Univ. Press, 1933), p. 100.
12. A. H. Silver, *Moses and the Original Torah* (New York: Macmillan, 1961), p. 46, n. 2.
13. G. Galil, "The Sons of Judah and the Sons of Aaron in Biblical Historiography," *Vetus Testamentum* 35(1985):488–495.
14. N. M. Sarna, *Exodus* (Philadelphia: Jewish Publication Society, 1991), p. 205.
15. M. Greenberg, "A New Approach to the History of the Israelite Priesthood," *Journal of the American Oriental Society*, 70(1950):41–47.
16. Y. Kaufmann, op. cit., p. 197f.

17. Ibid., p. 197.
18. A. Cody, op. cit., p. 29.
19. A. E. Glock, "Early Israel as the Kingdom of Yahweh," *Concordia Theological Monthly* 41(1970):558.
20. J. Milgrom, *Studies in Levitical Terminology, I* (Berkeley: Univ. of California Press, 1970), p. 10.
21. Ibid., p. 47.
22. M. Haran, *Temples and Temple-Service in Ancient Israel* (Oxford: Clarendon Press, 1978), p. 72.
23. E. Nielsen, *Shechem* (Copenhagen: G. E. C. Gad, 1959), p. 265, n. 2.
24. M. Greenberg, op. cit., p. 45.
25. G. E. Wright, "The Levites in Deuteronomy," *Vetus Testamentum* 4(1954):325–330.
26. J. E. Carpenter, *The Composition of the Hexateuch* (New York: Longmans, Green, 1902), p. 238.
27. M. Greenberg, op. cit., p. 45.
28. E. O. James, *The Nature and Function of Priesthood* (London: Thames and Hudson, 1955), p. 74.
29. Y. Kaufmann, op. cit., passim.
30. A. H. Silver, op. cit., p. 72.
31. B. Mazar, "The Cities of the Priests and the Levites," *Supplement to Vetus Testamentum*, Congress Vol., Oxford, 1959, pp. 193–205 (Leiden: E. J. Brill, 1960).
32. Ibid., p. 202.
33. M. Haran, "Studies in the Account of the Levitical Cities, I," *Journal of Biblical Literature* 80(1961):45–54.
34. B. Mazar, op. cit., p. 196.
35. Ibid., p. 195ff.
36. Ibid., p. 202.
37. Ibid., p. 205.

The Death of   13
Moses and Aaron

The Exodus journey was near its end when the people encamped at Kadesh-Barnea, where the eastern edge of the Sinai peninsula merges with the Negev region. We can sense the excitement and expectancy in the group as they prepare for the final leg of their journey into the Promised Land. It had been an eventful journey, as related in the Books of Exodus and Numbers. Despite several references to forty years as the period of wandering (Exod. 16:35; Num. 14:33; Deut. 2;7), the recorded events were all confined to a two-year period. Thirty-eight years thus remain unaccounted for. If the journey from Egypt to Canaan took forty years, the lack of documentation is inexplicable when contrasted with the myriad of narrative details that enliven the two-year span. Ibn Ezra considered these unattested years to be a blank page in the Book of Numbers, because there was so little of spiritual value left in the Exodus generation that had been condemned to die in the wilderness.[1] This interpretation assumes that the period of forty years is inviolate and then proceeds to rationalize the gap in time. It would be more reasonable to rely on the specific testimony of the Torah, where events of only two years are documented. The additional thirty-eight years, lacking in any event worthy of report, must be viewed as a separate tradition or a later gloss. In any event the number forty, used so commonly in the Bible, tends to be symbolic rather than actual.

It is unlikely that an anxious and petulant group could wander around the Sinai peninsula for forty years without experiencing major defections. Given the biblical description of the people's misanthropy, it becomes utterly fanciful to expect that they could have maintained group integrity for that period of time without demonstrable progress toward their goal. Also, survival conditions in the desert were marginal at best, and the ongoing search for replenishable food and water sources would have likely defeated a group that had previously partaken of abundance in agricultural Egypt. It is true that Bedouins have survived in the same deserts for millennia, but they were indigenous to the area and could control the very factors that were unfamiliar to the newly arrived Hebrews. Unless we can believe that the native Midianites supplied all their physical needs and that the emerging Mosaic order fulfilled their emotional lives, forty years of vagrancy is most improbable.

It is more reasonable to suppose that the events of the wandering period unfolded as generally presented in Exodus and Numbers but within the shorter time frame. As the Hebrews met and merged with other migratory bands, they contributed a loyalty and pride in their unique religious practices. Victory over the fearsome Amalekites, augmented by all able-bodied males in addition to the Levites, would have stimulated a sense of unity and purpose. Moses' conception of a single, omnipotent God who favored them by producing food, water, and victories must have struck a responsive chord in people unaccustomed to such favor. They were now no longer vulnerable to the vagaries of mercurial gods. Obeisance to one unseen power that responded to ethical and communally organized behavior was obviously preferable to groveling before competing deities. A "national" nucleus evolved slowly as the dominant Egyptian influence ebbed. The people soon felt strong enough to seek their destiny within the better land that tradition vouchsafed to them. It was time to make their move.

The hostility and contentiousness of the people against Moses did not diminish with time. In Num. 11:11–15 he is finally frustrated to the point that he presents God with an ultimatum: Either lighten his burden or put him out of his "wretchedness." God tells him to choose seventy of the wisest elders in the community and to bring them to the Sanctuary, where He will endow them with the same spirit that is in Moses. They will then be able to aid him in controlling the people's shortcomings. This event takes place in the second year and has a remarkable similarity to the episode that occurred early in the first year. Then Jethro had suggested that Moses find trustworthy men to deal with lesser problems, converting a disparate group of refugees into a cohort that had appropriate channels for maintaining discipline. This new group of "judges" suggests that a decentralization into tribal groupings was in progress, with monotheism as the coalescing thread.

The demise of Aaron and Moses within a short interval ordinarily should evince no surprise, especially as they were 123 and 120 years old, respectively (Num. 33:39; Deut. 34:7). Certainly the passing of the original leaders was necessary to make room for a more fraternal administration. Yet descriptions of their youthful vigor belie the implied deficiencies of old age and justify some skepticism about the traditions. The strange parallel circumstances of their deaths came just prior to the people's entrance into Canaan.

Aaron's death watch begins at Num. 20:24 where God says to Moses and Aaron, "Let Aaron be gathered to his kin: he is not to enter the land that I have assigned to the Israelite people, because you [Moses] disobeyed my command about the waters of Meribah." To understand this "transgression," we must return to the earlier verses in the same chapter, in which the people complained about thirst (Num. 20:2–5). Moses had appealed for help to God, who said, "You and your brother Aaron take the rod and assemble the community, and before their very eyes order the rock to yield its water" (20:8). But Moses instead "raised his hand and struck the rock twice with his rod. Out came copious water, and the community and their beasts drank" (20:11). The very next verse (20:12) contains God's judgment against them both: "Because you did not trust Me enough to affirm My sanctity in the sight of the Israelite people, therefore you shall not lead this congregation into the land that I have given them." That was to be Moses' reward for leading His people for forty years, hardly a classic example of justice in which the punishment fits the crime. Although both men approached God, it was Moses alone who committed the offense. Why, then, was Aaron punished? Obviously his death had to be given Divine justification.

The story of Aaron's demise contains other ambiguities. Moses, along with Aaron's son, Eleazar, took him, and "They ascended Mount Hor in the sight of the whole community" (Num. 20:27). Unless we believe that all the people were privy to God's intention to "gather Aaron to his kin," a more appropriate description might be that "they marched him up Mount Hor." God was supposed to have told Moses, "You can comfort him with the assurance that he is bequeathing his crown as an inheritance to his children, whereas you will not do so to yours."[2] The added punishment to Moses' children would seem irrelevant here except that it casually predicts their dismissal from the future history of Israel.

The incongruity of Aaron ascending the mountain to his foretold death in full cultic regalia has been called into question.[3] Perhaps he was enticed by the expectation that he would be performing a special rite on holy ground. Such an explanation is to be expected when rabbinic sources openly conjectured about the unnatural circumstances of his death. They describe how gently Moses tried to convey to his brother that he was about to die (although Aaron himself had heard God's sentence).[4] The removal of Aaron's ceremonial robes while he was still alive embarrassed later apologists. One legend states that a cave suddenly appeared at the mountaintop and that Moses invited Aaron to enter it. As Aaron did so, he was reminded that the cave might contain old graves, which would cause his priestly garments to become ritually unclean. Thus he was fooled into giving up his vestments.[5] At the mountain top "Moses stripped Aaron of his vestments and put them on his son Eleazar, and Aaron died there on the summit of the mountain" (20:28). Perhaps it was politically expedient for Eleazar to appear before the people, already enrobed as the successor priest, preempting what could have been a prolonged and divisive controversy. Although there can be no doubt that Aaron's death has undergone an intentional palliation, it certainly does nothing to enhance Moses' moral stature. In fact, the rabbinic exegesis that leaves Moses' role merely in question may be kinder to him than other alternatives.

If the obvious question of murder is unthinkable, motive becomes irrelevant. However, where objectivity demands that we entertain the idea of a violent crime against Aaron, reasonable motives must be advanced. In this case there are several, all speculative, but none illogical, given the context of Moses' relationship with Aaron and the Hebrews. If God could exact the ultimate punishment for a minor infraction at Meribah, how much more likely would it be that Moses, a mere human with natural jealousies, would nurse a desire for revenge, if only because of the golden calf? Moses reacted with forbearance to Aaron's many challenges for political leadership, but might he not have been determined to get rid of the troublemaker while still appearing to support the priestly family in the person of his malleable son, Eleazar?

A legendary scene suggests that the question of foul play was on everyone's minds when Moses and Eleazar returned to the valley. The people were angry when they saw that Aaron had not returned with them. Some thought that Moses had killed him because of jealousy at his popularity, whereas others were convinced that Eleazar did his father in to hasten his own succession. The people were about to stone them when Moses prayed for help and God again interceded.[6] It appears that another ambiguous episode has been immortalized by the deft invocation of God's help.

The need to understand Aaron's suspicious death is less compelling than the uncertainty of Moses' final day. The obituary of each man contains notable similarities: venue at the outskirts of Canaan, expiration alone on a mountaintop, and a plethora of apologetic exegeses. As the Exodus group approached the lower Jordan River valley, Moses was informed that he too was to ascend a mountain, Nebo in this case, where "[you] shall be gathered to your kin" (Deut. 32:50). The same reason—that he disobeyed God at Meribah—was given for his exclusion from the Promised Land. This "sin" is patently contrived, given the countless examples of Moses' absolute obedience to God's demands, and was very likely added by later tradition to obfuscate his awkward death.

Early in the wandering period in Sinai, when the people first complained of thirst at Rephidim, God told Moses to take his rod and "Strike the rock and water will issue from it, and the people will drink" (Exod. 17:6). It is common knowledge today, as it must have been then, that the cracking of porous limestone can often yield a flow of entrapped water. Therefore is it unreasonable that Moses, remembering the success at Rephidim, would attempt the same maneuver by "twice" striking hard at the rock of Meribah (Num. 20:11)? Note also that God specifically told Moses to take along his rod. Unless one wishes to believe in gratuitous miracles, it was as unlikely that Moses' words could bring forth water as it was for Canute's to reverse the tides.

Another reason offered apologetically for Moses' exclusion from the Promised Land suggests that he suffered vicariously for the sins of the people.[7] As part of his testament to them, Moses says, "Now the Lord was angry with me on your account and swore that I should not cross the Jordan and enter the good land that the Lord your God is assigning you as a heritage" (Deut.4:21). This variant interpretation upholds Moses' sanctity while projecting the blame onto the common people.

The most inexplicable aspect of Moses' relationship with Israel is the dramatic change that takes place after his death. That Israel's first and greatest leader could be disavowed in creedal literature for the next several hundred years belittles reason. We have already noted the dramatic disappearance of his progeny. Even King David, hardly an exemplar of goodness, appears to be more esteemed in Israelite literature than does Moses[8] and is certainly mentioned far more often by the Prophets and in Psalms.

Later references to events in the Exodus period seem to avoid acknowledging Moses' paramount role. In the entire book of Psalms, numbering 150, he is mentioned by name in only 3, and in 2 of these he is in the company of Aaron. In Psalm 119, the longest by far with 176 verses, a reference to God's laws or synonyms such as teachings, rules, precepts, words, commandments, etc., appears in each verse. But there is not a single reference to Moses' involvement in any of these, although he is traditionally considered to be the author of the Torah, "the Law of Moses." This seems to imply that outside of the Torah traditions, preexilic Israel repressed his role in the giving of the Law. Something of a profound nature must have happened at the end of Moses' life that radically altered the memory of him.

The Prophets are similarly silent. Amos ignores the role of Moses when he says, "And I brought you up from the land of Egypt, and led you through the wilderness forty years, to possess the land of the Amorite" (2:10). Isaiah 63:11 asks, "Where is He who brought them [His people] up from the sea along with the shepherd of His flock?" The only mention of Moses by Isaiah occurs in the next verse: "Who made his glorious arm march at the right hand of Moses." In Jeremiah 15:1 he is remembered by name just once, as a petitioner on Israel's behalf. But even then it is in conjunction with Samuel. Micah also has a single example: "and I sent before you Moses, Aaron, and Miriam" (6:4). The most traditional reference to Moses is found in Mal. 3:22: "Be mindful of the teaching of My servant Moses, whom I charged at Horeb with laws and rules for all Israel." Mention of "the Teaching of Moses" occurs twice in Daniel (9:11,13). However, these meager citations serve only to underline the almost total eclipse of Moses' historical persona.

Hosea, the only prophet from the northern territory of Israel, offers an occult acknowledgment of Moses' existence but without naming him. He alludes to Moses in 12:14 when he says, "But when the Lord brought Israel up from Egypt, it was through a prophet; through a prophet were they guarded." These lines suggest that even the simplest recognition of Moses' role had to be avoided. If people who ordinarily should have been grateful to the man who gave them immortality suddenly try to forget him, the process has guilt written all over it, and dark deeds must be suspected.

In 1922 German scholar Ernst Sellin hypothesized that Moses suffered a martyr's death after the "apostasy" at Baal Peor (Num. 25:1–8).[9] Sellin also concluded that in certain contexts the terms prophet, Ephraim, and Israel were equated with a single individual, Moses.[10] The last line of Hos. 13:1, "And so he died," indicates that Moses suffered a "violent atonement-death." Sellin sees an echo of the atonement-death in Deut. 1:37 and 4:21, where the P source allows Moses to die for his own sin at Meribah.[11]

Several hundred years after Hosea, an atavistic memory of violent death visited on previous Jewish prophets was still in evidence. How else are we to understand the words of Jesus in the Gospel of Matthew: "Alas for you, lawyers and Pharisees, hypocrites! You build up the tombs of the prophets and embellish the monuments of the saints, and you say, 'If we had been alive in our fathers' time, we should never have taken part with them in the murder of the prophets.' So you acknowledge that you are sons of the men who killed the prophets" (Mt. 23:29–31).[12] Here Jesus was mocking their false piety, but a linkage to the murder of prophets is explicit. The same charge is repeated in Lk. 11:47, 48. The degree of rancor that the Hebrews displayed toward Moses during his lifetime certainly sustains the likelihood that such a deed was possible.[13]

Sigmund Freud added the imprimatur of psychoanalytic theory to Sellin's concept that the Hebrews themselves killed Moses. It could certainly be anticipated that this sullen people, given to almost continuous confrontation, would sooner or later free themselves of their hated alien authority by a direct assault.

Freud believed that the deed was done much earlier in the Exodus period, probably before they reached Kadesh-Barnea. As soon as Moses was dead, they reverted to their original Canaanite rituals as in the episode of the golden calf. Actually the people might have killed Moses in any of the episodes of rebellion, but where religious recidivism symbolized by flagrant sexual excesses occurred as they were approaching Canaan, it is not unreasonable to accept the Torah's approximate chronology in localizing the time and place of his death.

Freud imagined the powerful effect that the patrician Moses made on the primitive Hebrews when he promised them that a universal and omnipotent God had chosen them to be His people as long as they were faithful to Him. It is likely that the stern image of this God soon merged with the obsessed and demanding man who was accomplishing what seemed at first impossible. When they killed Moses, they recapitulated the deed of killing the primeval father, the memory of which had to be repressed. One of Freud's major theses is that repression is an incomplete process, with isolated bits of guilt remaining accessible under certain circumstances. When any of these reach consciousness, they undergo radical change, freeing themselves of the guilt that caused the repression in the first place. Therefore the remembrance of the murder did not disappear completely, because people "retain an impression of the past in unconscious memory traces."[14]

Freud also postulated an interesting theory about the survival of monotheism among the Israelites, whereas it was rejected in Egypt shortly after Akhenaten died. A unique group of men arose in Israel, the prophets, who urged and cajoled the people and their leaders to return to and maintain the laws of Moses. These men were able to restore the honor of Moses' accomplishments without reawakening the memory of the lamentable deed. Freud felt that the guilt associated with the murder gave rise to the Messianic "wish-fantasy" that plays so great a role in both Judaism and Christianity.[15]

The reality of Moses' death can never be recovered with certainty. Nor should we seriously try to predict what differences in destiny a natural rather than a violent death might have produced. He was assigned a mythic birth to conceal an Egyptian pedigree, and it is not unthinkable that his heroic death alone on a mountaintop represents a violent death expunged.

Freud also believed that two persons by the name of Moses were ultimately rolled into a single figure. One was a "Midianite" Moses whose father-in-law was Jethro and who served the mountain-god Yahveh. This Moses was the leader at Kadesh but had no function in the Exodus. The other Moses was Egyptian with association to the Sinai traditions. Each man did not know of the other.[16] To round out the extreme range of scholarly positions is the suggestion that Moses existed never as a real person but only as a myth.[17]

However we assess the idea of a single, twinned, or even a denied Moses, it is generally accepted that his traditions were preserved in the northern, or Joseph, tribes, which had a more linear association with the Egyptian experience. The southern tribes more likely participated in the Kadesh experience. Some scholars still contend that the Levites of Judah transmitted the southern Moses traditions to the north during the monarchy period; others maintain that the bulk of the traditions always resided in the north and reached the south only later, through Deuteronomic circles. Because all the prophets except Hosea were from the south, it is possible that they did not have access to all of the Mosaic traditions. The psalms also are mainly of southern origin. George Widengren writes that "the importance of Moses is quite unaffected by the insignificant role he plays in literature of Southern origin in pre-exilic times."[18] It is certain, however, that as the Israelites matured in Canaan, south and north, they did so with a vaguely conspiratorial amnesia about the man who was responsible for their very existence.

Notes

1. J. H. Hertz, *The Pentateuch and Haftorahs*, 2d ed. (London: Soncino Press, 1969), p. 655.

2. H. Freedman and M. Simon, eds., *Midrash Rabbah* (London: Soncino Press, 1983), p. 767.

3. D. F. Zeligs, *Moses: A Psychodynamic Study* (New York: Human Sciences Press, 1986), p. 289.

4. L. Ginzberg, *The Legends of the Jews*, vol.3 (Philadelphia: Jewish Publication Society, 1911), p.324.

5. Ibid., p. 324f.

6. Ibid., p.327.

7. G. von Rad, *Deuteronomy* (London: SCM Press, 1966), p. 210.

8. G. Widengren, "What Do We Know About Moses?" in *Proclamation and Presence*, ed. J. I. Durham and J. R. Porter (Richmond: John Knox Press, 1970), p. 28.

9. E. Sellin, "Hosea und das Martyrium des Mose," *Zeitschrift für die Alttestamentliche Wissenschaft* 46(1928):26–33.

10. Ibid., p. 29.

11. Ibid., p. 31.

12. *The New English Bible* (New York: Oxford Univ. Press, 1976), p. 32.

13. R. P. Carroll, "Rebellion and Dissent in Ancient Israelite Society," *Zeitschrift für die Alttestamentliche Wissenschaft* 84(1977):176–204.

14. S. Freud, *Moses and Monotheism* (New York: Alfred A. Knopf, 1939), p. 149.

15. Ibid., pp.70–175, passim.

16. Ibid., p. 60.

17. E. Meyer, *Die Israeliten und Ihre Nachbarstämme* (Halle: Verlag von Max Niemeyer, 1906), p. 451, n. 1.

18. G. Widengren, op. cit., p. 44ff.

Settlement in Canaan: Israel Comes of Age

14

We have almost completed the historical recreation of Israel, needing only to place the people within the land. Migrations and the internal coalescence of various groups over 500–1000 years were the main source of proto-Israelites. They had all come to Canaan before the end of the Thirteenth Century, often by indirect routes. Of all the peoples who later constituted Israel, those who contributed its essence came from Egypt. A discarded religious concept that offered an ethical monotheism was reenergized by Moses, and the people he chose to carry that concept were fatefully moving into Canaan.

Possession of the Promised Land was their long-standing goal. God had vouchsafed it to the patriarchs, their putative ancestors, and Moses was the catalyst through whom the promise would be fulfilled. This idealization has to be seen as folkloristic, except to those persons who hold Scripture to be inerrant. Historical understanding requires more objectivity than mere hearsay can provide even if sanctified by thousands of years of repetition. However, yearning for land to validate one's existence has always been a human characteristic. In this case creedal election was merely an innovative etiology for a natural hunger. People who believed that they were chosen by God to occupy a specific land would not be long put off.

An objective analysis of the Israelite settlement is crucial in preparing a sound perspective for the later, more documented eras of Jewish history. To do this we must refocus on certain specific groups, all within or converging on Canaan, and whose relationship to Israel was at first tenuous. The time frame in which these peoples were active is uncertain. There are no direct, sequential relationships in the Scriptural narratives, and events seem to spring forth without a definite chronology. We shall have to create a rational explanation of the birth of Israel in Canaan while maintaining a chronologic uncertainty of hundreds of years. Groups of people appeared on the scene or disappeared without apparent reason, occasionally reappearing in altered configurations. They all became part of Israel sooner or later. The Torah portrays a tightly integrated twelve-tribe family of many generations, but overwhelming testimony suggests that casual mergers among many peoples over the centuries created the Israel of history.

The Egyptian Connection (Outsiders)

Poised on the northeastern edge of Sinai, the Exodus Hebrews had to decide on an approach to Canaan. Num. 13 describes a scouting expedition to the north made by representatives of the twelve tribes then residing in Kadesh-Barnea. Moses' charge to them was, "Go up there into the Negev and on into the hill country, and see what kind of country it is. Are the people who dwell in it strong or weak, few or many? Is the country in which they dwell good or bad? Are the towns they live in open or fortified? Is the soil rich or poor? Is it wooded or not? And take pains to bring back some of the fruit of the land" (13:17–20). The men explored as far north as the region of Hamath (in today's western Syria). They returned after forty days and reported that Hittites, Jebusites, and Amorites were in the hill country; Amalekites in the Negev; and Canaanites, who "dwell by the Sea and along the Jordan" (13:29). The spies were pessimistic about the wisdom of entering the land, saying, "The country that we traversed and scouted is one that devours its settlers." Of greatest concern were the Anakites, or Nephilim, "men of great stature" where "we looked like grasshoppers to ourselves, and so we must have looked to them" (13:32, 33). Caleb, here a Judahite, was alone among the scouts in venturing the contrary opinion that they should "go up" because they would "surely overcome it." (13:30). In a later verse (14:7) Joshua, also one of the scouts, agrees with him. But another tantrum by the Hebrews causes God to threaten to disown them again and to transfer the chosen peoplehood to Moses' own descendants. Moses dissuades Him for a second time and in Num. 14:13–19 offers a convoluted argument rebutting the promise that we suspect could never be honored, given his Egyptian nationality.

With God's blessing they defeat the Canaanites, destroying their city, Hormah (21:1–3), as the Midianites fought along with them (Judg. 1:16). The ancient city of Hormah has a well-documented history, mentioned in the Egyptian Execration Texts, as well as in the inscriptions of Amenemhet III.[1] It is also listed as one of the Simeonite cities in 1 Chron. 4:30. Its name is thought to come from the Hebrew word *cherem*, which means to ban, proscribe, or destroy, and is obviously etiological. The turbulence within the region seems to provide a rationale for the wide detour to the southeast that Moses would have to take to enter the Promised Land.[2]

The traditional center of the early southern tribes was Hebron, several miles to the north of Hormah. This city, associated with Abraham, was conquered by Caleb in some passages (Num. 14:24; Josh. 14:13, 14; Judg. 1:20) and by Judah in others (Judg. 1:10). Caleb, now a Kenizzite, married Ephrathah (1 Chron. 2:19), whose name is also that of the Judean clan from which David was descended (1 Sam. 17:12). Ephrathah was a place-name for later Bethlehem in the territory of Judah (Gen. 35:19; 48:7). Hur, now the son of this union, and his grandson, Bezalel, were also part of the Exodus group and were patronized by Moses (Exod. 17:12, 31:2, 3). Caleb's nephew Othniel, besides being the conqueror of the southern city of Debir (Judg. 1:11–13), becomes a "chieftain" of Israel (Judg. 3:9, 10). Many descendants of Jerachmeel, a brother of Caleb, are listed as Israelites in 1 Chron. 2:25–41. A tribal listing without a geographical location tends to be indicative of nomadism, although a relationship to the body of Israel can be surmised from 1 Sam. 30:26–29 "When David reached Ziklag, he sent some of the spoil to the elders of Judah . . . in Racal, in the towns of the Jerachmeelites, and in the towns of the Kenites." This action would have taken place some 200 years after the Exodus.

The foregoing data ineluctably lead to the conclusion that the Judahites and all their early relatives were at one time indigenous to the area of southern Canaan, including the Negev. It is also likely that some of them migrated to Egypt, integrating with other groups from Canaan. As these "fugitives" from Egypt encountered elements of their own clans, what could be more logical than a defection from the new group to rejoin the old? Perhaps in this process they introduced a proportion of Mosaic law into the native Yahvism of those who had never left the land. Thus an equivalence of spiritual standard may have been established between the peoples of the south and those who continued on to become the Israelites of central Canaan. It could also account for the strong Levitical associations with Judah. In order to understand the ascendant role of Judah in the history of Israel, it is necessary to see it as a large group of related, indigenous peoples occupying or converging on the land area of southern Canaan, unlike the "house of Joseph," which was a separate and relatively small number of people migrating from Egypt.

There is good reason to believe that the name Judah referred to a geographic region first and only later lent its name to the people who lived there. The same is also true of other tribes, such as Ephraim and Naphtali. Josh. 20:7 refers to "Kedesh in the hill country of Naphtali, Shechem in the hill country of Ephraim, and Kiriath-arba [Hebron] in the hill country of Judah." Roland deVaux believes that Judah became a tribal name at the time of King Saul and reached the acme of its power under favorite-son David.[3]

Throughout the Sinai trek, the people grudgingly maintained their integrity, probably because the keys to their physical survival were concentrated in the hands of a tightly organized leadership of Egyptian background. But subtle changes were taking place along the line of march. Chance encounters with nomadic groups that willingly joined them contributed important cultural and historical depth. The Midianites, by acknowledging and perhaps embracing the principles of monotheism, confirmed to the Hebrews the pragmatism and universality of their new faith. The people with Moses may have felt the stirring of a self-conscious pride that had not been present before. Again it was the Mosaic ideals held by the Exodus group that attracted the large numbers who later began to think and act as Israel.

The Exodus group, bound for central Canaan, pressed ahead on the only logical route left open to them after the report of the scouts and the hostility of the king of Arad (Num. 21:1). This route included a wide detour toward the Gulf of Aqaba and then northward along the eastern side of the Jordan rift. Moses' reported confrontation with the inhabitants along this route reflects another anachronism. He is reported to have petitioned the Edomites and Sihon, king of the Amorites (Moab), for peaceful passage through their respective territories (20:14–17, 21:21–23). Both refused him. However, strong archeological evidence suggests that these areas were mostly uninhabited in Moses' time. An Eighth Century inscription, found in present-day Jordan, describes a "Balaam, son of Beor," who was a "seer and prophet." It is quite likely that this was the same Balaam who was called on by the king of Moab to curse the oncoming Israelites in Num. 22–24. But because there was no Moabite kingdom in the Thirteenth Century, the real Balaam of the Eighth Century was retrofitted into the Exodus story to appropriate a dramatic resolution to the episode.[4] Moses meekly accepted the king's refusal of passage and detoured widely, which is understandable given the sapped condition of his flock. Significant defections to the southern tribes and psychological fatigue after two years in the wilderness must have taken their toll. Even the incipient rebellion in Num. 21:4–5 does not seem to carry as much rage as in previous episodes. Perhaps the people's earlier pessimism was beginning to fade with the awareness of a new strength coming from the Mosaic ideals.

The settlement of the Hebrew tribes in Canaan has been traditionally viewed as the result of a war fought at the behest of God. Conquest is the word most often used for the process described so clearly in Joshua and Judges 1–18. It seems to indicate that the displacement of the native Canaanites was achieved by an irresistible army, augmented by brilliant tactics and all foreshadowed by oracular encouragement. Support for an Israelite conquest of Canaan was proffered by archeological evidence in the early and middle part of our century.[5] Today, however, most scholars consider the evidence to be less than convincing.

After Moses' death within sight of the Jordan River, the remaining people of the Exodus group prepared to cross over into Canaan under Joshua's leadership. The conquest of the "promised" land was about to begin. But Josh. 1:12–15 clearly reflects the concern he had about his shrinking forces. He had to remind the men of Reuben, Gad, and the half-tribe of Manasseh that even though Moses had assigned them the Transjordanian land they were then traversing, they still had a prior obligation to help the other tribes achieve their Cisjordanian patrimony. All the men pledged their fealty with a consensual zeal that would have astonished Moses. However, it is doubtful whether their resolve was converted into action. Just how eagerly would the men of the tribes that just took possession of land that was to be theirs leave their wives, children, and livestock unprotected while they went some distance to secure the rights of their "brothers"? The Song of Deborah, one of the oldest traditions of Israel, slyly mocks the cowardice of Reuben and Gilead (Gad) in avoiding just such mutual assistance pledges (Judg.5:15–17). That these tribes had little consequence in the trajectory of Israelite history might be indicative of their estrangement from the others.

Joshua's entrance into Canaan is presented as the product of a continuing Covenantal relationship. The symbolic "Hand of God" is seen everywhere in the miraculous victories of the Israelite forces. In the first chapter God assures Joshua, "No one shall be able to resist you as long as you live. As I was with Moses, so will I be with you; I will not fail you or forsake you" (Josh. 1:5). At the eastern bank of the Jordan River the Levitical priests carried the ark at the head of the people, and when their feet entered the water, the flow ceased, "the waters coming down from upstream piled up in a single heap a great way off" and "all Israel crossed over on dry land" (3:16,17). Such hydraulic oddities should no longer come as a surprise. After all, if it could happen to the Red Sea, why not to a relatively placid river? In reality this episode does not necessarily represent a magical happenstance, as earthquakes in the seismically active Jordan rift valley have been known to interrupt the flow of the river. It last happened in 1927, when the limestone banks of the river collapsed and dammed it up.[6]

This biblical "miracle" was commemorated by twelve stalwart men, one from every tribe. Each man picked up a stone from the middle of the dry river bed where the priests with the ark stood and carried it to Gilgal, where the stones became part of the first cultic center. Twelve other stones were placed in the river so that when its flow resumed, there would be a "memorial for all time" (Josh. 4:4–9). But miracles and markers were not enough. Covenantal circumcision, which was supposedly practiced by the ancestors of this group before they left Egypt, seems to have been ignored in the wilderness. Therefore prior to their first attack, all the men were ritualized at Gibeath-haaraloth, known thereafter as "the Hill of Foreskins" (5:2, 3). This episode also suggests that blocs of new and uninitiated people had joined the group while they were en route to Canaan.

Joshua, whose career was beginning to resemble Moses' in many respects, assembled the Israelites after they had prevailed in the land. He reviewed their history and exhorted them to remain faithful to their God (Josh. 24:1–15). The Book of Joshua closes with his death and burial in Ephraim but not before some loose ends are tidied up. Joseph's bones (Moses was supposed to have taken them with him, remember?) were buried at Shechem in land that Jacob had bought from the children of Hamor. Also, Aaron's son and successor, Eleazar, was buried in land owned by his own son, Pinehas, indicating quite directly that the leading Aaronites accompanied the Exodus group into central Canaan rather than splitting off to live among the Judahites. Thus ended the chapter detailing the glorified fulfillment that Scripture had been promising. However, history rarely cooperates to provide such invariable and continuous success.

The Book of Judges follows Joshua and continues the colonization narrative of each tribe. The perspective of the conquest shifts from a "national" strategy to localized foci where the individual tribes are adjusting the boundaries of their own living spaces. The battles fought in both books imply that they all were part of a single, prolonged campaign. But when the same text is subjected to rigorous scrutiny, it cannot sustain the thesis of a rapid, overwhelming conquest.

The site of action first occurs within the tribal area of Benjamin in the central part of the country. Surprisingly only the cities of Jericho, Ai, and Gibeon are captured there, despite the reports of many battles won. In Josh. 10:16–43 the entire south of Canaan is conquered when the five Amorite kings of Jerusalem, Hebron, Jarmuth, Lachish, and Eglon are defeated in their bid to stop him. Only a single city in the north, Hazor, is taken. "Thus Joshua conquered the whole country, just as the Lord had promised Moses; and Joshua assigned it to Israel to share according to their tribal divisions. And the land had rest from war." This verse seems to exaggerate the situation that pertained at that time (11:23) and is flatly contradicted in 13:1–7, which lists the many territories that had not been conquered.

The first chapter of Judges is a reprise of the conquest in Joshua but with enough differences to suggest other sources. Modern scholars hold that Judges is not simply an account of secondary battles to complete the victories of Joshua but represents alternative traditions of those same events from different sources and times. These victories were the result of individual tribal efforts, often without the help of others.[7] The Canaanites retained significant amounts of land so that even after the advent of David and Solomon 200 years later, they continued to live side by side with the Israelites. Recently this categorical polarization of the two peoples was softened: "The sharp boundaries, which the use of the terms 'Canaanite' and 'Israelite' make possible, are wholly unwarranted and inapplicable."[8]

The conquest narratives that have been fundamental to the believing world throughout the Common Era rest on the credibility of Scripture. The idealization of dashing, irresistible attacks that conquered the land intact, just as God had promised, could have been created only by ethnocentric interests plus extensive glossing. Today the most logical view of the settlement of Israel in Canaan eschews a major military campaign with a single army-style force overwhelming city after city. The Canaanite city-states, with new technology built into their defensive perimeters and with highly developed offensive chariot skills, presented a most formidable opponent, especially against a fatigued and bedraggled horde lacking nearby bases for supplies or reinforcements. The Hebrews also could not have mustered the positive manpower ratio that is usually needed to mount a series of successful attacks.

* * *

Without an assault on the major cities of Canaan, how did the Israelites get possession of the land? Archeology has shown that there were an increased number of settlements, mainly in the central hill country around 1200 B.C.E.[9] Unfortunately the data are less specific in indicating who the inhabitants of those settlements were. The people who became Israel settled in Canaan over a period of several hundred years. Those who migrated into the land in continuing waves probably did so in relatively small numbers. This quiet introduction allowed them to occupy untended areas without presenting a threat to their neighbors.

Albrecht Alt suggested that these people, nomadic migrants seeking better, unclaimed land, were the Israelites.[10] However, there is no evidence of a large-scale immigration of the kind he postulated. The increase in population could have come as well from the flight of a native peasantry displaced by the political upheavals known to be going on in Canaan. Perhaps those who had always been linked to the soil had merely to change their political or religious colors to become Israelites. The patriarchal traditions then contributed a later eponymic status to the peoples who joined forces with those who nursed the spark of Mosaic monotheism. Folklore adapted from these groups was then emplaced around the heroic Moses/Joshua axis. This conflation of various aphoristic tales created the rich broth of Israel's historical epic but at the same time masked the specific source.

The welter of genealogical details offered in the Torah and 1 Chron. 1–9 about each tribe belabors the issue of unity within Israel. The number of discrepant references suggests a heterogeneous population, scrambling for shelter under the Israelite tent. Clan names of geographic origin are frequently duplicated within different tribal territories. Some names have a distinct northern Arabian or Canaanite ring.[11] Also, gaps appear in the chain of descent, especially in Judah and Benjamin.[12] These two tribes generally share a disproportionate emphasis as compared with the other ten tribes.[13] The impression is inescapable that there was extensive fragmentation of larger political entities, along with massive family movements into expanding clans, including the assimilation of Canaanite elements into Israel for generations after the arrival of the Exodus people and beginning, perhaps, before they arrived.

The tribe of Gad has the same name as the Canaanite god of luck, and Asher is the masculine of Asherah, the Canaanite goddess of fertility/love, suggesting a significant native influence.[14] Another example of Canaanite provenance for later Israelite names is found in the Egyptian topographical lists of Thutmose III. There a territory, or city-state, in pre-Israelite Canaan, called Jacobel, exists. The name appears again in the lists of Ramesses

II and Ramesses III, prompting Shmuel Yeivin to speculate that Jacob's change of name to Israel was prompted by an uncomfortably close association with Canaanites.[15]

It is tempting to identify the group led by Moses as the fountainhead of Israel. They were a mixture of wandering Hebrews, Egyptians, Egyptianized Semites, Midianites, and perhaps others, integrated only by a tenuous monotheism. Indeed there is no evidence before the Exodus group arrived in Canaan that the indigenous peoples showed any of the ethical proclivities that later characterized Israel. But did the incoming group led by Moses already bear that name? Here we must exercise caution before assuming that they did. An indisputable reference to Israel straddles the issue.

The famous stele of Pharaoh Merneptah, which lists his conquests in Canaan, among other places, was found at Thebes in 1896 and is closely dated to 1220 B.C.E. This so-called Israel Stele is the first extrabiblical reference that we have, and it attests to the reality of an Israel during the Thirteenth Century. The translation as given in Pritchard[16] is illuminating in the imagery of its victory paean.

> "The princes are prostrate, saying: 'Mercy!'
> Not one raises his head among the Nine Bows [The traditional phrase for the enemies of Egypt]
> Desolation is for Tehenu [Libya]; Hatti [the Hittite empire] is pacified;
> Plundered is the Canaan with every evil;
> Carried off is Ashkelon; seized upon is Gezer
> Yanoam is made as that which does not exist [three city-states within Canaan]
> Israel is laid waste, his seed is not,
> Hurru [the Hurrian kingdom] is become a widow for Egypt!
> All lands together, they are pacified;
> Everyone who was restless, he has been bound by the King of Upper and Lower Egypt." [The dual name was officially in use from the beginning of the XVIIIth Dynasty.]

Israel was the only named entity that had the determinative of an ethnic group. Therefore, Israel refers to a people rather to a geographic place, whereas the other names had determinatives of territorial units.[17] Scholars at one time thought that Merneptah's allusion to Israel's "seed" intimated the total destruction of its people. However, another interpretation yields a perception of an Israel that was not annihilated; the hieroglyphic sign used represents a kernel of grain with a plural suffix, a cliché that is contained in an almost identical reference to a Libyan victory inscription by Ramesses III.[18] Invaders commonly burned, carried off, or otherwise destroyed the grain supply that the defenders had stored to last until the next harvest. Thus deprived of their food supply, the populace would more readily submit to vassalage. The most information we can derive from this record is that an entity called Israel did exist somewhere in the Syro-Palestine area and that although it may have been pacified in Merneptah's campaign, it was not destroyed.

If Israel existed in 1220 as a group important enough to merit Merneptah's notice, one has to wonder how much older it was. The general date of the stele is fairly secure, but can we know for sure whether any of the Exodus group were already included among that Israel? Or did the immigrants from Egypt, led by Joshua and the later judges, join them and become Israelites by extension?[19] This would be the area where the traditions about Jacob/Israel were indigenous, and the name of god would have been El rather than Yahveh. Thus a population already living in Canaan and known as Israel is a very compelling fact. It was around this time, and probably in the central hill country of Canaan, that historical Israel came to the attention of the world.

As if to underscore the reality that poorly documented history cannot be presented in definitive chapters, the origin of Israel remains hostage to the most logical explanation. For almost 3000 years the Torah alone provided the history of Israel. But the rising level of intellectual sophistication and the tantalizing bits of data uncovered by scientific research and archeology demand that we continue to reevaluate the given episodes of that history. Most scholars agree that the Exodus migration had an enzymatic effect on Near Eastern religious practice, but the fact that there is no consistent, extrabiblical confirmation jeopardizes its historicity. It is difficult to believe that an Exodus group, even reduced from an estimate of millions to several thousand at most, could have eluded official notice. Yet Egypt did not record the specific departure of any Semitic group except for the Hyksos. One conclusion to be drawn is that the escape from Egypt involved even fewer persons than previously thought. Or perhaps the departure occurred in stages, all being welded together at a later time.

Recently there has been a tendency to review Egyptian records for any evidence of an eastward movement of Semites that might conceivably correlate with the biblical Exodus. The Anastasi VI Papyrus, dating from the reign of Merneptah, is a report of a customs official to the effect that he allowed the "Shasu tribes of Edom" to pass the fortress in "Tjeku" to feed themselves and their cattle in the "pools of Per-Atum (Pithom?)."[20] Although this document reflects a westward passage, it indicates that there was intermittent traffic by Semitic peoples. We may safely presume that such movement occurred in both directions, but perhaps there was less urgency in reporting people who were leaving the country to the east. In the Anastasi V Papyrus, another contemporary report, a frontier officer discusses the search for two escaped slaves (or servants) who "passed the walled place north of the Migdol of Seti Mer-ne-Ptah."[21] This report does not further characterize the two escapees, but it highlights the feasibility of surreptitious eastward movements into Sinai by small groups.

Another point of view suggests that there was an "expulsion" Exodus from Egypt in addition to the "flight" Exodus under Moses. The former movement, involving Judah, Simeon, and Levi, stopped at Kadesh-Barnea to mingle with the Calebites and Kenites and then proceeded to occupy parts of southern Canaan. The Moses group renewed contact with the others at Kadesh and then took the circuitous route east of the Arabah to central Canaan.[22] This concept offers a straightforward, if simplistic, explanation of the manifest differences between the southern and northern branches of Israel.

A generation ago it was popular to see the multileveled settlement in Canaan as the separation of the "Leah" tribes from the "Rachel" tribes. The earlier Leah tribes, predominantly Reuben, Simeon, Levi, and Judah, disrupted the political landscape of Canaan as part of the Hab/piru. Their unsuccessful depredations against the established Canaanite city-states explained the later banishment of Reuben to the east bank of the Jordan, the disappearance of Levi, and the absorption of Simeon into the now dominant Judah group. The Rachel tribes, on the other hand, consisting of Ephraim and Manasseh (the sons of Joseph) and Benjamin, were the Moses-led group that entered and occupied central Canaan. Benjamin ultimately became associated with Judah because of its more exposed southerly location. However, this neat construction does not account for the "hand-maiden" tribes. Gad, Asher, Dan, Naphtali, Issachar, and Zebulon did not occupy any central or southern land but instead formed a solid and separate northern tier from the Mediterranean coast to the Transjordan region. These tribes generally contributed very little to the Torah traditions and probably represent indigenous Canaanites who were later attracted to the new religious insights of the central and southern Israelites.

We must be cautious in accepting this stylized distribution by genealogy. The three southern tribes, dominated by Judah, and the three central tribes, led by Ephraim, were somewhat balanced by the northern group of six tribes. Yet when the monarchy split into two parts after Solomon's death, the ten northern tribes became Israel as against two for the southern entity, Judah.

Indigenous Peoples (Insiders)

The Torah traditions do not apply the term Israelite to people other than the supposed twelve-tribe Exodus group. But they do specifically name several other groups that occupied various hill-country areas. Most prominent besides the lowland-dwelling Canaanites were the Horites, Hivites, and Jebusites. In contrast, Kenites, Calebites, Kenizzites, Othnielites, Perazzites, and Jerachmeelites were peoples living in the southernmost parts of the land. We have already recognized many of them as generic Israelites, even though some traditions tried to maintain a genealogic distance. Until the Davidic dynasty brought the bulk of the countryside into a single political unit in the Tenth Century, these peripheral peoples lived in tension and mutual suspicion. The Hivites were prominent in the central region around Shechem and Gibeon (Gen. 34:2, Josh. 11:19), whereas the Hittites lived in the Hebron and Bethel/Luz areas (Gen. 23:2, Judg. 1:26). The Jebusites, who were probably related to the Hittites, occupied the Jerusalem area but perhaps only after Judah "put it to the sword and set the city on fire" (Judg. 1:8). It is thought that these ethnic enclaves had been migrating from Syria and Anatolia for a long time but in greater numbers since the Hittite empire collapsed.[23] The Sea Peoples, including the Philistines, invaded the eastern Mediterranean, beginning in the Twelfth Century.

Egyptian documents of the XIIth Dynasty (2000–1800 B.C.E.) reveal that Canaan was developing a pattern of urbanization into city-states mainly in the coastal lowlands, where agriculture could flourish, and along the sea coast for trade with the Mediterranean basin. It is very likely that areas surrounding the city-states were not actively patrolled and therefore were accessible to the seminomadic peoples approaching from the western and northern fringes of the Arabian Desert. Canaan had been prosperous and without significant social or political turmoil for several hundred years. By the Fourteenth Century the situation had become volatile, resulting from the combination of an indifferent suzerain Egypt, a large Hab/piru presence, and the immigration of a seminomadic population. Pressure from these groups of people was felt mainly along the periphery of the land and in the hill country.[24]

The particular importance of the patriarchs to later Israel is in their association with certain areas of Canaan where they set up *matseboth* (stone pillar shrines). Originally these were territorial landmarks constituting proprietary ownership—essentially "promised" land to their descendants. There is no definite time frame for any of the founders, but it is virtually certain that they all lived in specific areas associated with their names, not necessarily at the same time but prior to the Egyptian experience. Martin Noth feels that although Judah and the Galilean (northernmost) tribes did not contribute their own ancestors to the patriarchal history when they joined the confederation, the sum total of their individual traditions far outweighed the contribution by any individual patriarch.[25]

The patriarchal stories became particularly strong within central Canaan when the "house of Joseph" (the Exodus tribes) augmented the Jacob memory. It is around this tribal cluster that much of the history of early Judges revolves. The primary cultic center was in Ephraim, and Benjamin contributed the first king of Israel, Saul.

When the early Israelite history had to turn its focus on the Egyptian stage, an outstanding individual was recognized in Joseph. Treated as a near-patriarch in Genesis, in which his legendary deeds are acknowledged, his biography occupies one-quarter of the text. This is equal to the space devoted to Abraham and Jacob combined and certainly much more than to Isaac. Although prominent in Genesis, Joseph all but disappears from Exodus and other Scriptural references. For most of his life he was the most powerful man in Egypt, second only to pharaoh. But in later tribal lists his presence is intimated only by references to a "house of Joseph." His sons, however, removed by a generation from the stigma of an Egyptian origin, assume the same vague Israelite nationality accorded to their putative uncles. This suppression of an overt Egyptian provenance parallels the disappearance of Moses and his descendants from further biblical leadership.

In Deut. 26:5 the phrase "a fugitive Aramean was my father" could include each patriarch but settles on Jacob as the sire of twelve sons. This primary eponymic linkage was set because he was associated primarily with Shechem and Bethel, where the first fixed shrines had been placed (Gen. 12:6–8). The southern tribal descendants of Abraham and Isaac, of the Hebron and Beersheba sanctuaries, respectively, then advanced their traditions, coordinated in the maturing confederation's saga. The kindred traditions carried in the communal memory, along with the worship of a single God, prompted Noth to propose the term "amphictyony" for the Israelite grouping.[26] Originally it referred to the support and defense of a common shrine by related tribes in ancient Greece. But the term applies to Israel only in the broadest sense and after their settlement on the land.

It is not unlikely that some of the so-called Galilean tribes— Asher, Naphtali, Issachar, and Zebulon—started out as Sea People who were driven inland by later forces. The tribe of Dan first carved out a territory near the south-central coast adjacent to the Philistines but ultimately had to migrate to the extreme north, even beyond the Galileans. One theory suggests that these Danites were a branch of the *Danuna*, one of the Sea Peoples related to the Philistines. Another theory holds that Dan was a later amalgamation of Israelite and Canaanite elements associated with Dinah (the daughter of Jacob who was raped by the Shechemite prince in Gen. 34:2). This outsider origin may account for the lack of support that Dan received from the other tribes in its contention with the Philistines for land.[27] However, it is clear from the uncertain provenance of the foregoing names that most of the Israelite tribes were "outsiders" at one time or another.

Political ferment and unique topography were dominant factors in the Israelite settlement of Canaan. In the Amarna Age and afterward local princelings contended for space and power, totally indifferent to the consequences on their long-suffering people. The independent city-state was usually centered within a heavily fortified walled city from which supporting agricultural land radiated. Scattered between fields were the open villages of the workers. These Canaanite principalities were concentrated in the fertile lowlands, coastal areas, and to a lesser extent on the Transjordan steppe. The hill country, running like a spiny skeleton down the length of the land west of the Jordan River, was sparsely settled. However, this mountain barrier was penetrated by two east-west valleys where city-states also bristled. One was the Jezreel Valley, anchored by Acco on the seashore and Bethshean in the east. The other extended toward Jerusalem from Jaffa on the coast. Both valleys effectively divided the agriculturally less desirable uplands into three isolated segments: Galilee in the north, the central highlands, and the Judean hills in the south. It was precisely in these three rugged areas that the Israelites of Joshua, Judges, and 1 Samuel (circa 1200–1000) concentrated their settlement efforts. Many of the simple unwalled villages of the early Iron Age have been found here, especially on the eastern slopes.[28] We cannot be certain that these villages were occupied by proto-Israelites coming from Egypt, but the biblical description of their approach from the eastern side of the Jordan River and the dates (late Thirteenth to early Twelfth Century) coincide very well.

It appears that the newcomers advanced into the central hills as close to the Canaanite centers as they could without arousing them to war. Israel Finkelstein found that most of the villages reflected the lifestyle of seminomadic people, although there was also evidence of contact with the material culture of Canaanite cities "especially in pottery."[29] From the central hills there was expansion southward into Judah and northward into Galilee. However, the sites excavated in the south could also have been settled by indigenous peoples.[30]

Canaanite society had been rigidly organized with a regent or hereditary king at the apex since the days of the Hyksos. An intermediate class of *maryannu* constituted a privileged military aristocracy, which also provided the state with a ministerial and entrepreneurial elite. The peasantry, either free or indentured, and referred to as *chupshu*, supported the pyramid from the bottom. At first glance it appears that this societal form existed with some variations throughout the ancient Near East and was quite stable in good times. But this fertile spot of land, a prize to be ground up between the millstones of Egypt and Asia, would not enjoy extended peace or independence for long.

The aging of the Eighteenth Dynasty allowed Egypt's grip on Canaan to falter, unleashing the pent-up cupidity of the local tyrants. A long period of strife ensued, during which the peasants traditionally suffered the most, and covetous outsiders saw opportunity. The rapid growth of Israel beyond the natural increase of the Exodus group suggests that either there was a continuous inflow of new people or they were being augmented extensively by native Canaanites. Population estimates for this early period are unknown, but Salo W. Baron bravely attempts to extrapolate numbers while admitting that both the sources and the derivative process might be flawed. During the century before the destruction of the Temple (587 B.C.E.), about 2.5 million people lived in "Palestine," including small enclaves of Samaritans, Nabataeans, and Hellenic peoples. The Roman emperor Claudius (41–54 C.E.), had a census taken of his Jewish subjects, who were then found in every region pacified by Rome. A belt of settlement extended from the Near East around the Mediterranean Sea to western Europe. The figure Baron offers is 6,944,000, which means that there were more than 4 million Jews living outside the traditional homeland. Because there must have been 1 million living in Babylonia and other places outside of Roman control, the total population of Jews in the world came to roughly 8 million, a truly astonishing number.[31] One wonders whether the 603,550 Exodus figure given in Num. 1:46 was not a similar attempt by the early scribes to extrapolate a reasonable number, using the population of Israel at the time of writing.

One approach to the settlement concept assumes a peaceful infiltration by seminomadic tribes into the sparsely inhabited hill areas. Albrecht Alt first offered this theory in 1925. As their numbers increased, they expanded farther into the hill country, compressing the earlier arrivals. Their choice of the underpopulated hinterlands avoided confrontation with the Canaanite city-states, but in time their former grazing practices yielded to agricultural imperatives. Alt also postulated a second stage of territorial expansion that brought them into conflict with the Canaanite communities in the lowlands.[32] The fighting took place much later, near the end of the period of Judges, when there was more tribal cooperation. He states, "Its final conquest was yet to come, when the Israelite states turned wholeheartedly to a policy of expansion, at the beginning of the first millenium B.C."[33]

As reasonable as the theory appears to be, it is not without weakness. A critical question remains unanswered: Where could the large numbers of people have come from, since the Egyptian contingent was so small? Except in small, isolated groups, evidence of these Arabian nomads coming in from the eastern desert is entirely lacking. This issue is pointedly raised in the comment, "The romantic image of the Syro-Arabian desert as a vast womb, producing wave upon wave of Proto-Semites, is as demographically fallacious as it is long-lived in historiography."[34]

The incredibly rapid expansion of Israel's population, following settlement by a group that carried a unique message from Egypt, still must be explained. If the two explanations—a conquest by incoming Semites from Egypt, as described in Joshua and Judges, and a generally peaceful infiltration and sedenterization by nomadic peoples, as suggested by Alt—are seriously flawed, how did the expansion occur? George E. Mendenhall proposed a concept of settlement that was at once bold and innovative. Would not the native Canaanites who were already there be the most logical candidates? He suggested that all the elements contributing to the massive augmentation of Israel within Canaan were already resident in the land: No large-scale immigration was needed to provide the astonishing demographic growth. Mendenhall thought of it as a self-contained upheaval, a "peasant's revolt."[35] The political, social, and economic dislocation of the Amarna Age in Canaan triggered a rootlessness that lasted for several generations. When the Exodus group appeared in their midst, bearing traditions of God's benevolent miracles and an outlook of infinite possibilities, the disenfranchised natives recognized a revolutionary theme and flocked to join them.

Under the stress of weakening imperial control, the chupshu, like all peasants in history, had few alternatives against the oppressive forces. They could withdraw from the hated regime, taking the land for themselves, or if such redress proved impossible, they could leave the village to seek a more congenial society.[36] Sooner or later either choice would have led them to approach other disestablished people, including the earliest Israelites. Many factors known to favor a peasant revolt obtained during the years of Israel's realization.

The Canaanite peasant-farmers worked the fields surrounding the walled city. It is not known whether they were mostly freemen on their own land or serfs. As long as the city-state organization was stable, the roles of the king, the professional soldier/executive/entrepreneur class (maryannu), and the peasants (chupshu) were well defined and mutually accepted. However, in those times the peasants always benefited least from the self-serving socioeconomic policies of the princely overlords. The anarchy and political instability of the Amarna Age struck hardest at this marginal group. Material contained in the Amarna letters and the Ras Shamra/Ugarit data describe their personal vulnerability. Living in the rural areas well outside of the central city, their homes and persons bore the brunt of initial attacks. As pawns in the mindless intermural conflicts, they were subject to the levy (an arbitrary tax imposed by the rulers, usually to finance a war), and/or the corvée (an impressment for unpaid labor or soldiery). This happened so often in this period that the balance in their lives became even more precarious. If they managed to crowd into the walled city, they would be viewed as parasites and would be the first to feel the siege effects. Significant numbers of them became estranged from the established society of the Canaanites, and desertion or making common cause with the enemy was widespread.[37] Many of them joined those consummate outsiders, the Hab/piru. We cannot be certain that they were invariably welcomed into the fighting bands, given the separate motives and objectives of each group. However, the peasants who joined them and had previous military service "fought with a certain pride of craft and with a deep self-interest."[38]

Another recognizable group of Canaanite peasants lived in the hill country during the latter half of the Second Millennium. These were people who found conditions there to be more favorable than in the lowlands. These people were not necessarily in revolt against political pressures but rather saw economic opportunity there, as did the Hab/piru. Apparently this happened mostly in periods of urban decline or stress. The definite settlement shift that occurred early in the Iron Age was set in motion by disruptions during the Late Bronze Age.[39] One author writes that "a significant number of the peasants had formed coalitions led by dissident regents and members of the military aristocracy."[40] It seems that more than the peasant class were disenchanted with life among the city-states.

The presence of so many disenchanted peoples in the hill country did not seem to challenge the state's interest except in periods of expansion. Although their historical attachment to Canaan as a homeland was generally of shorter duration than that of the peasant-farmer, they should not be thought of as foreigners or strangers. The Hab/piru, as an underprivileged class, were widely distributed throughout the ancient Near East, whereas the Shasu, as subsistence shepherds, represented most of the seminomadic people of the arid steppes around Canaan. Despite appellative differences, these people were indigenous to the area for at least a millennium. "The emergence then of the Israelites as a dominant group in the late Bronze Age should not be considered so much an incursion of new peoples from outside of Canaan but rather the emergence of the peasants of Canaan within the land."[41] Thus Canaanite peasantry were easily the numerically largest element forming Israel.

The pastoral nomads are best understood as a subset of Canaanite agriculture, although their contribution was more adjunctive than integral. A single species of domesticated animal,

such as sheep, goats, cattle, or asses, might be the focus of a specific group, although there were also mixed herds. Within each
year some changes of location were necessary. When grasses and
other plants were lush, usually in the spring, the entire group, or
a part of it, would lead their animals to graze in the hills until
there was no more edible growth. Then they would return to
their former locations. Occasionally they sought out new areas
that would be more receptive to them and their animals. They
purchased and sold necessities there and even engaged in some
seasonal agricultural activity themselves before repeating the
cycle. By arrangements with the landowners, they grazed their
animals on the stubble of a harvested field, thus dressing and fertilizing it in return for the fodder. People who were involved
with pastoral nomadism usually came to this occupation because
there was insufficient tillable land to support the whole group.[42]
An example of this transhumance is found in the Joseph story, in
which a portion of the community, in this case his brothers, had
taken the flocks to a distant, hilly region for grazing while Jacob
and his retainers stayed in the lowlands (Gen. 37:12–17). However, pastoral nomads were not necessarily landless. They often
engaged in some agricultural work on land of their own or that
of others or were part of a community that did.[43] Raiding or banditry was also common to these groups, and therein is another
possible association with the Hab/piru.

Although pastoral nomads might have been an element in
any community, they were more likely to be found in the countryside than in urban areas. The Canaanites probably accepted
them as part of the city-state social structure, even though their
migratory habits made them less reliable as citizens. But if their
interests were ignored often enough by the ruling class, they
could easily transfer their loyalty and support to other people
who had already detached themselves from established society.
Thus they joined those people already waiting to challenge the
cities for control of the plains. One scholar sees the ancient
Near East conflict to be "between city and village," not between

"village farmer and the shepherd who may be typically blood-brothers."[44]

Until recently conventional wisdom assigned categorical definitions to each component group, fostering the impression that they were distinctly different from one another in all parameters. The Amoritic origin of the Canaanites was thought to contrast with the Shasu's North Arabian genesis and the multicentric ethnicity of the Hab/piru. Today this strict and arbitrary categorization has been softened to acknowledge many commonalities. Yet their mutual involvement serves to underline the appeal of Israel's election and its widespread success in attracting converts from the world's aggrieved.

A recent trend in academic circles sees the formation of Israel as a conjunction of indigenous groups whose similarities outnumbered their differences. An "Asiatic mode of production" applicable to Canaan has been described wherein the peasants of a village owned the productive land communally. Although they were subject to the exploitative forces of a strong centralized state, they retained a communal village structure.[45] Such an organization would have been far more democratic than one within the walled city. It would also have congruence with the tribal structure of Israel. If this point is accepted, it becomes irrelevant whether the aggregation of Israel arose primarily from one element or the other. What really characterized Israel was that "it constituted a very broad alliance of extended families, protective associations, and tribes that managed to throw off the central authorities and take over formerly state-operated socio-economic, military, and religious functions at the village and tribal level."[46] It is less important whether the source of this revolutionary process was from people who brought it in from the outside or from peasant groups within the main Canaanite political umbrella.

There is support for both positions if we understand that the frame of reference includes several hundred years, as well as a broad geographic area of which Canaan was merely the center. A considerable group of seminomadic pastoralists from within

Canaan or its fringes settled into underpopulated zones during the latter half of the Second Millennium. Early in the Iron Age the majority of the people occupying the rude villages were indigenous, although not necessarily part of a "peasant's revolution" against the city-state establishment.

* *
*

We have now seen that many peoples were involved in the complex process that changed the Canaanite world sufficiently to allow the emergence of Israel. No demographic statistics are available for that time, but it stands to reason that the indigenous peasants, farmers, seminomadic pastoralists, and the ubiquitous Hab/piru made up the bulk of the population from which Israel grew. Their conventional religious practices were variants of local polytheisms, probably little changed from that of previous generations.

The Exodus group, carrying the seed of the new religion, was very small in comparison with the other peoples who were competing for place within the larger whole. How, then, could the exacting ethical standards of the smallest group become the surviving characteristic of the nation of Israel? Was the dynamic monotheism of the more recent immigrants preferable to the tired practices of the regional El religions? Or were the people being drawn primarily to the manifest power and pervasive justice of the Covenant? Likely both reasons were appreciated by different groups at various times. But to understand the questions better, we must review what it was that the fugitives from Egypt brought to bear on the popular imagination of the poor and dispossessed of Canaan.

If the major spiritual hurdle from polytheism to monotheism was taken in Egypt during the Amarna period, it is probable that further ethical modifications evolved over the next few generations by those who were touched by Akhenaten's vision. Moses might have been such a believer. He formulated the Decalogue as a simple yet practical code by which all people could approach God and one another in fairness and trust. Moses subsequently recognized that the Yahveh cult of Sinai was a pragmatic vehicle for carrying this message. After accepting the strict morality of Moses, albeit tentatively, the Exodus people were flattered by the realization that others could be moved by the same principles. When they reached Canaan, having witnessed the spread of their modified Yahvism to many southern peoples along the way, their faith became the central force in Israel. The drifting, disestablished poor could perceive the grandeur of it and rushed to embrace the concept that offered them order, justice, and equality at no cost but to affirm and practice its rules.

The Exodus group proposed an all-powerful God to whom everything animate and inanimate ultimately belonged.[47] This appealed to reason and belied feudal order. The Levitical leadership, living in the midst of the people, contrasted favorably with the remote and secretive priesthood of the various Canaanite cults.[48] Those who accepted the Covenant bound themselves to behavior that renounced violence against one another, although it was permitted against others if authorized by God. Based on reciprocal self-interest and protected by Law, such transfigured relationships were almost unimaginable in the traditional society of Canaan.

Up to this point we have identified several elements of Near Eastern peoples, all with certain characteristics in common and spanning a lengthy period of time. Because of the obliquity of the data from which our information comes, it is not clear how synchronous they were. What is certain is that most elements could be found in Canaan, beginning at the Amarna Age. To some degree they all sought the reality of land tenure wherever they could prevail. A lack of political warrant in the lands where they resided must have turned their loyalties in the direction of new allies, leaving a residue of hostility toward the repressive host society. In this context there was a degree of correspondence among all the named groups. They felt themselves to be more or less permanent outsiders despite having resided in the land for a considerable period. Similarities in orientation and need allowed this confluence of peoples to become the wellspring of a twelve-tribe nation even though convergence did not necessarily result in a solid political unity. Nationality in the usual sense did not come easily or quickly to Israel. When the death of Solomon resulted in the Dual Monarchy, its proximate cause was the persistent and competitive parochialism that still existed among the tribal groupings.

The few people who experienced the Exodus under Moses provided the exponential influence on the rest of Israel. One author characterized the new nation as "an amalgam of Palestinian peasants who traced their lineage back to Amorite Mesopotamia, 'a fugitive Aramean', and the charismatic leadership of Moses in Sinai."[49]

This was Early Israel.

Notes

1. B. Mazar, "Arad and the Family of Hobab the Kenite," *Journal of Near Eastern Studies* 24(1965):297–303.
2. R. de Vaux, "The Settlement of the Israelites in Southern Palestine and the Origins of the Tribe of Judah," in *Translating and Understanding the Old Testament*, ed. H. T. Frank and W. L. Reed (Nashville: Abingdon Press, 1970), p.111.
3. Ibid., p.131ff.
4. G. W. Ahlström, "Another Moses Tradition," *Journal of Near Eastern Studies* 39(1980):65–69.
5. W. H. Stiebing, *Out of the Desert?* (Buffalo: Prometheus Books, 1989), p.151.
6. R. G. Boling, *Joshua: Anchor Bible Series* (Garden City, NY: Doubleday, 1982), p.168.
7. S. Yeivin, *The Israelite Conquest of Canaan* (Istanbul: Nederlands Historisch-Archeologisch Instituut in Het Nahige Oosten, 1971), p. 6f.
8. T. L. Thompson, *Early History of the Israelite People* (Leiden: E. J. Brill, 1992), p. 311.
9. Ahlström, op. cit., p. 65.
10. A. Alt, *Essays on Old Testament History and Religion*, transl. R. A. Wilson (Garden City, NY: Doubleday, 1967), p. 228.
11. S. Yeivin, op. cit., p. 15.
12. Ibid., p.13.
13. Ibid., p.17.

14. Ibid., p.19.
15. Ibid., pp.11–21 passim.
16. J. B. Pritchard, *Ancient Near Eastern Texts*, 3rd ed. (Princeton: Princeton Univ. Press, 1969), p. 378.
17. S. Yeivin, op. cit., p. 28.
18. C. de Wit, *The Date and Route of the Exodus* (London: Tyndale Press, 1959), p.10.
19. G. W. Ahlström, "Where Did the Israelites Live?" *Journal of Near Eastern Studies* 41(1982):133–138.
20. J. B. Pritchard, op. cit., p. 259.
21. Ibid., p. 259.
22. R. de Vaux, op. cit., p.118.
23. B. Mazar, "The Early Israelite Settlement in the Hill Country," *Bulletin of the American Schools of Oriental Research* 241(1981):75–85.
24. B. Mazar, *The Early Biblical Period* (Jerusalem: Israel Exploration Society, 1986), p. 6.
25. M. Noth, *The History of Israel* (New York: Harper and Row, 1960), p.125ff.
26. Ibid., p. 88.
27. S. Yeivin, op. cit., p.19.
28. I. Finkelstein, *The Archeology of the Israelite Settlement* (Jerusalem: Israel Exploration Society, 1988), p.18.
29. Ibid., p. 347.
30. Ibid., p. 326.
31. S. W. Baron, *A Social and Religious History of the Jews*, vol.1 (New York: Columbia Univ. Press, 1952), p.168ff.
32. A. Alt, "The Settlement of the Israelites in Palestine," in *Essays on Old Testament History and Religion*, transl. R. A. Wilson. Garden City: Doubleday, 1967, pp.173–221.
33. Ibid., p. 202.
34. M. L. Chaney, "Ancient Palestinian Peasant Movements and the Foundation of Premonarchic Israel," in *Palestine in Transition*, ed. D. N. Freedman and D. F. Graf (Sheffield: Almond Press, 1983), p. 43.
35. G. E. Mendenhall, "The Hebrew Conquest of Palestine," *Biblical Archeology*, 25(1962):66–87.
36. J. M. Halligan, "The Role of the Peasant in the Amarna Period," in *Palestine in Transition*, ed. D. M. Freedman and D. F. Graf (Sheffield: Almond Press, 1983), p.17.
37. N. K. Gottwald, *The Tribes of Yahweh* (New York: Orbis Books, 1979), p. 482f, passim.
38. Ibid., p. 484.

39. R. B. Coote and K. W. Whitelam, *The Emergence of Early Israel* (Sheffield: Almond Press, 1987), p. 48.
40. J. M. Halligan, op. cit., p. 23.
41. J. M. Halligan, op. cit., pp.15–24.
42. G. E. Mendenhall, op. cit., p. 69.
43. N. K. Gottwald, op. cit., p. 438.
44. G. E. Mendenhall, op. cit., p. 71.
45. N. K. Gottwald, "Early Israel and the Canaanite Socio-Economic System," in ed. Freedman and Graf op. cit., pp.25–37.
46. Ibid., p. 30.
47. M. L. Chaney, op. cit., p. 64.
48. Ibid., p. 67.
49. A. E. Glock, "Early Israel as the Kingdom of Yahweh," *Concordia Theological Monthly* 41(1970):587.

Glossary

ab initio. From the beginning.

acolyte. An attendant or an assistant, especially at a religious service.

adumbrate. To vaguely indicate the future; to foreshadow.

Akkad. An ancient Near Eastern land in the lower Tigris-Euphrates valley just north of Sumer. This area became the earliest known Semitic kingdom.

alluvial. A type of soil made up of silt, clay, sand, or gravel and usually deposited by rivers.

Amarna. A region on the east bank of the Nile River midway between Thebes and the delta; the site of the ancient city of Akhetaten.

Amorites (Amurru). Semites who lived in the western horn of the Fertile Crescent.

amphictyony. A loose association of peoples who recognize some common interest.

amphora. A vaselike clay container (with two handles at the cylindrical neck and a small base) used for food and liquid storage in the ancient Near East.

anachronism. A mix-up in time; an event that is not assigned to a proper date or era.

analogic. Pertaining to a similarity, or correspondence, between two otherwise dissimilar objects or concepts; a mathematical association.

anathema. Something that is odious or distasteful; a ban or curse, often accompanied by excommunication.

Anatolia. The region that coincides with Asia Minor, or modern Turkey.

animism. A belief that spirits may become disembodied from their objects and take up residence in others.

anthropomorphism. The presentation of things in human form; indicates the humanized form of a deity.

apotheosis. Elevation to a God-like status; deification.

apotropaic. The ability to ward off evil (spirits).

appellative. Relating to the naming or designation of an object or person.

Aramaic. The language of the Arameans, commonly spoken by Jews after the Exile and well into the Talmudic Age.

Arameans. Semites who lived during the latter half of the Second Millennium in the land of Aram, which is today's eastern Syria.

archetype. The original form, or model, from which all similar things are patterned.

Aryan. An early race of people living in Iran and India who spoke a language from which the Indo-European languages derive.

Asia Minor. See Anatolia.

Assyria. An ancient Semitic empire of Mesopotamia originally situated in the north-central part of the Tigris-Euphrates valley.

atavistic. The reversion to an earlier form; throwback.

Ba'al. The great god of the West Semites; also an owner, master, or husband among humans.

Babylonia. A successor Semitic empire to Akkad and Sumer in Mesopotamia of the Second Millennium.

Bedouin. A nomadic group of Semites who traverse large areas of the Arabian desert today, just as they did in biblical times. See Shasu.

brideprice. A gift of value given to the bride's family on behalf of the groom.

Bronze Age. An era in which bronze was used for tools and weapons. In the Near East it was around 3000–1200 B.C.E.

Canaan. The name given to a vaguely defined land area, mainly west of the Jordan River, and including much of present-day Israel and Lebanon.

canon. The authoratative list of books that make up Scripture.

Cappadocia. In Asia Minor a region located in the east-central part of modern Turkey.

chimera. An illusion or fantasy; an impossible hope.

Cisjordan. A geographic term for land west of the Jordan River. See Transjordan.

C.E. (Common Era). The period of time when Jewish and Christian culture influenced Western civilization; it begins arbitrarily at year 0.

concatenation. The linking together, or uniting, in a series.

conflate. To combine several elements into a single text; to bring together.

cosmogony. A speculative theory on the origin of the universe.

covenant. An agreement, or compact, to perform a function for an appropriate consideration.

cultural homogenization. The merging of esthetic standards and behavior of various groups into a single, or common, pattern.

cuneiform. Triangular or wedge-shaped marks that when combined in different patterns created a pictographic form of writing.

Decalogue. Literally ten words; more commonly the Ten Commandments.

demarche. A course of action; a diplomatic maneuver.

demography. The study of the human population with reference to its statistical aspects.

dialectic. The nature of logical argumentation; discussion and reasoning by dialogue.

dimorphic. A thing that appears in two forms.

diurnal. Related to activities occurring in a single day.

Documentary Hypothesis. An explanation of the various tradition sources in the Torah. The present-day hypothesis postulates four main sources: J (Jahwist), E (Elohist), D (Deuteronomic), P (Priestly).

droit du seigneur. A Medieval custom whereby the feudal lord can demand the first sexual right from any vassal-bride on her wedding night.

Dual Monarchy. The two separate Israelite kingdoms that formed from the disintegration of Solomon's empire: Israel in the north and Judah in the south. See Israel; Judah.

El (Elohim). The head god in the Canaanite pantheon; (plural form used extensively in the Torah to denote the God of Israel).

Elamites. A non-Semitic people who lived east of the Tigris River in what today is western Iran.

Enlightenment. A widespread eighteenth-century rationalist movement that emphasized more liberal social, political, and religious practices.

epiphany. A manifestation or perception of an essential reality, usually sudden.

eponym. The name of a person, real or legendary, after whom a tribe or place was known.

ethnocentrism. The attitude that culture/race, presumably one's own, is most important.

etymology. A branch of linguistics that deals with the origin and history of words. See philology.

eucharistic. Giving thanks, usually by a celebratory act.

evanescent. Something that vanishes like vapor; transient.

Execration Texts. Documents from ancient Egypt in which curses and imprecations directed at enemies were thought to be effective.

exegesis. The explanation and critical interpretation of a text. See hermeneutics.

Exile. The period of fifty years (circa 586–538) when a significant portion of the Judean population was forcibly removed to Babylonia.

ex nihilo. Out of nothing.

exculpatory. Absolving, acquitting, exonerating.

factitious. An artificial standard, or convention, imposed by human will rather than by natural means.

fecundity. The ability to be productive, especially in offspring but also in ideas and agriculture.

fratriarchy. An early family, or clan, order whereby the oldest consanguinous male was the leader of the group.

gentilic. The name for a tribe, or a group of people descended from a common ancestor.

gestation. The process of conceiving; also carrying or developing an idea in the mind.

gloss. An explanation of an obscure text; an annotation.

habeas corpus. In common law a concept that requires a body to be brought to court as proof before trial; also, the certainty of evidence.

Hab/piru. A class of people, widespread throughout the ancient Near East, who were politically disenfranchised and rootless; outcasts. There is a strong probability that they were related to the early Hebrews.

haggadah. The nonlegal, legendary, and narrative part of rabbinic literature.

Hammurabi. The great law giver of Babylonia who lived in the first part of the Second Millennium.

henotheism. The belief in, and worship of, one god without denial of the existence of other gods.

hermeneutics. The process of interpretation; a branch of theology that deals with biblical exegesis. See exegesis.

hieroglyphics. In ancient Egypt a system of sacred writing that used pictorial characters as script.

historiography. The writing of history from available material and synthesizing it into a credible narrative.

Hittites. A non-Semitic people who created a powerful empire in Asia Minor and northern Syria in the Second Millennium.

Hurrians. A non-Semitic people, probably from the shores of the Caspian Sea, who conquered a portion of northern Mesopotamia and spread westward into Syria. See Mitanni.

Hyksos. A Semitic people, probably with a significant Hurrian infusion, who are best known for their control of the Nile delta during the Seventeenth Century.

inchoate. Imperfectly conceived or formed; rudimentary.

indentured. A person bound by contract to serve another person for a period of time.

Indo-European. A language root that gave rise to the speech of Europe, the Indian subcontinent, and other parts of Asia.

inductive. A form of logic whereby reasoning from particulars leads to a general conclusion.

inerrancy. Free of error; the concept of infallibility with regard to the Old and New Testaments, especially among fundamentalists.

Iron Age. The period of circa 1200–300, when tools and weapons were made of iron.

Israel. The northern segment of the Dual Kingdom, made up of the ten northern tribes that disappeared after the Assyrian conquest in 722 B.C.E. In a broader sense it is the institution from which Jews and Judaism descended.

Judah. The southern segment of the Dual Kingdom, consisting of the tribes of Judah and Benjamin. It was broken up with the Babylonian Exile in 586 B.C.E.

Kassites. A non-Semitic people of the northern Zagros mountains region who destroyed the First Babylonian Empire and ruled there around the middle of the Second Millennium.

Kenite Hypothesis. A theory that suggests that the Kenites (Midianites) were the original worshippers of Yahveh, contributing that name for God to Moses and his followers.

legerdemain. Skillful; adroit; sleight of hand.

levirate. Pertains to the old Israelite custom whereby a brother must marry his deceased brother's widow.

lingua franca. A common language used by diverse peoples to carry on commerce or diplomacy.

lists (King-, Omen-, etc.). Records kept in ancient societies as a form of primitive history.

Mari. An ancient Babylonian city on the Euphrates River where a cache of clay tablets was discovered. These documents covered events in the first half of the Eighteenth Century.

Masoretic Text. The definitive Hebrew text of the Scriptures, wherein the vowels were fixed, dating to around the ninth century C.E.

matrilinearity. The process of tracing descent through the maternal line.

Mesopotamia. The region bound generally by the Tigris and Euphrates Rivers.

metaphysics. The branch of philosophy that concerns the nature of reality and its relation to what is beyond the perception of the senses.

midrash. An exposition of Scriptural texts in a mainly discursive manner.

millennium. A period of 1000 years.

Mitanni. A kingdom with a large Hurrian population in the northern part of Mesopotamia during the middle centuries of the Second Millennium.

mnemonic. A code used for improving memory.

monotheism. The belief in a single God to the exclusion of all others.

Near East. A region of southwest Asia, with Iran in the east, Turkey in the north, Arabia in the south, and Egypt in the west. It has also been referred to as the Middle East, but its definition is both vague and variable.

New Testament. The second part of the Christian Scripture (following the Old Testament) and dealing with the life of Jesus and the Apostles.

nexus. A connection, or linkage; a series tied together.

nomadism. A condition whereby people have no fixed residence, wandering from place to place.

numinous. Something that shows holiness or an exaggerated spirituality; supernatural.

Nuzi. A city to the northeast of Mesopotamia that was populated by Hurrians in the early Second Millennium.

oblation. A religious offering; a sacrifice or gift.

Old Testament. The Hebrew Scripture, made up of Torah, Prophets, and Writings. The last section contains Psalms, Proverbs, Job, The Song of Songs, Ruth, Lamentations, Ecclesiastes, Esther, Daniel, Ezra, Nehemiah, and 1 and 2 Chronicles.

ontogeny. The course of development of an individual organism. See phylogeny.

oracle. A shrine, or occasionally a person, containing a manifestation of divinity and that can reveal occult knowledge.

palliation. The reduction, or moderation, of an extreme position.

pantheon. All the gods claimed by a group.

papyrus. A tall aquatic plant found along river banks in the Near East, especially in Egypt, from which paper was made in ancient times.

paradigm. A clear or typical example of a process.

parricide. The murder of a close relative.

parturient. About to give birth; at the point of producing something.

pathognomonic. Distinctively characteristic of a condition.

Pentateuch. Greek for the first five books of the Old Testament. See Torah.

penumbral. Shadowy, unclear.

pericope. A selection from a text; commonly used for Scriptural verses.

phagocytize. To engulf foreign or extraneous material.

Philistines. People who occupied much of the southern coast of Canaan from the end of the Second Millennium and were persistent antagonists of the Israelites. Thought to have been a segment of the Sea Peoples, Philistines were skilled in the uses of iron.

philology. The study of language and literary activity. See etymology.

Phoenicians. A Semitic people, Amorites, who occupied the coast of what is now Lebanon for most of the Second Millennium and later. Intrepid sailors, they colonized much of the Mediterranean shore.

phylogeny. The evolution of a species or a related group rather than of an individual; also, the history of the development of something. See ontogeny.

pictography. The art of recording or expressing ideas by picture symbols; diagrammatic representation.

polemic. Controversy or disputation; argument over a strongly held issue.

polytheism. The belief in multiple gods.

preternatural. Existing outside of natural experience; occult, mysterious, transcendental.

primogenitor. The first, or earliest, ancestor.

primordium. The elementary matter out of which something arises; earliest, or rudimentary, beginning material.

primus inter pares. First among equals.

prolegomenon. A preliminary observation or an introductory discourse.

proselyte. A person who has changed from one sect or religion to another; a convert.

Proto-. A prefix indicating an early, or original, stage in development; beginning, first formed.

Ptolemaic Egypt. The period of Egyptian history (323–30 B.C.E.) when the country passed into the hands of Ptolemy I (Soter) and his successors, after the death of Alexander the Great.

radix. A primary source; a root, or base, as in a system of numbers.

Ras Shamra. See Ugarit.

recidivism. The repeated or habitual tendency to relapse to an earlier behavior, especially in crime.

recondite. Hidden, concealed; not readily understood.

redaction. The process of selecting or adapting textual material; also, to revise or edit.

sacerdotal. Refers to priests or priesthood

SA.GAZ. Another name that equates with Hab/piru.

sarcophagus. A coffin, commonly of stone.

Scripture(s). The sacred writings of the Old and New Testaments; the Bible.

Sea People. Predatory raiders and settlers who attacked the shores of the Near East in the last two to three centuries of the Second Millennium. They are thought to have come from the islands and western coastal regions of the Mediterranean Sea.

sedenterization. The process of becoming firmly attached to the land; settling.

seminomadism. The condition of people who move about at certain seasons but remain at one place during a part of the year; seasonal migrants. See transhumant.

Semitic. Essentially a linguistic, rather than an ethnic, designation. The language began and was rooted in the ancient Near East.

Septuagint. The Greek version of the Hebrew Bible translated in Alexandria in the Third Century.

shaman. A person using magic to divine or control events.

Shasu. The name used by the Egyptians for groups of nomadic Semites.

status quo ante. The situation that existed previously.

stele. An upright block or pillar, usually with a text inscribed on it.

steppe. A vast treeless plain, frequently in an arid zone.

Sumerians. The first known people in southern Mesopotamia. Their origin is uncertain, but they were not Semites. Ultimately they were overrun and absorbed by the more northerly Akkadians/ Babylonians.

suzerain. A feudal overlord; a ruler of dependencies.

symbiosis. A relationship whereby two different units exist together in mutual benefit.

syncretism. A combination, or fusion, of different elements; a reconciliation of divergent principles or beliefs.

syncytium. A single mass with many nuclear centers.

Tannaim. Sages and teachers who lived in Palestine from the beginning of the Common Era to the third century. They were responsible for the compilation of the Mishna (the first part of the Talmud).

tectonic. Relating to the structure of the earth's crust.

tell. In the Near East an ancient mound that usually contains remnants of successive layers of habitation.

terminus a quo. A point of origin; the onset of a period of time.

terminus ad quem. The end point in a given period of time.

thaumaturgy. The performance of wonders or miracles; magic.

theogony. The account of the origin of a deity.

theophany. The manifestation of God to man; a wondrous event.

theosophy. The knowledge and understanding of God and divine matters, often based on mystical references.

titulary. A listing of titles and honors.

Torah. The first five Hebrew books of the Old Testament: Genesis, Exodus, Leviticus, Numbers, and Deuteronomy. See Pentateuch.

transhumant. The seasonal movement of people and livestock for food, often between highlands and lowlands. See seminomadism.

Transjordan. The name for the land east of the Jordan River. See Cisjordan.

Ugarit (Ras Shamra). A very ancient city on the coast of Syria that was populated by Amoritic Semites during the Second Millennium.

Urartu. A non-Semitic people of eastern Asia Minor, near Lake Van, who were most prominent in the centuries around 1000 B.C.E. They are thought to be the antecedents of today's Armenians.

vector. A direction or force, often related to or resulting from other forces.

xenophobia. The fear and hatred of anything or anyone foreign.

Chronology of the Ancient Near East

Many dates within the period covered by this book cannot be calculated precisely and therefore must remain approximate. The following chronology has relevance only for placing specific persons and events along a common historical continuum.

DATE (B.C.E.)	ASIA	EGYPT	CANAAN/ISRAEL
4000	Sumerians in place		
3000		Eygptian empire founded	
3000–2200	Early Bronze Age		
2600–2200		Old Kingdom/ IV–VI Dynasty	
2500–2200	Akkadians in power		
2300	Sargon I, Akkadian king		
2200–1500	Middle Bronze Age		
2200–1700	Babylonian empire replaces Akkadians		
2200–2000		First Intermediate Period/ IX–XI Dynasty	
2000–1650		Middle Kingdom/ XI–XIII Dynasty	
1900–1200	Hittites in Asia Minor and the Near East		
1900			Canaanites in place
1700–1200	Kassites overcome and dominate Babylonians.		
1700–620	Assyrian empire		

DATE (B.C.E.)	ASIA	EGYPT	CANAAN/ISRAEL
1650–1550		Second Intermediate Period/Hyksos Kamose (1555–1550)	
1550	Mitanni/Hurrians in place		
1550–1000		New Kingdom/ XVIII–XX Dynasty	
		Ahmose (1550–1525)	
		Amenhotep I (1525–1500)	
		Thutmose I (1500–1490)	
		Thutmose II (1490–1480)	
		Thutmose III (1480–1425)	
		Hatshepsut (1475–1460)	
		Amenhotep II (1425–1400)	
		Thutmose IV (1400–1390)	
		Amenhotep III (1390–1350)	
	THE	Amenhotep IV/ Akhenaten (1350–1335)	
	AMARNA	Smenkhkare (1335–1333)	
		Tutankhamen (1333–1323)	
	AGE	Aye (1323–1320)	
		Horemhab (1320–1305) Ramesses I (1305)	
		Seti I (1305–1290)	
		Ramesses II (1290–1225)	
		Merneptah (1225–1215)	
1500–1200	Late Bronze Age		
1400			Hab/piru in Canaan
1250–1200		Exodus period (probable)	
1220		Merneptah's "Israel" stele	
1200–1000			The period of Judges

DATE (B.C.E.)	ASIA	EGYPT	CANAAN/ISRAEL
1200–300	Early Iron Age		
1010–930			The Israelite monarchy
			King Saul (1010-1000)
			King David (1000-970)
			King Solomon (970-930)
965			Solomon builds the Temple
930–722			The Dual Monarchy (Israel and Judah)
722			Assyria conquers Israel. The ten tribes of Israel are "lost."
620	Babylonia conquers Assyria.		
587–586			Babylonia conquers Judah, the Temple is destroyed, and the Exile begins.
539–538	Persia conquers Babylonia.		Persia releases the Exiles, but not all return home. The Diaspora has begun.

Bibliography

Ackerman, J. S. "The Literary Context of the Moses Birth Story (Exodus 1–2)." In *Literary Interpretations of Biblical Narratives*, edited by K. R. Gros Louis, J. S. Ackerman, and T. S. Warshaw. Nashville: Abingdon Press, 1974.

Aharoni, Y. *The Land of the Bible*. Philadelphia: Westminster Press, 1979.

Ahlström, G. W. "Another Moses Tradition." *Journal of Near Eastern Studies* 39 (1980), pp. 65–69.

_____. "Where Did the Israelites Live?" *Journal of Near Eastern Studies* 41 (1982), pp. 133–138.

Albright, W. F. "Abram the Hebrew: A New Archeological Interpretation." *Bulletin of the American Schools of Oriental Research* 163 (1963), pp. 36–54.

_____. "Moses in Historical and Theological Perspective." In *Magnalia Dei: the mighty acts of God*, edited by F. M. Cross, W. E. Lemke, and P. D. Miller, pp. 120–131. Garden City, NY: Doubleday, 1976.

Aldred, C. "Egypt: The Amarna Period and the End of the Eighteenth Dynasty." *Cambridge Ancient History Series*, vol. 2, part 2. Cambridge: Cambridge Univ. Press, 1970, pp. 49–97.

_____. *Akhenaten*. London: Thames and Hudson, 1988.

Alt, A. *Essays on Old Testament History and Religion*. Translated by R. A. Wilson. Garden City, NY: Doubleday, 1967.

Anderson, G. W. *The History and Religion of Israel*. London: Oxford Univ. Press, 1966.

Baikie, J. *The Amarna Age*. New York: Macmillan, 1926.

Baines, J., and J. Malek. *Atlas of Ancient Egypt*. Oxford: Equinox, 1980.

Baly, D. *The Geography of the Bible*. New York: Harper and Row, 1974.

Baron, S.W. *A Social and Religious History of the Jews*. New York: Columbia Univ. Press, 1952.

Beit-Arieh, I. "Canaanites and Egyptians at Serabit." In *Egypt, Israel, Sinai*, edited by A. F. Rainey, pp. 57–67. Tel Aviv: Tel Aviv University, 1987.

Berger, M. *Moses and His Neighbors*. New York: Philosophical Library, 1965.

Bietak, M. "Canaanites in the Eastern Delta." In *Egypt, Israel, Sinai*, edited by A. F. Rainey, pp. 41–56. Tel Aviv: Tel Aviv University, 1987.

_____. "Comments on the 'Exodus.'" In *Egypt, Israel, Sinai*, edited by A. F. Rainey, pp. 163–171. Tel Aviv: Tel Aviv University, 1987.

Bimson, J. J. *Redating the Exodus and Conquest*. Sheffield: Almond Press, 1981.

Boling, R. G. *Joshua: Anchor Bible Series*. Garden City: Doubleday, 1982.

Bonnel, R. G. "The Ethics of El-Amarna." In *Studies in Egyptology*, edited by S. Israelit-Groll, pp. 71–97. Jerusalem: Magnes Press, 1990.

Bowden, G. "Painted Pottery of Tayma and Problems of Cultural Chronology in Northwest Arabia." In *Midian, Moab and Edom*, edited by J. F. Sawyer and D. J. Clines, pp. 37–52. Sheffield: JSOT, 1983.

Bradshaw, M. A., A. J Abbott, and A. P. Gelsthorpe. *The Earth's Changing Surface*. London: Hodder and Stoughton, 1978.

Breasted, J. H. *Ancient Times: A History of the Early World*. Boston: Ginn, 1916.

Bright, J. *Early Israel in Recent History Writing*. London: SCM Press, 1956.

_____. *A History of Israel*. 2d ed. Philadelphia: Westminster Press, 1972.

Buber, M. *Moses*. London: East and West Library, 1946.

Budge, E. A. W. *Babylonian Life and History*. New York: Cooper Square Publishers, 1975.

Butzer, K. W. *Early Hydraulic Civilization in Egypt*. Chicago: Univ. of Chicago Press, 1976.

Carpenter, J. E. *The Composition of the Hexateuch*. New York: Longmans, Green, 1902.

Carroll, R. P. "Rebellion and Dissent in Ancient Israelite Society." *Zeitschrift für die Alttestamentliche Wissenschaft* 84 (1977), pp. 176–204.

Cassuto, U. *A Commentary on the Book of Exodus*. Jerusalem: Magnes Press, 1967.

Chaney, M. L. "Ancient Palestinian Peasant Movements and the Formation of Premonarchic Israel." In *Palestine in Transition*, edited by D. N. Freedman and D. F. Graf pp. 39–90. Sheffield: Almond Press, 1983.

Childs, B. S. "The Birth of Moses." *Journal of Biblical Literature* 84 (1965), pp. 109–122.

Coats, G. W. *Moses, Heroic Man of God*. Sheffield: JSOT Press, 1988.

_____. "Despoiling the Egyptians." *Vetus Testamentum* 18 (1968), pp. 450–457.

_____. "Moses in Midian." *Journal of Biblical Literature* 92 (1973), pp. 3–10.

Cody, A. *A History of the Old Testament Priesthood*. Rome: Pontifical Biblical Institute, 1969.

Cody, E. "Jethro Accepts a Covenant with the Israelites." *Biblica* 49 (1968), pp. 153–166.

Coffman, J. B. *Commentary on Exodus*. Abilene, TX: A.C.U. Press, 1985.

Conroy, C. "Hebrew Epic: Historical Notes and Critical Reflections." *Biblica* 61 (1980), pp. 1–30.

Copisarow, H. "The Ancient Egyptian, Greek and Hebrew Concept of the Red Sea." *Vetus Testamentum* 12 (1962), pp. 1–13.

Cross, F. M. *Canaanite Myth and Hebrew Epic*. Cambridge: Harvard Univ. Press, 1973.

Cully, R. C. "An Approach to the Problem of Oral Tradition." *Vetus Testamentun* 13 (1963), pp. 113–125.

Daiches, D. "The Quest for the Historical Moses." Robert Waley Cohen Memorial Lecture, 1974.

_____. *Moses, Man in the Wilderness.* London: Weidenfeld and Nicolson, 1975.

Daube, D. *The Exodus Pattern in the Bible.* Westport, CT: Greenwood Press, 1963.

David, R. *Cult of the Sun.* London: J. M. Dent, 1980.

Davies, G. I. *The Way of the Wilderness.* Cambridge: Cambridge Univ. Press, 1979.

_____. "The Wilderness Itineraries." *Tyndale Bulletin* 25 (1974), pp. 46–82.

de Vaux, R. "The Settlement of the Israelites in Southern Palestine and the Origins of the Tribe of Judah." In *Translating and Understanding the Old Testament*, edited by H. T. Frank and W. L. Reed, pp. 108–134. Nashville: Abingdon Press, 1970.

_____. *The Early History of Israel.* Philadelphia: Westminster Press, 1978.

de Wit, C. *The Date and Route of the Exodus.* London: Tyndale Press, 1959.

Dothan, T. "The Impact of Egypt on Canaan During the 18th and 19th Dynasties in the Light of the Excavations at Deir el-Balah." In *Egypt, Israel, Sinai*, edited by A. F. Rainey, pp. 121–135. Tel Aviv: Tel Aviv University, 1987.

Draffkorn, A. E. "Illani/Elohim." *Journal of Biblical Literature* 76 (1957), pp. 216–224.

Dumbrell, W. J. "Midian—A Land or a League?" *Vetus Testamentum* 25 (1975), pp. 323–337.

Dundes, A. "The Hero Pattern and the Life of Jesus." In *In Quest of the Hero*, pp. 179–223. Princeton: Princeton Univ. Press, 1990.

Edwards, A. J. and S. M. Head *Red Sea: Key Environments.* New York: Pergamon Press, 1987.

Emerton, J. A. "Priests and Levites in Deuteronomy." *Vetus Testamentum* 12 (1962), pp. 129–138.

Encyclopedia Brittannica, Micropaedia, vol. 9, 15th ed (1975), p. 35.

Feldman, L. H. *Jew and Gentile in the Ancient World: Attitudes and Interactions from Alexandria to Justinian.* Princeton, NJ: Princeton Univ. Press, 1993.

Fensham, F. C. "Did a Treaty Between the Israelites and the Kenites Exist?" *Bulletin of the American Schools of Oriental Research* 175 (1964), pp. 51–54.

Finkelstein, I. *The Archeology of the Israelite Settlement.* Jerusalem: Israel Exploration Society, 1988.

Foulke-ffeinberg, F. X. *Moses and His Masters.* Edinburg: Cui Bono Books, 1990.

Freud, S. *Moses and Monotheism.* New York: Alfred A. Knopf, 1939.

Galil, G. "The Sons of Judah and the Sons of Aaron in Biblical Historiography." *Vetus Testamentum* 35 (1985), pp. 488–495.

Gardiner, A. H. "The Ancient Military Road Between Egypt and Palestine." *Journal of Egyptian Archeology* 6 (1920), pp. 99–116.

Garfuncle, Z. "Geography." In *Sinai*, edited by B. Rothenberg, pp. 41–60. New York: J. J. Binns, 1979.

Giles, F. J. *Ikhnaton*. Rutherford, NJ: Farleigh Dickinson Press, 1970.

Ginzberg, L. *The Legends of the Jews*, vols. 2 and 3. Philadelphia: Jewish Publication Society, 1911.

Glock, A. E. "Early Israel as the Kingdom of Yahweh." *Concordia Theological Monthly* 41 (1970), pp. 558–605.

Glueck, N. *The Other Side of the Jordan*. Cambridge: American Schools of Oriental Research, 1970.

Goedicke, H. "The End of the Hyksos in Egypt." In *Egyptological Studies in Honor of Richard A. Parker*, edited by L. H. Lesko, pp. 37–48. Providence: Brown Univ. Press, 1986.

Gordon, C. H. *Before the Bible*. New York: Harper and Row, 1962.

Gottwald, N. K. *The Tribes of Yahweh*. New York: Orbis Books, 1979.

_____. "Domain Assumptions and Societal Models in the Study of Pre-Monarchic Israel." *Supplement to Vetus Testamentum* 28 (1974), pp.89–100.

_____. "Early Israel and the Canaanite Socio-Economic System." In *Palestine in Transition*, edited by D. N. Freedman and D. F. Graf, pp. 25–37. Sheffield: Almond Press, 1983.

_____. *The Hebrew Bible—A Socio-Literary Introduction*. Philadelphia: Fortress Press, 1985.

Gray, J. *The Canaanites*. London: Thames and Hudson, 1961.

Gray, M. P. "The Habiru-Hebrew Problem in the Light of the Source Material Available at Present." *Hebrew Union College Annual* 29 (1958), pp. 135–202.

Greenberg, M. "A New Approach to the History of the Israelite Priesthood." *Journal of the American Oriental Society* 70 (1950), pp. 41–47.

_____. *The Hab/piru*. New Haven: American Oriental Society, 1955.

_____. "Response to Roland de Vaux's 'Method in the Study of Early Hebrew History'." In *The Bible in Modern Scholarship*, edited by J. P. Hyatt, pp. 37–43. Nashville: Abingdon Press, 1965.

Haldar, H. *Who Were the Amorites?* Leiden: E. J. Brill, 1971.

Hall, H. R. "Yuia the Syrian." *Proceedings of the Society of Biblical Archeology* 35 (1913), pp. 63–65.

Halligan, J. M. "The Role of the Peasant in the Amarna Period." In *Palestine in Transition*, edited by D. N. Freedman and D. F. Graf, pp. 15–24. Sheffield: Almond Press, 1983.

Halpern, B. *The Emergence of Israel in Canaan.* Chico, CA: Scholar's Press, 1983.

Haran, M. "Priests and Priesthood." *Encyclopedia Judaica,* vol. 13, pp. 1070–1086. Jerusalem: Macmillan, 1971.

_____. "Studies in the Account of the Levitical Cities, I." *Journal of Biblical Literature* 80 (1961), pp.45–54.

_____. *Temples and Temple-Service in Ancient Israel.* Oxford: Clarendon Press, 1978.

Har-el, M. *The Sinai Journeys.* San Diego: Richfield, 1983.

Hari, R. *New Kingdom Amarna Period.* Leiden: E. J. Brill, 1985.

Harper's Bible Dictionary. Edited by P. J. Achtemaier. San Francisco: Harper and Row, 1985.

Hay, L. S. "What Really Happened at the Sea of Reeds?" *Journal of Biblical Literature* 83 (1964), pp. 397–403.

Heidel, A. *The Gilgamesh Epic and Old Testament Parallels.* 2d ed. Chicago: Univ. of Chicago Press, 1949.

_____. *The Babylonian Genesis.* 2d ed. Chicago: Univ. of Chicago Press, 1951.

Herrmann, S. *Israel in Egypt.* Naperville, IL: Allenson, 1970.

Hertz, J. H. *The Pentateuch and Haftorahs.* 2d ed. London: Soncino Press, 1969.

Hollis, F. J. "The Sun Cult and the Temple at Jerusalem." In *Myth and Ritual,* edited by S. H. Hooke, pp. 87–110. London: Oxford Univ. Press, 1933.

Holy Bible, Revised Standard Version. New York: Thomas Nelson, 1952.

Hort, G. "The Plagues of Egypt." *Zeitschrift für Alttestamentliche Wissenschaft* 70 (1958), pp. 48–59.

Huizinga, J. "A Definition of the Concept of History." In *Philosophy and History: Essays Presented to Ernst Cassirer,* edited by R. Klibansky and H. Paton, pp. 1–10. New York: Harper Torchbooks, 1963.

Hunt, I. *The World of the Patriarchs.* Englewood Cliffs, NJ: Prentice-Hall, 1967.

James, E. O. *The Nature and Function of Priesthood.* London: Thames and Hudson, 1955.

Josephus, F. *Jewish Antiquities.* Translated by H. St.J. Thackeray. Cambridge: Harvard Univ. Press, 1978.

Kalimi, I. "Three Assumptions About the Kenites." *Zeitschrift für Alttestamentliche Wissenschaft* 100 (1988), pp. 386–393.

Kalisch, M. *A Historical and Critical Commentary on the Old Testament—Exodus.* London: Longman, 1855.

Kase, N. G., A. B. Weingold, and D. M. Gershenson. *Principles and Practice of Clinical Gynecology.* 2d ed. New York: Churchill Livingstone, 1990.

Kaufmann, Y. *A History of the Israelite Religion.* Translated and abridged by M. Greenberg. Chicago: Univ. of Chicago Press, 1960.

_____. *The Biblical Account of the Conquest of Canaan.* Jerusalem: Magnes Press, 1985.

Kempinski, A. "Some Observations on the Hyksos (XVth) Dynasty and Its Canaanite Origins." In *Pharaonic Egypt*, edited by S. Israelit-Groll, pp.129–137. Jerusalem: Magnes Press, 1984.

Kenyon, K. M. *Digging up Jericho.* London: Ernest Benn, 1957.

Kinross, P. B. *Between Two Seas: The Creation of the Suez Canal.* London: John Murray, 1968.

Klopfenstein, M. A. "Exodus, Desert, Mountain of God." In *Sinai*, edited by B. Rothenberg, pp. 17–40. New York: J. J. Binns, 1979.

Knauf, E. A. "Midianites and Ishmaelites." In *Midian, Moab and Edom*, edited by J. F. Sawyer and D. J. Clines, pp. 147–162. Sheffield: JSOT, 1983.

Kramer, S. N. *From the Tablets of Sumer.* Indian Hills, CO: Falcon's Wing Press, 1956.

Lewis, B. *Semites and Anti-Semites.* New York: Norton, 1986.

Lewy, J. "Habiru and Hebrews." *Hebrew Union College Annual* 14 (1939), pp. 587–623.

_____. "A New Parallel Between Habiru and Hebrews." *Hebrew Union College Annual* 15 (1940), pp. 47–58.

Littauer, M. A. and J. H. Crouwel. *Chariots and Related Equipment from the Tomb of Tutankhamun.* Oxford: Griffith Institute, 1985.

Malamat, A. "Israelite Conduct of War in the Conquest of Canaan." In *Symposia Celebrating the 75th Anniversary of the Founding of A.S.O.R. (1900–1975)*, edited by F. M. Cross, pp.35–55. Cambridge: American Society of Oriental Research, 1979.

Matthews, V. H. *Pastoral Nomadism in the Mari Kingdom.* Cambridge: American Schools of Oriental Research, 1978.

Mazar, B. "The Cities of the Priests and the Levites." *Supplement to Vetus Testamentum*, Congress Volume, Oxford, 1959, pp. 193–205. Leiden: E. J. Brill.

_____. "Arad and the Family of Hobab the Kenite." *Journal of Near Eastern Studies* 24 (1965), pp. 297–303.

_____. "The Historical Background of the Book of Genesis." *Journal of Near Eastern Studies* 28 (1969), pp. 73–83.

_____. "The Early Israelite Settlement in the Hill Country." *Bulletin of the American Schools of Oriental Research*, vol.241 (1981), pp. 75-85.

_____. *The Early Biblical Period.* Jerusalem: Israel Exploration Society, 1986.

McCarthy, D. J. "Plagues and Sea of Reeds: Exodus 5–14." *Journal of Biblical Literature* 85 (1966), pp. 137–158.

Mendenhall, G. E. "Covenant Forms in Israelite Tradition." *Biblical Archeologist* 17 (1954), pp. 50–76.

_____. "Response to Roland de Vaux's 'Method in the Study of Early Hebrew History'." In *The Bible in Modern Scholarship*, edited by J. P. Hyatt, pp. 30–36. Nashville: Abingdon Press, 1965.

_____. "The Hebrew Conquest of Palestine." *Biblical Archeology* 25 (1962), pp. 66–87.

Meyer, E. *Die Israeliten und Ihre Nachbarstämme*. Halle: Verlag von Max Niemeyer, 1906.

Milgrom, J. *Studies in Levitical Terminology, I.* Berkeley: Univ. of California Press, 1970.

Miller, J. M. *The Old Testament and the Historian*. Philadelphia: Fortress Press, 1976.

Midrash Rabbah, vol. 6. Edited by H. Freedman and M. Simon, London: Soncino Press, 1983.

Morgan, R., with J. Barton. *Biblical Interpretation*. New York: Oxford Univ. Press, 1988.

Morgenstern, J. *The Fire Upon the Altar.* Chicago: Quadrangle Books, 1963.

Moscati, S. *Ancient Semitic Civilizations*. London: Elek Books, 1957.

Murnane, W. J. *Ancient Egyptian Coregencies*. Chicago: The Oriental Institute, 1977.

Naville, E. *The Route of the Exodus*. The Victoria Institute, 1891.

Nielsen, E. *Shechem*. Copenhagen: G.E.C.Gad, 1959.

_____. "The Levites in Ancient Israel." *Annals of the Swedish Theological Institute* 3 (1964), pp. 16–27.

The New English Bible. New York: Oxford Univ. Press, 1976.

Noth, M. *The History of Israel*. New York: Harper and Row, 1960.

Oates, J. *Babylon*. London: Thomas and Hudson, 1986.

O'Doherty, E. "The Conjectures of Jean Astruc, 1753." *Catholic Biblical Quarterly* 15 (1953), pp. 300–304.

Oren, E. D. "The Ways of Horus in North Sinai." In *Egypt, Israel, Sinai*, edited by A. F. Rainey, pp. 69–119. Tel Aviv: Tel Aviv University, 1987.

Osman, A. *Stranger in the Valley of the Kings*. London: Souvenir Press, 1987.

Payne, E. J. "The Midianite Arc in Joshua and Judges." In *Midian, Moab and Edom*, edited by J. F. Sawyer and J. Clines, pp. 163–172. Sheffield: JSOT Press, 1983.

Perepelkin, G. *The Secret of the Gold Coffin*. Moscow: Nauka, 1978.

Pfeiffer, R. H. and W. G. Pollard. *The Hebrew Iliad*. New York: Harper, 1957.

Pixley, G. V. *On Exodus*. Maryknoll, NY: Orbis Books, 1987.

Pond, S. and G. L. Pickard. *Introductory Dynamic Oceanography*. New York: Pergamon Press, 1978.

Posener, G. "Syria and Palestine." In *The Cambridge Ancient History*, vol. 1, part 2. 3rd ed. Cambridge: University Press, 1971, pp. 532–559.

Pritchard, J. B. *Ancient Near Eastern Texts*. 3rd ed. Princeton: Princeton Univ. Press, 1969.

Raglan, F. R. "The Hero: A Study in Tradition, Myth, and Drama." In *In Quest of the Hero*, pp. 89–175. Princeton: Princeton Univ. Press, 1990.

_____. *The Hero: A Study in Tradition, Myth, and Drama*. London: Methuen, 1936.

_____. *The Hero: A Study in Tradition, Myth, and Drama*. New York: Vintage Books, 1956, p. 173.

Rainey, A. F. "Review of 'Redating the Exodus and Conquest' by J. J. Bimson." *Israel Exploration Journal* 30 (1980), pp. 249–251.

Rank, O. *The Myth of the Birth of the Hero*. New York: Journal of Nervous and Mental Disease Publishing Co., 1914.

Redford, D. B. The Literary Motif of the Exposed Child." *Numen* 14 (1967), pp. 209–228.

_____. "The Hyksos Invasion in History and Tradition." *Orientalia* 39, fascicle 1 (1970), pp. 1–51.

_____. *A Study of the Biblical Story of Joseph*. Leiden: E. J. Brill, 1970.

_____. *Akhenaten, the Heretic King*. Princeton: Princeton Univ. Press, 1984.

_____. "An Egyptological Perspective on the Exodus." In *Egypt, Israel, Sinai*. edited by A. F. Rainey, pp. 137–161. Tel Aviv: Tel Aviv University, 1987.

Reik, T. *Listening with the Third Ear*. New York: Farrar, Straus, 1954.

Robinson, T. H. *A History of Israel*, vol. I. Oxford: Clarendon Press, 1932.

Rosmarin, T. W. *The Hebrew Moses: An Answer to Sigmund Freud*. New York: Jewish Book Club, 1939.

Rothenberg, B. *Timna*. London: Thames and Hudson, 1972.

Rowley, H. H. "Early Levite History and the Question of the Exodus." *Journal of Near Eastern Studies* 3 (1944), pp. 73–78.

_____. *From Joseph to Joshua*. London: Oxford Univ. Press, 1950.

_____. *From Moses to Qumran*. New York: Association Press, 1963.

Rowton, M. B. "The Topological Factor in the Hapiru Problem." *Assyriological Studies* 16 (1965), pp.375–387.

_____. "Dimorphic Structure and the Problem of the Apiru-Ibrim." *Journal of Near Eastern Studies* 35 (1976), pp. 13–20.

Saggs, H. W. F. *The Might That Was Assyria*. London: Sidgwick and Jackson, 1984.

Sarna, N. M. *Exploring Exodus*. New York: Schocken, 1986.

_____. *Exodus*. Philadelphia: Jewish Publication Society, 1991.

Säve-Söderbergh, T. "The Hyksos Rule in Egypt." *Journal of Egyptian Archeology* 37 (1951), pp. 53–71.

Schofield, J. N. *The Religious Background of the Bible*. London: Thomas Nelson, 1944.

Sellin, E. "Hosea und das Martyrium des Mose." *Zeitschrift für die Alttesta-mentliche Wissenschaft* 46 (1928), pp. 26–33.

Shils, E. "Tradition." *Comparative Studies in Society and History*, New York: Cambridge Univ. Press, vol. 13 (1971), pp. 122–159.

Silver, A. H. *Moses and the Original Torah*. New York: Macmillan, 1961.

Silver, D. J. *Images of Moses*. New York: Basic Books, 1982.

Snaith, N. H. "The Sea of Reeds: The Red Sea." *Vetus Testamentum* 15 (1965), pp. 395–398.

Speiser, E. A. "I Know Not the Day of My Death." *Journal of Biblical Litera-ture* 74 (1955), pp. 252–256.

_____. "The Biblical Idea of History in Its Common Near Eastern Setting." *Israel Exploration Journal* 7(1957), pp. 201–216.

_____. *Oriental and Biblical Studies*. Philadelphia: Univ. of Pennsylvania Press, 1967.

_____. *Genesis*. Garden City, NY: Doubleday, 1986.

Stiebing, W. H. *Out of the Desert?* Buffalo: Prometheus Books, 1989.

_____. "The Amarna Period." In *Palestine in Transition*, edited by D. N. Freedman and D. F. Graf, pp. 1–14. Sheffield: Almond Press, 1983.

Taylor, J. G. *Yahweh and the Sun*. Sheffield: Sheffield Academic Press, 1993.

Tcherikover, V. *Hellenistic Civilization and the Jews*. Philadelphia: Jewish Pub-lication Society, 1959.

Thompson, T. L. *The Historicity of the Patriarchal Narratives*. New York: Wal-ter de Gruyter, 1974.

_____. *Early History of the Israelite People*. Leiden: E. J. Brill, 1992.

Tobin, V. A. "Amarna and Biblical Religion." In *Pharaonic Egypt*, edited by S. Israelit-Groll, pp. 231–274. Jerusalem: Magnes Press, 1985.

Van Seters, J. *The Hyksos*. New Haven: Yale Univ. Press, 1966.

_____. "The Terms 'Amorite' and 'Hittite' in the Old Testament." *Vetus Tes-tamentum* 22 (1972), pp. 64–81.

_____. *Abraham in History and Tradition*. New Haven: Yale Univ. Press, 1975.

_____. *In Search of History*. New Haven: Yale Univ. Press, 1983.

von Rad, G. *Deuteronomy*. London: SCM Press, 1966.

Waddell, W. G. *Manetho*. Cambridge: Harvard Univ. Press, 1940.

Waterman. L. "Moses the Pseudo-Levite." *Journal of Biblical Literature* 59 (1940), pp. 397–404.

Weigall, A. E. *The Life and Times of Akhenaten*. London: William Blackwood, 1910.

Westermann, C. *Genesis*. Translated by D. Green. Grand Rapids: Eerdmans, 1987.

Widengren, G. "What do we know about Moses?" In *Proclamation and Pres-ence*, edited by J. I. Durham and J. R. Porter, pp. 21–47. Richmond: John Knox Press, 1970.

Wildavsky, A. *Moses as a Political Leader.* University, AL: Univ. of Alabama Press, 1984.

Wilson, I. *Exodus: The True Story.* San Francisco: Harper and Row, 1985.

Wiseman, P. J. *New Discoveries in Babylonia about Genesis,* 1936. (Now offered as *Ancient Records and the Structure of Genesis.* New York: Thomas Nelson, 1985.)

Wright, G. E. "The Levites in Deuteronomy." *Vetus Testamentum* 4 (1954), pp. 325–330.

Wyld's Official Map of the Suez Maritime Canal. London: James Wyld, 1869.

Yadin, Y. *The Art of Warfare in Biblical Lands.* New York: McGraw-Hill, 1963.

Yahuda, A. S. *The Language of the Pentateuch in Its Relation to Egyptian.* London: Oxford Univ. Press, 1933.

Yeivin, S. "The Age of the Patriarchs." *Rivista degli Studi Orientali* 38 (1963), pp. 277–302.

———. *The Israelite Conquest of Canaan.* Istanbul: Nederlands Historisch-Archeologisch Institut in Het Nabije Oosten, 1971.

Yerushalmi, Y. H. *Freud's Moses.* New Haven: Yale Univ. Press, 1991.

Zabkar, L. V. "The Theocracy of Amarna and the Doctrine of the BA." *Journal of Near Eastern Studies* 13 (1954), pp. 87–101.

Zeligs, D. F. *Moses: A Psychodynamic Study.* New York: Human Sciences Press, 1986.

Index